Testers and Testing

The Sociology of School Psychology

Carl Milofsky

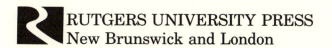

RUTGERS UNIVERSITY PRESS
New Brunswick and London

Library of Congress Cataloging-in-Publication Data
Milofsky, Carl.
    Testers and testing : the sociology of school
    psychology / Carl Milofsky.
           p.   cm.
    Bibliography: p.
    Includes index.
    ISBN 0-8135-1407-X
    ISBN 0-8135-1408-8 (pbk.)
    1. School psychologists—United States—Case
studies.
2. Intelligence tests—United States—Case studies.
3. Discrimination in education—United States—
Case studies.
4. School psychology—United States—Case
studies.   I. Title.
LB3013.6.M55   1989
371.2'022–dc19   88-28293
                                                 CIP

     British Cataloging-in-Publication information
                    available

This book is dedicated to my parents,
Bernard and Ruth Milofsky

Contents

Figures

Tables

Acknowledgments

This has been a transcontinental project. Parts of this work have been done on both coasts and in the Midwest. As a result of these journeys, I have enjoyed fruitful relationships with so many people who have taken an interest in this project that I cannot hope to tell them all how much I have learned from their help.

Fred Strodtbeck, of the Department of Sociology at the University of Chicago was instrumental in helping me obtain a postdoctoral fellowship from the Alcohol, Drug Abuse, and Mental Health Administration of the U.S. Government and in helping me find a place to work at the University of Chicago. Without his help this project would not have happened.

This project continues work I began as a graduate student at Berkeley where, as part of the Childhood and Government Project at Boalt Law School, I worked with Gale Saliterman on David Kirp's research investigating the implementation of procedures of due process in schools, especially in special education. Peter Kuriloff of the Department of Education at the University of Pennsylvania was one of Kirp's collaborators during that time. Once I moved to the East Coast, Peter repeatedly came to my aid on this project, and he has been a good friend. Similarly, Barbara Heyns, one of my teachers at Berkeley, became a continual source of advice, help and support when she moved nearby to Harvard and New York University.

Data for this book was collected in the metropolitan Chicago area while I was a postdoctoral fellow at the University of Chicago. Dan Lortie was my sponsor in the Department of Education and helped me enormously. Arthur Stinchcombe, a teacher at Berkeley and a colleague at Chicago, laid out some of the basic organization theory ideas upon which this study is constructed. He also helped me gain access to the National Opinion Research Center, where Celia Homans and Ron Hirsch gave me valuable help designing the survey instrument. Bob Slater and Mitch Pressman, then graduate students in the Department of Education at the University of Chicago, also provided great help with the survey portion of the study. Slater also did most of the historical research on the Bureau of Child Study of the Chicago Public Schools.

This project was only possible because people working in public school systems in and around Chicago were interested in talking about schools, helping me meet others who also liked to share ideas and who let me watch them at work. Pat Allen provided my entrée into the Chicago public schools. He was a courageous man, and his death left Hyde Park a poorer place. Cora Passin was a key person who helped me gain access to school psychologists in Chicago in very difficult times. In the suburbs, the senior psychologists of the two cooperatives I visited, Stanford MacDonald and Faye Coultas, were both key informants and vital facilitators. I would thank the other psychologists who helped me so much but I fear violating my promise of confidentiality.

In some respects the data collection phase of this book was the easiest part of the research. This project proved difficult to write up because I have intended it to speak to multiple audiences—school psychologists, educational policy analysts, sociologists, and practitioners with little technical training in sociology. Framing the concepts so they address issues important to all of these groups and constructing the text so that all would find it readable and valuable has been a struggle.

Fortunately, most of the writing for this book took place at Yale's Institution for Social and Policy Studies, an environment perfectly suited for this multidisciplinary effort. Members of the Education Group at ISPS were my intellectual "family" and their help was enormous. Working with Seymour Sarason, the person I consider the most insightful observer of the special education scene, was a dream I had as a graduate student. I cannot think of a more interested, informed colleague to have for this sort of project. Ed Lindblom, David Cohen, Judy Gruber, Dick Murnane, Ed Pauly, and Janet Weiss taught me about educational policy analysis and got me thinking about issues I had never encountered in my sociological training.

John Simon, Paul DiMaggio, and Jim Rosenbaum read parts of this material and helped me out with their legal and sociological understanding of schools. Ed Ziegler and Nancy Apfel, members of the Bush Center for the Study of Childhood in the Department of Psychology, provided a special psychological boost. Stan Merrill, a sociology student friend from Chicago and a colleague at Yale, gave me the most friendly, supportive introduction to computer work I can imagine and helped enormously with the analysis of this data. Miriam Klein was a wonderful secretary and a good friend.

In Lewisburg, Pennsylvania, I also was fortunate to have friends and colleagues who have provided help and support in this project. Sandra Elion has been the greatest help with her friendship and her accurate intuitions about how schools, teachers, and children function. John Kendrick has been a continual source of encouragement. Marc Schloss, Jacqueline Sallade, and Michael Gross read nearly completed versions of the manuscript and gave me vital last-minute advice about how to sharpen the focus of the book. Yvonne Wetzel has piloted the computer and in her masterly way has given me secretarial help.

Finally, my family has been supportive and encouraging through stressful times. Having a new title to put on their bookshelves is a small return for so much love.

Intelligence Testing and Race in the Public Schools

Intelligence is a valuable commodity in our society. It may be a source of status, achievement, and wealth if one has it or of profound stigma if one does not. Ours is a technological society that demands cognitive sophistication for success, if not for survival. Economists in particular have argued that our society is a meritocracy in which wealth and status are earned by those possessing the most sophisticated skills.[1] Other observers, however, argue that intelligence is more important as a cultural symbol that legitimates status and power after it is achieved than as a determinant of wealth and success.

Critics of meritocratic thinking argue that intelligence in itself is not, in fact, crucial for job success. If we control for socioeconomic background and the number of years of education people have completed, actual intellectual ability and cognitive performance make little contribution to job status. School success, furthermore, is more strongly predicted by social class background and by deportment than by IQ scores. In this perspective, IQ is important mostly as a means of selecting those with middle-class attributes and justifying exclusion of others from opportunities to achieve high status.[2]

Debate has raged for decades about whether intelligence really explains success or whether the primary ways we have of determining intelligence—school achievement and psychometric measures of cognitive performance—are culturally biased in favor of white middle-class people and against minorities and the poor. Oddly, most of this argument has been abstract. Economists have built elaborate predictive models. Genetic psychologists have fine-tuned their estimates of the heritability of IQ.[3] Sociologists and others have bitterly fought back, complaining about the inadequacies of twin studies and the misinterpretation of the interaction term in the heritability equation.[4] Intelligence tests tend to be treated as fixed, unchanging, and objective. What people fight over is their interpretation.

Few people who take part in this debate ask how intelligence is actually determined in the day-to-day affairs that shape people's lives. IQ tests, as they are administered in a laboratory, may or may not be culturally biased. Whether they are "objectively" biased is irrelevant if the people who administer tests and make decisions in schools about intellectual status ignore laboratory guidelines or use tests to legitimate a foregone conclusion. Biased instruments may be used in a culturally sensitive manner, and rigorously culture-fair instruments may be used unethically. We can only know how and why tests are used if we go to the field and look at what people actually do when they give tests and how the results of those examinations are used in institutions like the public schools or the workplace.

This book is an empirical study of one group of people responsible for allocating intellectual status: public school psychologists working in Illinois. School psychologists are central actors in the process by which students are placed in special education classes, classes that serve both the intellectually talented and the intellectually flawed. School psychologists are important because they are primarily responsible for administering individual intelligence tests. Although IQ tests are not the only psychometric instruments school psychologists use and data from other specialists is also used in determining special class assignments, some studies have found that intelligence tests, of all the data used, are most predictive of what a child's special class assignment will finally be.[5] Tests, and the testers who administer them, are pivotal to the process.

The relationships between tests, intellectual ability, and social status are the key issues in this book. This examination is worth study because decisions about when to test, how to test, and how to interpret and report test results are complex. In practice, testing usually departs from laboratory norms. Because psychometric instruments are designed to be finely tuned research devices, the departures I report in this book mangle methodological subtleties that make tests powerful in the lab.

For some readers, the fact that school psychologists do not religiously follow standard test norms may invalidate the occupation and its work. I will try to show that such rejection would be too hasty. I am convinced that good school psychology requires creative use of tests. If this is the case, however, the question arises as to how we can tell competent, responsible testing from that which is incompetent and irresponsible.

The only way to make this distinction is to learn the many details about the contexts in which school psychologists work and about the dilemmas that confront them when they are asked to examine children in schools. Consider the following two case examples, for instance.

Crystal Thompson: A Psychologist in the Ghetto. Crystal Thompson is a black woman in her mid-fifties who is one of three school psychologists serving in a decentralized neighborhood school district in Chicago, a district that serves a black area on the South Side. Although there are a few middle-class neighborhoods in the district, Thompson is assigned to schools in the poorer neighborhoods. I accompanied her to one of these schools on a day given over to staffings. That is, a number of children had been placed in or referred to be considered for assignment to classes for the educable mentally handicapped (EMH; Illinois used EMH rather than *retarded*) or for reassignment. Mrs. Thompson and other members of the diagnostic team had already examined these children and now, in a marathon meeting, decisions would be made about each student.

Mrs. Thompson had tested these children in rapid-fire fashion on earlier days, when I had not been present. She explained that the district with its two high schools and seven elementary schools has about fifteen hundred students in special education classes. She and the other two psychologists must reexamine all of them each year and carry out examinations of all new children referred for special education. This means she must test more than three hundred children each year, and for many of them she must complete her job of testing in less than two hours—breakneck speed, if one takes test norms seriously.

The situation she works in seemed pretty discouraging to me. She is assigned to some of the most desperate neighborhoods of Chicago. This day we were in the Richard J. Daley Elementary School, a modern building with several boarded-up windows that sits in its glass-strewn playground in the middle of a field of burned-out apartment buildings.

We arrived early and sat down in an empty classroom, waiting for others to arrive. As people drifted in they chatted casually, waiting for the formal meeting to start. Because it involved many children already assigned to EMH classes, this staffing was primarily a planning session for the special educators, and it included special teachers and members of the interdisciplinary diagnostic team that served the Daley School. The interdisciplinary team included a special teacher, a speech pathologist, the school nurse, and the school social worker. In addition to the team members, the people present were Tom James, the administrator for special classes in the region of the city in which Crystal Thompson's local school district is located, and two teachers of EMH classes.

Tom James asked Mrs. Thompson if she remembered Mr. Tompkins, the learning disability teacher who had been at the Daley school two years before. One of the students they were to discuss began his special education career in Mr. Tompkins's class. Mr. James laughed as he recalled that Tompkins never seemed to do any teaching at all. Mr. James came into the classroom one day and found the teacher asleep on the couch, ignoring the students. James had become so enraged that he finally spent an entire week sitting in the back of the classroom demanding that Tompkins submit detailed lesson plans and teach from them. Tompkins requested a transfer and left at the end of that semester. Mrs. George, the EMH teacher in the junior high school to which Daley sends students, asked ruefully if Mr. James had considered doing the same with Lenny Schmidt, one of the current learning disabled teachers at Daley. Thompson leaned over and whispered to me that they have constant problems finding teachers trained to teach in the special education classes of this district.

At the beginning of the meeting, Mrs. Thompson introduced each case and provided a quick overview of the case background. Team members then discussed any new information they had and decided whether the student's assignment should be changed for the coming year.

Nick was the first student discussed. He was put in an EMH class in February after a child study had been conducted in the fall. He had been tardy frequently and had a tendency to read from right to left instead of from left to right. He also was reported to have trouble getting along with classmates who were more agressive than he. Mrs. Dale, the EMH teacher at Daley, reported that Nick seemed to be getting along better with his peers since he has been in the EMH class.

Mrs. Thompson gave a brief history of Nick's personal background. He lived with his grandmother in rural Arkansas until a year previously, when he moved to Chicago to live with his mother. His IQ was listed as 73–verbal, 51–performance, 63–full scale. His achievement was at the third grade level, although he was thirteen at the time. The reasons for referral emphasized his tardiness, withdrawn behavior, and defacement of property. All of this suggests, Mrs. Thompson said, that the boy has had trouble adjusting to the move from country to city. One would expect depressed school performance given his rural background and family changes, she explained. This theory was supported, she speculated, by Nick's quick responsiveness to Mrs. Dale. Everyone quickly agreed to retain him in the EMH class for the coming school year. The whole discussion took about four minutes.

The group then raced through several other cases. Throughout the meeting, Mr. James was relaxed, courtly, flirtatious, and complimentary to the two EMH teachers. The party atmosphere this group generated contrasted starkly with Mrs. Thompson's manner.

She seemed hurried, hassled, and a little confused. Although she emerges as the person taking care of most of the administrative details in the session, she seemed to have incomplete knowledge at best about what was actually happening in the classes. She did not seem to know how many classes there were, how many children were involved, or what the teachers were trying to accomplish prescriptively with particular students. It seemed as though Crystal Thompson's job was quite removed from the school and from the real issues involved in defining students' problems and determining what their needs were. She appeared mostly preoccupied with being sure that the many forms required for special education placement were completed and filed in the appropriate administrative office. It seemed as though the other people were at the meeting only to help Mrs. Thompson attend to these unpleasant administrative details.

Earlier, Mrs. Thompson had told me that she was frustrated with the formality of her work. She had been working in the neighborhood district for twelve years, having taken the job mainly because she wanted financial security after her husband died. She now was desperately unhappy because the local superintendent put pressure on her to do most of the paperwork for special education classes in the district at the same time he demanded a heavy load of testing from her. Mrs. Thompson feels trapped in her job and unable to change her situation.

As she talked about her life, some bitterness with the Chicago schools became apparent. She began her professional life as a teacher and had received her teaching certificate in high school chemistry. Unable to obtain a full-time job in Chicago, she had been assigned, as a long-term substitute, to teach general science and math in one of the inner city high schools. That she had a "temporary" assignment was amusing to her, because she continued in that position for several years while she did graduate work in psychology. Eventually, the principal, knowing of her graduate work in psychology, asked her to set up programs for the gifted and the EMH in the high school. This work encouraged her to continue with her graduate work, and she eventually completed her master's degree in school psychology. To her frustration, she could not get a job as a school psychologist in Chicago for several years. Her impression was that the district, in the 1950s, just would not hire a black to be a school psychologist.

She maintained her identity as a psychologist by working in private clinical practice in the late 1950s and early 1960s. Meanwhile, she was promoted to be head of special education in her high school while also serving as a counselor. These responsibilities involved her in a heavy load of administrative work, work she did not much enjoy but did well. What she did like was the opportunity her position provided to work with new teachers and to help them set up their programs.

Once the Bureau of Child Study began employing blacks as psychologists, Mrs. Thompson changed jobs and became a school psychologist. She took on her current load of administrative responsibilities after the school system had entered a retrenchment period and threatened to reduce the term of school psychologists from twelve months of work to nine and a half months. Administrative work guaranteed her a full twelve months of employment. Unfortunately, her assignment also included an overwhelming amount of testing and paperwork.

Henry Jones: A Psychologist in a Suburban Ghetto. On the day I observed Henry Jones, he was doing early childhood screenings in South Poletown with children referred from Headstart programs in the town. South Poletown is one of the poorest municipalities in the ACORN Special Education Cooperative area and the residents are nearly all black. The children from that area have a reputation for having limited educational skills, in part, Mr. Jones told me, because the school system offers relatively few services.

The early childhood screening program he was administering during my observation period is part of a state-wide initiative to test children and is a program provided in most of the ACORN districts. In this case, however, the screening has special importance because Mr. Jones is both the school psychologist for South Poletown and the head of the ACORN early childhood program for children with developmental disabilities.

Jones had worked at ACORN for about five years when I interviewed him. Although he is one of the youngest psychologists working for the cooperative, Jones works with noticeable assurance. During his graduate work, he had participated in research to develop a new psychometric instrument for discovering learning disabilities in young children. Now he is working in a setting where those research skills have direct application.

When I arrived at the South Poletown Community Service Center where the screenings were being conducted, Mr. Jones was doing an evaluation of Rena, a three-year-old. I observed the evaluation process that was repeated over and over throughout the day. First he tested manual dexterity and perception of shapes. He asked her to copy a circle, which she did. Next, at his request, she tried to pile eight or nine blocks in a tower of admirable height. He then asked her to move her thumb without moving her hand, something she could not do. She could, however, touch each of her fingers to her thumb.

The test went on in this way as Mr. Jones asked Rena to carry out a variety of tasks. As he asked her to climb steps, attempt to copy pictures, or complete puzzles, he muttered under his breath, "Well, what am I supposed to do with this? She can't do this puzzle but probably her mother never does puzzles with her. How am I supposed to tell the difference between a practice effect and a real disability?" He was saying these things partly for my benefit to impress upon me that when working with a low-income population, testing becomes an especially slippery process. The tests are geared to provide objective measures of performance as though they tap some global sort of cognitive ability. But when parents do not play with their children in ways that develop the skills that are tested for, it is difficult to tell whether inability to perform is biological or cultural.

When the session was over, Mr. Jones took Rena back to her classroom and then said to me, "Well, that's what we do all day." He said that Rena is functioning at her age level, which is all he looks for, but he thinks she does not pay attention or follow directions very well. The speech therapist will have more to say about that than he. He commented, ruefully, that psychologists are supposed to answer questions about the children's social and affective development but they cannot usually tell much. The children might not respond well in the test setting, but this may be because they cannot or because they are used to folowing directions only when their mothers yell at them.

Mr. Jones left for a moment and returned with Madonna. As I watched the psychologist work with this small child, I noticed that he was not very pleasant to her. He later explained that this was intentional. He is behavior-modification oriented and is interested in exploring what kinds of rewards motivate the children he sees. He takes a practical and analytic approach to rewards and punishments. When he is firm or supportive, he thinks of himself as being like a doctor who listens to someone's heart. For the doctor, the heartbeat is somewhat disassociated with the way he relates to the person. Although Mr. Jones may seem hard-hearted at times, this is inextricably involved with his effort to systematically explore what actions on his part will make a child perform on a test, and especially what will lead a passive child to perform. He is as likely to be friendly and warm if that seems to be what a child needs to work well. His mode of interaction with a child is something he has to manipulate if he wants to understand how a child will perform upon entering school or if he wishes to determine why a youngster has been identified as a problem student.

After Mr. Jones struggled with Madonna for a while, the school nurse came by and asked, "Is this the one who does not talk?" She looked at Madonna for a moment and then continued, "Yes, I have her sister in the other room. A year and a half I've been working with that one and I haven't heard a word. The mother makes them sleep in the living room and then makes them be quiet all of the time. She never gives any warmth. I think Madonna is just scared of adults."

Mr. Jones looked at the child for a moment and said, "No, that's not it. She was sitting there crying when I first came into the room. As soon as she saw me she came over to me to get comforted. She wouldn't do that if she were scared."

The nurse said, "She never gets comfort at home. I have one of my nursing students working with the mother and we never see any cuddling."

Mr. Jones replied, "Well, maybe she is getting it from someone else. She sure has learned not to say, 'I want to be cuddled.' At the same time, she knows she doesn't have to say a thing if she cries loudly enough. She expects someone to pick her up."

This patter of conversation between Mr. Jones, other staff members, and the children continued throughout the day. I was amazed by how well the staff people seemed to know the students, how openly they talked with each other, and with the sensitivity Mr. Jones brought to observing the children. He also brought intense intellectual curiosity to his work. Each child was a fresh puzzle, and all of the staff people seemed comfortable with him, even though Mr. Jones has a somewhat brusque manner. They seemed to respect his knowledge and his sensitivity, and they expected him to listen to their ideas. The critical exchange I witnessed between him and the nurse seemed to be a routine procedure among colleagues who trust each other enough to disagree.

Crystal Thompson and Henry Jones exemplify two different approaches to school psychology and to the business of testing. Mrs. Thompson seemed trapped in her work and isolated from the children. Testing was a routine administrative activity for her that was disconnected from the schooling process, rushed and formalized. Mr. Jones, in contrast, treats testing as a creative, interpretive process that cannot be separated from the setting in which he is working and the special characteristics of the children he sees. To his mind, tests are not an objective measure to be counted on for a fixed number that will guide him in making a routinized administrative decision. This is the perspective that seems to dominate Mrs. Thompson's work environment. Mr. Jones instead uses tests to build an understanding of the children he sees so that he can work more effectively with the other staff members.

Although these cases do not include much detail about how Thompson and Jones actually did their testing, detail that must wait until a later chapter, the two short descriptions suggest that neither psychologist always goes "by the book." Their deviations from what might be standard practice in a laboratory have sharply different motivations and equally different implications for the children they examine.

For Mr. Jones, tests are limiting. He has to take them with a grain of salt because they do not tell them much about the reasons children fail tasks. Test results are incomplete. Because his job is to learn as much as he can about a child, he uses tests to the extent that they are useful to him in developing and testing hypotheses about whether a child is in trouble and why he or she might be failing to complete necessary tasks. Mr. Jones might give fragments of tests or use parts of tests in unconventional ways if they will help him build his understanding of a subject.

Mrs. Thompson uses tests to administer an objective measure and obtain a score that will tell whether a child is eligible for EMH class or must be retained in the mainstream. She has learned to streamline the process of giving tests so that she can complete a maximum number in a short period of time. She has no time to sit back and wonder about why a child is failing, try three or four methods of improving rapport with her subjects, or discuss with other members of the interdisciplinary team about why a particular child performs as he or she does. She does not seem inclined to that sort of speculation, anyway.

A formalized approach to testing, like Mrs. Thompson's, magnifies any cultural biases that are built into tests. Treating test results as though they are objective and true makes one blind to whatever distortions and inaccuracies are built into the instruments. Furthermore, hurried testing leaves little time for building rapport with children or for using the diagnostic process as a means of formulating and testing hypotheses about subjects. Practice effects, the anxieties children bring to the test session, discomfort with the formality of the test setting, and other factors often interfere with subjects' objective performance.[6] Ignoring these elements will tend to produce lower test scores. Searching out those same factors can allow a psychologist to learn much about a child's learning style and his or her reasons for having trouble in school.[7]

We shall see in coming chapters that this difference between a formalized testing style and one that treats the evaluation as a creative discovery process is a matter of importance in school psychology. The occupation is split between people who, like Mrs. Thompson, treat their testing work as formal, objective, withdrawn, and administrative and those who believe their job is to intervene and change schools and children. If formalized testing styles magnify the cultural biases built into tests, then it is unfortunate that black children in Illinois are significantly more likely to receive this sort of psychological evaluation when they are referred for placement in special education classes.

A major task of this book is to demonstrate the presence of this troublesome racial difference in the way public schools test children and to explore the reasons for its existence. The race effect is a by-product of a profound difference that exists between school psychology as it is practiced in large cities—Chicago, in this study—and in smaller, newer suburban school districts. Of the psychologists who reported to me that they worked with many black children, most worked in Chicago. The working conditions Mrs. Thompson described, conditions that foster rapid testing and an administrative approach to the work, apply to both white and black children in the city.

The race differences in testing practices might be dismissed as an unfortunate product of bureaucracy in education. It is a truism that urban education is in crisis and that small, wealthy suburban school districts often are in a better position to provide students with high-quality education. Where school psychology is concerned, however, bureaucracy, strictly defined, turns out not to be the main cause of formality in evaluation procedures.

Chicago schools are dramatically different from most of those in the suburbs, but it is not accurate to describe the difference in terms of greater bureaucracy. Bureaucracy suggests organizational formality, hierarchy, supervision, rationalsim, and other qualities related to self-conscious control of an organizational system by a small group of top administrators.[8] Psychologists in Chicago, like those in the suburbs, report an almost complete absence of control or supervision. To be sure, psychologists worry about what regular school officials and administrative superiors want them to do. We saw this with Crystal Thompson. But in fact other educators rarely tell psychologists what to do. They do not keep track of school psychologists' time schedules, and they let psychologists determine their own productivity levels. Even in Chicago the psychologists acknowledged that they could do group therapy with children if they wished rather than carry on the intense diet of testing that characterizes their role.

The organizational climate they work in has a tremendous impact on how school psychologists do their work, but in the last analysis psychologists control how they will work. They choose to do little but test, defining their role as an administrative one or, alternatively, to see their role as one focused on doing genuine psychology in the schools. Understanding why black children receive formalized testing while many white children receive creative, investigative evaluations cannot be explained by just saying that the black children go to city schools. We need to know why urban school psychology is so rigid and formalized in contrast to that which goes on in so many suburban school districts.

The question this book seeks to answer is why different styles of school psychology have emerged and why there are essentially two distinct public school systems where special education is concerned. Although the question seems to imply a detailed comparison of urban schools with those outside of cities, this is a false analytic trail.

Upon close examination, school psychology in Chicago turns out to be narrow, formalized, routine, and dull. The frantic anxiety we saw in Crystal Thompson is extreme, but when I interviewed Chicago school psychologists I saw others with little variation from the main pattern of her work. Most Chicago practitioners do little but test children. They do their work rapidly and in relative isolation from the schools, teachers, and children they serve. They do not try to actively change schools. Rather, they see their job as one of providing support and help when asked. This pushes them into a role that is defined by the expectations of the regular school staff. Because educators believe school psychologists are testers, that is what they ask school psychologists to do.

School psychology outside of the city is more complex because it is active. Practitioners tend to resist the passive, reactive role that dominates in the city. Many of the people I spoke to resist the idea that learning problems reside *within* the children they study. Those problems are transactional and they arise within the context of school and family life. Sometimes the reasons a child is seen as a problem have more to do with breakdowns in the adult social systems in which that child is entangled than with the child's behavior. Suburban school psychologists are more inclined that their urban counterparts to address these adult problems and to avoid blaming student failure only on something contained inside the child's head.

Nonurban school psychologists tend to have an active orientation toward their work, but the regular educators they serve usually share with urban regular educators a narrow definition of the school psychologist's role. A major task of this book is to show 1) what it means for a psychologist to be active rather than passive, 2) a variety of ways that psychologists may implement an active orientation, and 3) how psychologists address the strategic problems involved in building an active role when regular educators expect them to provide narrow, specific services.

This detailed description of how school psychologists can build an active role, despite being somewhat peripheral to the most visible business of schools, teaching children in regular classrooms, is itself an original contribution to the literature on psychology in schools. In terms of the overall structure of my argument, however, the extended ethnographic descriptions of psychologists at work is something of a digression from the central analytic theme of the book. It is essential to the discussion but there is danger that the reader, becoming immersed in tales of school psychologists at work, will forget why we entered this territory in the first place.

The point of departure for this book is a concern with the relationship between race and testing in schools. That concern emerges from the broader political and social policy debate about how testing and student classification should proceed in schools. Intelligence tests have been sharply criticized over the past quarter century, and there have been elaborate procedural reforms in special education in an effort to minimize the effects of test bias in the student evaluation process. This book demonstrates that those reforms have had little impact where it counts the most, in cities. Going beyond that demonstration, this book explains why those reforms have not worked. It also gives an exploratory analysis of how schools would have to change for minority children to receive fair evaluations of their intellectual abilities and services that would appropriately address their school problems.

A History of Special Education

To understand this book's argument, readers need to know more about special education, intelligence testing, and the role of school psychologist. Programs for the mentally retarded, gifted, emotionally disturbed, and physically disabled, with instruction in self-contained classrooms, have existed in one form or another since the turn of the twentieth century. The most famous effort to locate the retarded and to address their special needs was Binet's project, sponsored by the Paris public schools. That resulted in his invention of the individual intelligence test in 1904. Binet's work was not isolated, however. The Chicago Public Schools sponsored a similar project, launching the Bureau of Child Study in 1894. Special education programs existed in many large cities from the first decades of this century. However, programs were generally small and there was no systematic approach to the treatment of children. In some districts school officials placed immigrant children they thought were immoral in special classes, while in others children with severe physical and intellectual disabilities were placed in special classes.[9]

Special education remained sporadic and unsystematic until after World War II. Beginning in the late 1940s, many states passed laws mandating programs for the mentally retarded in public schools. This period launched a time of exponential growth continuing until the late 1970s. At the outset, the programs that grew were mainly those that were already established. Thus, programs for the mentally retarded in major cities grew during the 1950s. They primarily enrolled students from the upper elementary grades who were low income, black, and male.[10]

As the civil rights movement grew in the late 1950s and early 1960s, criticism of programs for the retarded grew because their enrollments heavily overrepresented blacks. In the late 1960s, a number of lawsuits were initiated that sought to enjoin schools from arbitrary placement of minority children in classes for educable mentally retarded children. Several lawsuits challenged the rights of schools to use individual intelligence tests as part of the procedure for evaluating black or Chicano children during the special education placement process. The San Francisco schools were ordered to stop using tests in *Larry P. v. Riles,* and sociologist Jane Mercer undertook the development of a test of individual competence that would not be culturally biased. Her social adaptation scale was adopted as a standard evaluation instrument in California.[11]

At the same time that special education programs were being attached as ethnically biased and culturally imperialist, parents—primarily middle-class ones—began to demand programs for the "learning disabled." These are children who supposedly have normal intelligence but fail to learn because they are unable to process certain kinds of information. Some children cannot process instructions given aurally. Some children write in mirror vision. Other children are hyperactive and overstimulated by normal classroom activities. Learning disability programs tend to be less stigmatizing than those for the retarded because children are not considered intellectually subnormal. Their failure to learn flows from a conflict between their idiosyncratic learning styles and the institutional rigidities of public schools.[12] It is asserted that these children need special classes so they can learn how to work around their particular disability and thereby achieve within the narrow instructional program public schools of necessity offer in the "mainstream."

Learning disability theory has been strongly challenged.[13] However, by partially replacing classes for the retarded and by providing a rationale by which middle-class children could be incorporated into special education, learning disability programs allowed special education to continue expanding and reduce the visibility of minority children assigned to special education classes. Throughout the late 1960s and early 1970s, learning disabilities programs grew—especially in suburban school districts—until they became the largest special education programs (see Table 1). Programs for the mentally retarded became proportionately smaller compared with total special education enrollments.

Programs for the retarded also became targets of procedural reforms. Law suits initiated by civil rights activists forced school districts in Pennsylvania to seek out handicapped children who were not being served by public school programs and to remove from special classes children who did not require services. Other states introduced legislative reforms that reproduced provisions of the Pennsylvania consent decree. Then in 1975 the federal government passed the Education for All Handicapped Children Act (PL 94-142), which incorporated important aspects of the Pennsylvania law.[14]

Pivotal to this whole program of reform have been the ways children are identified as candidates for special education; the manner in which they are given educational, psychological, and physical examinations; and the processes by which decisions are made about which students should be placed in special classes. Most children in special classes are mildly handicapped—speech impaired, educable mentally retarded (EMR—the same as Illinois' EMH category), or learning disabled (LD) (see Table 1). Typically, EMR and LD children are hard to distinguish from nonhandicapped children. They are not spontaneously identified as handicapped by members of their families or by people in their communities.[15] Furthermore, school officials do not see them as handicapped until they begin to fail in the classroom. Even then, it is difficult to reliably separate those children who are handicapped from those who are not.[16]

In response to this uncertainty, federal law PL 94-142 mandated that a multidisciplinary team, composed of a school psychologist, a social worker, a nurse, a speech pathologist, and a special educator, should evaluate each child. Together they are to provide an evaluation that takes into account family background, psychological characteris-

TABLE 1. **Students Served in Special Education Programs in the United States**

	1963	*1970*	*1980*
All public school students	37,405,303	41,934,376	37,702,370
All handicapped children served	1,682,351	2,968,000	3,234,337
Percentage change	—	+76%	+9%
Children served as a percentage of all children	4%	6%	7%
Speech impaired	—	1,224,000	908,241
Learning disabled	—	648,000	1,262,535
Mentally retarded	—	728,000	658,082
Emotionally disturbed	—	253,000	182,931
Hard of hearing	—	41,000	28,740
Deaf	21,000	17,850	
Crippled (orthopedically impaired)	—	30,000	39,119
Partially sighted and blind	—	23,000	17,330
Other (other health impaired, deaf-blind, multihandicapped)	—	—	43,404

Sources: Kenneth Simon and W. Vance Grant, *Digest of Educational Statistics, 1972* (Washington, DC: National Center for Educational Statistics, 1973); W. Vance Grant and Leo J. Eiden, *Digest of Educational Statistics, 1981* (Washington, DC: National Center for Educational Statistics, 1982); and W. Vance Grant and Thomas D. Snyder, *Digest of Educational Statistics, 1983–84* (Washington, DC: National Center for Educational Statistics, 1985).

tics, physiological anomalies, and an analysis of educational problems. This evaluation provides the information by which school personnel should decide whether to assign children to special classes. If they do assign children, the evaluation should provide the basis of a teaching prescription called an Individualized Educational Plan (IEP).

The Importance of School Psychologists and of Testing

In my experience, multidisciplinary teams have rarely provided the rich, in-depth information envisioned by the federal law. In most districts I have observed, the special education classification process has become elaborately formalized. Many children have to be evaluated and processed by a small number of people. Federal law requires that extensive records be kept, so members of interdisciplinary teams spend most of their time compiling and maintaining records rather than working with children and trying to solve their problems. In an earlier book, I described an evaluation session in California,[17] which also represented the process I observed in this study of Illinois, as the example of Crystal Thompson showed. Children often are discussed by committees for three to five minutes before decisions are made and new cases are taken up. Naturally, there are exceptions to this rapid decision process. But even districts in which children are evaluated with some care are under constant pressure to keep up with paperwork and to maintain formal procedures.

The formalization of evaluation focuses greatest attention on those measures of a student's performance that seem most objective and that are easiest to summarize as indicating health or pathology. Intelligence tests are powerful because they impress both teachers and parents with their objectivity, accuracy, and authoritativeness. Information gathered by social workers, nurses, and teachers is seen to be softer, more judgmental, and more dependent on the particular history of cases. It is difficult to collect such information when one is in a hurry. Once collected, the information is easier for hostile parents to challenge. Although one goal of the federal legislation has been to attack excessive reliance on intelligence test scores alone, as a school system's special education procedures become more formal, officials rely more on intelligence test scores in deciding whom to place in special classes.

Where my observations are impressionistic, Berk, Bridges, and Shih demonstrate unequivocally that intelligence test scores are the only significant predictor of whether children in the Chicago public schools would be placed in classes for the mentally retarded.[18] Thus, although the introduction of interdisciplinary teams may help emphasize that educators should use many kinds of data to understand the causes of student problems, the reality is that decisions depend on intelligence tests and the practices of those who administer them: the school psychologists.

Testing

The public hears about two kinds of tests that are routinely used in public schools: group tests and individual tests. Group tests, often administered by teachers in their classrooms or in the school cafeteria, measure student achievement. They are the tests given to whole grades every several years to measure overall achievement in a school district.

Individual tests, like the Stanford Binet or the Wechsler Intelligence Scale for Children, are administered privately by school psychologists or other professional test administrators and measure intelligence. Some sociological research uses group tests to investigate relationships between schooling and social class. We also read about results in the newspaper from such group tests when school districts compare their students with others around the country.

Individual tests are preferred by most psychologists who investigate student performance. They allow the examiner greater control over the test setting and better opportunities to manage problems with student rapport. They also give testers more flexibility in matching test batteries to student abilities, especially with those students who are difficult to examine. Psychologists normally administer four or five different tests to children during a child-study session, including projective and achievement tests and individual intelligence scales. Hundreds of these tests are available, and a broadly informed psychological examiner is likely to select special tests to fit the particular qualities difficult children present.

Although individual tests take more time and are more personalized than group tests, they still, compared with other ways of gathering data, are a relatively quick way to collect information about children. They help psychologists cope with their need to examine many children in a short period of time. Normally, practitioners serve two thousand to four thousand children, often in several schools, and the average psychologist conducts between one hundred and two hundred child studies per year. With such a load it is hard to learn much about a student that is independent of the information provided by school personnel.

Individual tests help overcome this problem because they allow a lot of information to be gathered in a short period of time. My respondents argued that the test setting provides a standardized environment that allows a psychologist to compare the particular child at hand to the many others he or she has observed over time. Extreme variations are thrown into sharp relief. In a couple of hours one can roughly understand how a child works and some things about his or her emotional makeup. Psychologists can explore reasons a child might be having problems before seeking information from teachers, principals, and parents, people whose perceptions of a child may be colored by conflict, anger, and defensiveness.

Time Allocation and Transactional School Psychology

Whether a student fails in school usually depends on the way the school functions on an organizational level, as well as whatever a child does to attract the concern of educators. The main job of the school psychologist is to learn why a child has been referred and whether a special class placement makes sense. That decision may rest more on what the psychologist thinks are the strengths and weaknesses of a child's teachers, principal, school, and family than on cognitive or emotional attributes of the child. Detailed psychological studies have limited usefulness in schools because most educators either will not understand them or do not use them.[19] Furthermore, despite the rhetoric of PL 94-142 that special education programs should be prescriptions worked out in closely coordinated teams, the psychologists in this study rarely had ongoing contacts with special teachers and did not believe their recommendations had much effect on the teaching children they studied would later receive.

The measure of quality in school psychology is whether practitioners take the time to learn about the interactive background of a case as they conduct a child study. When a psychologist knows the school personnel from working with them an a continual basis, it may not take very long to learn the organizational history of a case. One becomes adept at picking up current gossip in the teachers' room or elsewhere. Psychologists also may work with teachers and principals to alleviate staff conflicts. These contacts make it easy to fit a child's problems into the bigger picture of the school.

Psychologists can quickly pick up essential details about what I will call the "politics" of a case, but not all of them do. Questioning the motives behind student referrals, deciding that one should confront a teacher who seems to be having personal problems, and assuming that one has a right and an obligation to give advice to a principal or to a superintendent are activities one might perform to deal with the politics of a case. They require a transactional understanding of schools, self-confidence, and an aggressiveness many psychologists do not possess. Avoiding unpleasant confrontations becomes easy when one is busy. As one's case load increases, there is less and less time to give to each child. As time becomes more precious, psychologists tend to become focused on completion of the specific, concrete tasks required of a testing session.

The time structure of a psychologist's work role, thus, becomes a critical variable in explaining how sensitive practitioners are to the transactional aspects of student problems. Psychologists who report spending six or seven hours on each case and those who report spending only two or three do their jobs in radically different ways. The latter become so busy that they do not have time to learn much about the background of a case.[20] Given the conventions of test-giving in schools, the former will generally have some time left over after administering their tests, which will allow them to talk to people. Time devoted to different tasks becomes, for the researcher, an important diagnostic test of organizational behavior and, in turn, of the likelihood that individual psychologists are being careful when they test.

Black children, taken as a group, receive substantially and significantly more rapid testing than do white children. The data I present here show that, in Illinois, school psychologists serving blacks average less total time 1) administering tests to black children, 2) writing reports about the results of their testing sessions, and 3) attending meetings to discuss case dispostions than do those serving whites. In fact, they spend less time *in total* on these three tasks than the norms that govern test administration suggest they ought to spend on only the *first* task (administering the test batteries).[21] The psychologists I studied spend between two and three times as much time testing each white child as they spend testing each black. Test results are less accurate when they are administered to "nonmodal" children, anyway.[22] The rushed testing black children receive makes erring even more common. The differences between the intellectual performance of black and white children that we hear about are distorted and probably exaggerated as a result.

The Marginality of School Psychologists

Because school psychologists have a nearly exclusive mandate to be the IQ testers for schools, it is easy to see why they are key actors in making special education whatever it is. Yet blaming school psychologists for racial overrepresentation in special education classes or for hurried examination of minority students recommended for placement might seem to exaggerate their importance. School psychologists are minor cogs in large machines.

One might argue, for example, that children are placed in special education classes because school systems and educational policymakers have for the last eighty years supported and paid for these classes. If classes exist, children will be placed in them. In support of this idea, I showed in an earlier book that once special classes are available, the teachers and principals in regular classrooms make decisions about what kinds of children should be referred. Special class teachers get ready to receive whatever troublesome children might be sent along.[23] The school psychologist is a gatekeeper, usually removed from the day-to-day life of schools or of special classes. He or she processes children, sometimes in large numbers and often under considerable pressure to move children from one setting to another. School psychology is a minor occupation in a huge administrative system, and it is hard for school psychologists to keep a finger in the dike for long. If the regular school staff wants to move children into special classes, it is hard to stand up against educators who may work in desperate conditions and who wish to make quick use of whatever extra resources are available. Who protects the conscientious school psychologist? No one.

One might conclude that, facing these organizational pressures, it would be easy for school psychologists to become bureaucrats, aimlessly pushing paper and blaming others for certification decisions they make each day. If tests are carelessly administered and results are skewed, perhaps it is the system that is at fault and not the tester. That answer is too easy, however, and this book will show why.

When we accept that intelligence tests might be used as diagnostic instruments and that, even if they are culturally biased, they can be used profitably to examine and diagnose intellectual performance problems of clients, we also acknowledge that the psychometrician at his or her best is an artist of sorts. Tests are instruments of creativity. They provide a standardized setting for observation that allows a sensitive person to compare the immediate subject with hundreds of other people similarly observed and to learn, more quickly than is possible with other methods, important things about individual psychodynamics. Also creative is the way data is passed on and explained to other professionals or to family members. The psychologist not only forms an opinion of the client for him- or herself, but attempts to convince others that this picture is accurate and that certain decisions for the client should follow.

The Dual Special Education System: Urban and Suburban

About one-third of the school psychologists I observed and interviewed recognized this creativity and described their work as political. It is political in the following sense. Convincing other people in the referral process to accept recommendations one would make based on having studied a child requires some tactical and strategic planning concerning how to handle people and how to shape their perception of events. Most psychologists who make up the other two-thirds of my sample eschewed a creative or political role for themselves. This is a crucial division within the occupation that strongly correlates with the way testing is carried out in schools. People who see their work as political and creative test more slowly and do more diverse kinds of work during an average month than do people who reject that role. I shall argue that they do a better, fairer, more sensitive, and therapeutically or educationally more effective job than people who see testing in narrower terms and define their role simply as being the tester for the schools.

There also is a demographic split among school psychologists, which mirrors their philosphical split. Those who resist the creative-political view of testing work in large cities—Chicago, in this study— and they are overwhelmingly more likely to be the people asked to test minority children.[24] Psychologists who see their work as creative and political are more likely to work in suburbs and to serve white children. This split in the occupation captures a profound organizational difference between urban and suburban or nonurban education. The division is so deep that I think we need two different theories of education and school administration to make sense of them. We have two school systems, not one. Psychologists in city schools are heavily pressured to be good soldiers, and it is not too surprising that they capitulate.

Yet the differences between urban and nonurban school psychology are not just organizational. In urban schools, psychologists are overwhelmingly former teachers. In nonurban schools, there is heavy representation of people trained only in psychology who happen to work in schools. Having different backgrounds, the members of the two groups also have sharply different philosophies about what their work is about, whom they are serving, and how they ought to spend their time. These values translate into different work practices.

The Illegitimate Politics of School Psychology

Although this contrast in styles explains differences in the ways children of different races are evaluated and placed in special education classes, its ethical conflicts are what make school psychology worth studying as an occupation. Individual psychometric tests embody the psychological doctrine of "individual differences." Tests are presented as devices for carefully describing the unique features of individual personalities and styles of performance. To use tests objectively, according to this perspective, one must be methodologically rigorous. One must carefully follow the exact procedures recommended by those who have developed the instruments so that the internal consistency of the instrument and the validity of the measures are maintained and so that in comparing one's subjects to the test norms no sampling bias creeps in.

Many of the school psychologists I met, and Chicago's Bureau of Child Study as an institution, are deeply committed to the notion that tests objectively measure student attributes in ways that can and should inform educational decision making. This not only is an ideology strongly held by some practitioners, it also is a primary basis for psychologists' legitimacy in schools. As Berk, Bridges, and Shih show, IQ test scores are the most effective predictor of placement outcomes for students referred for evaluation as potentially mentally retarded.[25] One psychologist commented to me, "Testing is our bread and butter. It is how other educators explain to themselves what we are doing in schools." Even if they are skeptical about the absolute accuracy of test results, many psychologists feel obliged to embrace the myth to purchase the trust of other educators.

Despite this connection between methodological rigor and a concern for individual differences, when one studies the details of what school psychologists do, their work is most "individualized" when they bring to each case an awareness of the organizational or systemic contexts in which student problems are defined. As I showed in my previous book, it is not uncommon that referrals for psychological evaluation made by teachers and principals are rooted in school staff problems or in school-family conflicts.[26] In a less troubled setting, the child's behavior might be quite manageable. A school psychologist who only looks at the individual referred, the child who is judged a problem by some authority figure, is in danger of becoming a weapon wielded against the student by an already formidable school staff. This actually is broadly acknowledged among academics who teach and write about school psychology.[27]

Thus, there is irony in school psychology. To the extent members of the occupation are publicly most concerned with individual differences and objective measurement, the individual is treated as an entity distinct from context. Yet objective student characteristics are expressed in many different ways, depending on the transactional settings that exist in school, family, and community. School psychology can only attack student problems effectively when its practitioners develop heightened awareness of organizational dynamics in schools.

Concerned publicly with the individual alone, this organizational focus is not a legitimate function for school psychologists. They must be surreptitious when they try to discover and explain the "real" causes of a child's misbehavior during the process of evaluation and referral that precedes placement in a special education class. School psychologists cannot have much impact on schools even when they are attuned to the interactional basis of student failure, yet they, more than any other occupational role in the schools, witness the conflicts that undermine public education.

This book is not about those conflicts, since being aware of them represents a perspective on schools that underlies research rather than the analytic target of a particular investigation. As an organizational sociologist, one of the attractions of this research for me has been working with subjects who so often adopt a sociological perspective. But I am more interested in what school psychologists do with the ambiguity of their role—Merton would call it their ambivalence—and how they use it to either liberate or restrict themselves.[28] Because there are two clear poles, one represented by city school psychologists who have become bureaucrats rapidly testing children and the other by psychologists who see themselves as clinicians whose practice is in schools, it becomes important to ask why people migrate philosophically in one direction or the other.

We explore here that contrast and seek to learn what administrative arrangements encourage workers to work in a creative, independent way on one hand, and an automatic, rule-bound way on the other. Understanding this contrast should help us better understand how we might more effectively reform schools. As Stinchcombe has argued, it is central to understanding differences in manufacturing productivity.[29] It also is central to better understanding problems of bureaucratic indifference to the broader public interest.

The Illinois School Psychology Project

Data for this book was gathered while I was in residence doing postdoctoral research in the Department of Education, University of Chicago, in 1977 and 1978.[30] I observed school psychologists at work in the city of Chicago and in two cooperatives that served between ten and twenty suburban school districts outside the city. I also interviewed thirty-three of them, and this provides most of the case material. Pseudonyms are used throughout the book. After I finished with this intensive observational and interview study, I sent a mail questionnaire to all psychologists in the state of Illionis (see appendix). Because I had extremely limited resources for this study, I had to use follow-ups judiciously. I divided the state into three regions, or cohorts—urban Chicago, "downstate" (outside the metropolitan area), and suburban

Chicago. I concentrated my follow-up efforts on Chicago and its sub-urbs. The response rates were 43 percent for urban Chicago, 41 percent for downstate, and 47 percent for the metropolitan area, with an overall rate of 44 percent (225 out of 514). Despite limited resources, these rates compare reasonably well with those achieved with similar populations and in mail surveys generally.[31]

Many of the ideas for this project came from an earlier ethno-graphic study I conducted of special education classes in California elementary schools.[32] In important respects, this is an attempt to study more systematically and in a more quantitative form issues I identified in that earlier study. Results of this study are more compelling because they recapitulate and confirm observations I made in another state.

Further data supporting the arguments of this study are con-tained in the research of David Kirp and Peter Kuriloff.[33] While a graduate student at Berkeley, I was a research assistant for Kirp, and when I taught at Richmond College–CUNY and planned this study, I consulted with Kuriloff about a similar study he was conducting of Pennsylvania school psychologists. Although I have not rigorously tested the conclusions from this study on Kuriloff's data, his data tables for Pennsylvania support my Illionis conclusions.

As we enter the 1990s, one might object that the data for this study are too old to accurately inform a commentary on problems of testing and special education policy. There is no reason to think that conditions surrounding special education have changed since 1978, however. The major policy innovation was the Federal Education for All Handicapped Children Act passed in 1975, which mandates proce-dures for examining children and placing them in special education classes. The administrative machinery for enforcing the federal legisla-tion was in place at the time of the study.

One conclusion of my work is that provisions of the Federal Act will only be effective if they are enforced, because there are strong incentives at the school and district level to subvert them. Shortly after I left the field, the Chicago Public Schools went bankrupt, making resources even less available than they were at the time of my work. Once the Reagan administration took office, federal enthusiasm for enforcing provisions of PL 94-142 declined. Meanwhile, public opposi-tion to enforcement of the Act for fiscal reasons is more commonly heard.[34] There has been no increase in the amount spent on special education or on the number of children enrolled in programs in recent years.[35]

The stasis in special education policy suggests that this study was done at the high-water mark of concern for equity and due process in special education. It is likely that conditions have since deteriorated. If the age of my data introduces biases, they are in the direction of making my results unduly optimistic about conditions in special education. Because some of my conclusions are critical, this optimistic bias is acceptable.

The Structure of the Book

Chapter One introduces the role of the school psychologist, describing the special education selection process and showing that there are substantial differences in the way that process is applied to black and to white children. This chapter also shows that those differences mostly have to do with radical differences in testing practices between cities, where most blacks live, and in nonurban school districts.

Chapter Two describes the nature of the testing process in detail. This both introduces readers to the day-to-day life of school psychologists and lays out a key variable for this study: the time structure of school psychologists' work. In chapters One and Two I will argue that because the time structure of school psychology is so strongly controlled by the process of testing, psychologists will have difficulty continuing to give the requisite amount of time to each test if the volume of testing is allowed to increase.

In Chapter Three I begin discussing how psychologists work to avoid the acceleration of testing described in the first two chapters. In this portion of the book, I argue that although there are sharp differences in testing practices between city and suburb, this is not explained by differences in the structure of direct administrative control to which psychologists are subject. Individuals choose their rate of testing. The task is to understand how organizational conditions and personal characteristics shape this choice. The focus of this chapter is on the difference between an active and a passive approach to one's work in a bureaucracy. People who create a role for themselves are more successful at avoiding an acceleration in their testing work than are psychologists who are reactive to their surroundings. Thus, activeness is a key factor in explaining differences in testing practices.

Chapter Four shows how an active orientation leads to a number of strategies by which psychologists shape and expand their role. Key to the strategies psychologists use for role creation is covert action. Psychologists use deception and distortion in an effort to influence others in schools to accept their recommendations. One of the questions this raises is how does violation of the norms of testing for purposes of enhancing the strength of one's argument about how a case should be resolved differ from situations in which rushed testing violates those same norms.

Chapter Five argues that these normative violations have to be seen in relationship to the professional values psychologists bring to their work. There are two professional orientations or segments in the occupation; rushed testing is concentrated in what I call the school-oriented segment. Members of the other segment tend to bring a more transactional approach to their work and seem more likely to bend the rules to influence school politics and case outcomes. Norms that govern testing should not be treated as rigid controls. Rather, they are malleable and open to interpretation. School-oriented people who justify hurried testing claim that tests are objective, scientific measures, and that one can shorten them, just as one could shorten a ruler, without changing their capacity to measure. This reasoning ignores the ambivalence professional psychologists voice about the accuracy of tests given without attention to the context of administration. Clinical psychologists tend to view tests as instruments of creativity and discovery, and it is more in this spirit that profession-oriented psychologists violate formal norms.

Although professional values encourage organizational activism and an artful approach to testing, Chapter Five ends by rejecting the notion that any particular values inform the professional orientation I describe. Professionalism focuses on an organizational process, not on content or substance. Chapter Six shows what this process means by describing the structure of control in ACORN, a special education cooperative. Chapter Seven summarizes the arguments of the book.

CHAPTER 1

The Role of the School Psychologist

School psychologists are marginal actors in public schools. When the main purpose of the schools—teaching children in regular instructional programs—conflicts with the formal responsibilities of the school psychologist, there is pressure to subordinate the specialized, peripheral interests of these practitioners to the greater institutional problems central to the success of the whole institution. In this, school psychologists face the same problem confronted by all of those who work in special education and, indeed, in any of those programs on the "periphery" of public education.[1]

The notion that there is a core of public school activity contrasted with its periphery is ironic. A substantial amount of money is spent on peripheral programs like interscholastic athletics, adult education, student extracurricular activities, school libraries, bilingual and multicultural programs, in-service instruction, and special education. The tremendous increases in state and federal funding and in student enrollments over the past twenty years have made school psychology and special education the major areas of growth in public schools, growth made more significant by the fact that the institution of education has otherwise been suffering through a period of retrenchment. School systems can hardly pretend any longer that they could do without special education. A large portion of the school population is involved in the array of programs I am calling peripheral. Many people consider their involvement in specific programs to be critical parts of their school experience.

Important as they may be to students, peripheral programs come under pressure to subordinate the stated primary responsibilities of their programs or of their role to the needs and demands of the core. They are subject to attack during times of fiscal crisis. Some programs, interscholastic sports and adult education, for instance, have been eliminated. The attacks have been more subtle in special education. The attempt to meet core program needs undercuts the peripheral programs. In some districts, the activities and goals of special classes and support personnel can be, and routinely are, diverted to support the needs of mainstream classroom programs. Special education stops being special.[2]

Because these programs are viewed as secondary in importance, we—researchers and the public—do not know a lot about them, partly because social scientists who study the overall dynamics of educational institutions tend to accept the governing dogma of public education. Either the social scientists ignore the dynamics or they consider that research focused on peripheral programs is unimportant.[3] Yet nearly any scheme one might offer to reform or improve schools will propose creating new programs that are partly independent of regular instructional programs. Any such programs are likely to find some of their goals at odds with those of the regular instructional program—if only because they propose to repair the failures of that program.

Thus, although peripheral school programs have received little research attention, effective school reform requires a better understanding of how people who work in these areas cope with the marginality of their organizational role. One set of questions asks how these programs may be defended against fiscal reductions and other kinds of frontal attack on their legitimacy and continued existence. A more subtle group of questions recognizes that being peripheral carries advantages as well as handicaps. In many districts, however, school psychologists are key behind-the-scenes actors consulting with higher-level administrators on major policy issues, helping to resolve potentially explosive conflicts across levels of the organizational hierarchy, and providing freelance consultation to classroom teachers on any program development problems or potentially explosive interactional problems that they confront in class. The questions to be answered here have to do with the strategic advantages and disadvantages inherent in peripheral roles and how one may wield maximal influence operating in a low-profile position.

Questions about how to enhance the influence of peripheral roles partly involve power issues. The core-periphery metaphor is attractive because it suggests why one set of programs in the core, perhaps no larger in budget or staff, can so dominate the other programs in an institution. In any battle, those forces that occupy central ground find it easier to coordinate their movements and isolate and dominate a fragmented opponent. Although regular educators may resent this martial imagery, people in marginal programs routinely worry about conflict, threat, and dangers to their security that might arise were they to run afoul of prominent people in the regular school program. With these worries, it may be difficult for them to define their school role as a simple reflection of the impersonal descriptions of tasks and technical expertise associated with their job titles. The content of their role tends to be shaped by the demands and intimidation that flow from the core programs.[4] It is important to ask what power resources are available to those in marginal roles so that they can neutralize the corrosive effects on their work roles of demands made by members of the core.

If the contrast between core and periphery were only a matter of conflict, it would be relatively simple to guarantee autonomy to small programs. All one would have to do is place these programs in a separate building, give their administrators independent fiscal authority, and impose draconian legal controls that would prevent the raiding of the peripheral treasury by core institutional officials.

In reality, peripheral programs must usually coordinate their work closely with the regular program, and to a greater or lesser extent their success and effectiveness are dependent on the successes of the core program. If students are always truant, athletic programs will have trouble attracting participants. If many students are failing or disrupting classes, then special programs aimed to help out a minority are likely to have trouble finding criteria that tell which students are most worthy of help. Large numbers of needy students will inevitably be neglected.

Special educators in troubled districts often have to decide whether to serve the students who fail most spectacularly in the regular program and most desperately need help—for the sake of both the students and their teachers—or whether to help those children most likely to benefit from the focused technology of the special program. A program that chooses only students it can easily teach may find all of its work destroyed later when those students return to a disrupted, chaotic regular school program. Effectiveness in most peripheral programs—or at least in the special education programs school psychologists serve— depends on an orderly regular school program for its own success.

This book discusses the problems and strategies of those who fill a marginal role. A large part of this discussion concerns the sources of leverage available. We will see that this leverage is related in part to the kind of school system people work for. It also is related to the amount of interpersonal support marginal-role members give to each other and to their personal determination to chart a course independent of that urged on them by representatives of the regular school core "culture."

What School Psychologists Do

School psychologists are part of the special education apparatus in most schools. Special education programs include classes for exceptional students on both ends of the ability continuum—gifted and handicapped—although most of the programs serve children with some sort of physical, cognitive, or emotional impairment. These handicaps vary in severity and, consequently, the children involved are to differing degrees isolated from regular school classes. The majority of handicapped children attend special classes only part of the time. They are enrolled in regular classes but go to special classrooms located in the same buildings that serve children in the mainstream. This is more true today than it was twenty years ago when most mildly handicapped children were removed entirely from the regular school program and where many severely handicapped children were excluded entirely from public schools.

Table 1 showed national enrollment trends in special education enrollments with about 8½ percent of all students in special classes by 1980. Enrollment growth has flattened out during the 1980s and has remained about constant through the decade.

The two largest groups of special education students are the speech impaired and the learning disabled. If breakdown statistics were available for 1963, we would see that learning disabled programs are a new innovation, with the category introduced only in the late 1950s. In earlier days, many students who today are in classes for the learning disabled would have been placed in classes for the mildly retarded, if they were included at all. Classes for the speech-impaired are of relatively minor importance for my discussion since these classes generally only involve removal of students from class for a few hours per week and participation is rarely stigmatizing or long-lasting.

Classes for the learning disabled, mentally retarded, and emotionally disturbed are different because children usually are removed either for the academic instruction portion of the day or they are in special classes full time. Special classes often are held in regular classroom buildings to facilitate movement back and forth between regular and special classes—this is called mainstreaming. However, the special classes are normally set off from the regular classrooms in an unused portion of the school or in portable classrooms placed on the playground.

For children with more severe handicaps, there are independent special education schools that draw students from larger cachement areas than those of the regular schools.

Generally, special education teachers who work in regular school buildings are employed by the special education department of local school districts. Self-contained special schools generally are run as an independent special education organization. In suburbs and rural areas, these independent organizations are special education cooperatives (Illinois), intermediate units (Pennsylvania), or education service centers (Connecticut).[5] In large cities like Chicago, the special education organization comprises one or more separate departments that operate as units equivalent to the division of primary or secondary instruction.

This complex administrative arrangement means school psychologists may have any of several administrative locations. About two-thirds of the people I surveyed work in primary, secondary, or unified regular school programs. They spend most of their time physically in regular school buildings, and it usually means their time is spent helping to process students into and out of special education classes. This is the group of psychologists I shall talk about most in this book.

Of the remaining school psychologists, 22 percent are employed directly by special education cooperatives, 12 percent work entirely for special schools, and 3 percent work as supervisors or administrators. Psychologists who work in special schools usually work with teachers to design programs or work individually with students. Psychologists who work for special education cooperatives may work in special schools and do administrative work. More likely, they service several regular school districts, each too small to employ their own psychologist, and do the same sort of work as psychologists who work wholly in regular schools.

When psychologists work in regular schools, they serve a student population of from one thousand to six thousand with the mean being about three thousand students. If they work at the high school level, this generally works out to two or three schools. At the elementary level, psychologists routinely serve from four to seven schools. Two-thirds of the psychologists serve four or more schools.

Because their efforts are so diluted, school psychologists have little time to devote to any one child. They are, at best, occasional visitors to the schools they serve. This is especially true of those psychologists who serve elementary schools—they may visit each school one day per week or even once every other week, with one additional day per week taken up in office work at the administrative center.[6] High school psychologists are more stable because they have fewer buildings to cover. They also may have a lighter testing load than do elementary school psychologists, since learning disabled and educable mentally retarded children usually are identified in the third through fifth grades.[7] By the time students reach high school, most special education students have already been classified for years and do not require extensive diagnostic workups. They also are moving into a system that routinely tracks the majority of students so that no unusual administrative procedures of the kind elementary schools undertake are required to provide them with special instruction. Thus, high school psychologists are more likely to work intensively on the problems of particular students or on some long-term school program.

The Special Education Selection Process

Most school psychologists who work in regular schools, and especially those who work at the elementary level, participate in an almost continual process of examining students who have been referred for or already placed in a special education program. That process is elaborate. Jane Mercer studied it and reported that there is an extensive winnowing that goes on before children are referred for thorough evaluation.[8] Generally, children are not referred until they have caused concern for regular teachers over a span of several years, during which time they may have been held back. Eventually, teachers and principals, sometimes in consultation with the local special teacher, complete a form requesting a child study.

A child study is an examination by members of an interdisciplinary team that includes a school social worker, school nurse, speech or special education teacher, and a school psychologist. Each specialist gathers data relevant to his or her specialty, and then they collectively discuss a recommendation to the regular school staff and to a child's family. Although a number of professionals make up this team, the Berk, Bridges, and Shih study of Chicago placement practices reported that IQ test scores were by far the most significant predictor of a student's case disposition.[9] Because IQ testing is the province of the school psychologist, the psychological evaluation appears to be the most consequential part of the child study process. In practice, local variation is found here, especially as one moves from city to suburb, that depends on the orientation of the psychologist and the relative influence of the different members of the special education team.

Ideally, the interdisciplinary team is a diagnostic unit. The team receives a verbal or written report from a school principal stating the reasons for referral. These reasons usually focus on a child's classroom or playground problems, so it falls on the interdisciplinary team to look for underlying causes of problems. The social worker normally interviews the family, the nurse reviews the child's physiological history, the speech pathologist or special teacher reviews the child's pedagogical difficulties, and the psychologist evaluates the cognitive and emotional functions of the child. Because other educators are not trained observers in these specialties, one might expect a substantial number of children referred to present simple learning failures with no identifiable social, physiological, or psychological problem. This is suggested in Mercer's finding that in the 1960s sample, only about 10 percent of the children referred for evaluation in Riverside, California, were actually placed in classes for the retarded.[10]

Psychologists I surveyed reported a placement rate much higher than Mercer's, suggesting that diagnosis and careful sorting of students was a less important part of their work. Among 60 percent of the psychologists, at least one-half of the children referred to them are actually placed in special education classes. In Chicago, about one-quarter of the psychologists report placing over 80 percent of their referrees. This fit with my impressions as I observed psychologists. A large number of the children who are referred receive routinized treatment. In an earlier study, I observed an interdisciplinary team in California that disposed of cases at a rate of about one a minute. These represent cases for which some sort of agreement has been reached beforehand between regular and special education staff about what should happen. The child studies performed in these cases are often quickly administered and are almost perfunctory. Other cases are much more carefully considered, sometimes because all participants are concerned about a child, or because some districts always examine cases carefully. Staff members hope to gain new insights through a thoughtful evaluation.

Referrals may be made primarily because of school politics. I spoke with one principal who referred thirty students a semester—about ten times the number the special class could admit—because he wanted people "downtown" to know how tough things were in his school. Other principals, as a placating move, might refer a child a particular teacher cannot stand. The team may be presented with more students than it can carefully evaluate or place, some of whom are referred without explanation. In these instances, the team may spend considerable time discussing the cases just trying to figure out what the regular staff wants done.

The Marginality Factor

Where does marginality fit into this process? Ideally, a diagnostic team will be child-centered. It will try to learn why a child has been referred, what the most appropriate setting is for that child, and what sort of programming would be most helpful. From the team perspective, certain children are especially needy of their help—children with serious psychodynamic problems, extreme psycholinguistic disorders, or children with serious physical disabilities. There is no assurance, however, that these children will be the ones referred. Children with serious emotional or communication disorders may respond in regular classrooms by withdrawing or by compensating for their difficulty by excelling in areas unrelated to their disabilities. In either case, teachers may then feel that other, more aggressive, children ought to receive special education services first.

This presents two problems for the special team. First, what can it do to educate the regular school staff about the problems most appropriately served by special education? Can it convince them to refer the kinds of students special educators think they can help most? Second, given that regular educators refer students who are disruptive, what leeway does the team have to refuse special class placements for these children?

The law mandates that the interdisciplinary team not place children in special classes if they could function adequately in a regular class. In reality, interdisciplinary teams usually place children to the extent that there are openings in special classes. If all of the children referred are discipline problems, then the special class will be filled with discipline problems. Few school districts mount serious efforts to screen the regular school population in search of those students who would most benefit from special education services. After children are evaluated by the interdisciplinary team, the team rarely conducts follow-up studies to see whether the treatments it has prescribed are carried out. There is a mandated annual case review for all placed children, but usually this is a perfunctory study. Forty-two percent of the psychologists I surveyed report following up on students less than 25 percent of the time; 63 percent follow up less than 50 percent of the time.

Ideally, the interdisciplinary team would be more involved with problem children in two ways. First, team members would have an ongoing relationship with regular school staff members so they could discuss cases as teachers begin to encounter problems. Early involvement allows them to help teachers find ways to combat difficulties and maintain children in regular classes. This involvement would also allow specialists to participate in preselecting students for a more extensive diagnostic review. Second, team members would work closely with special education teachers to help design and revise problems and to coordinate their reintegration into the main stream.

This can happen only if psychologists are released from their gatekeeper roles and are allowed to work on a freelance basis with teachers and principals as problems arise. Some psychologists do have this freedom. About half the psychologists I surveyed spend less than one-quarter of their time at work testing children. Nearly 60 percent spend between 25 percent and 50 percent of their time working with teachers in some capacity.

There is, however, a powerful tendency for testing to crowd out other activities. As people give more tests, their time becomes more structured with mandated activities making up the child study process. The more tests psychologists and other members of the interdisciplinary team give, the less time remains for informal conversations with teachers about children. This reduces the human touch in the child study process and emphasizes the application of impersonal measurement instruments. The process becomes more routinized, formally bureaucratic, and automatic.

Testing and Race

The psychologists I interviewed report a steady pressure from regular school staff for them to increase the volume of testing they carry out. This sometimes happens because an atmosphere of crisis pervades the regular program, and its staff hopes to use special classes to relieve itself of difficult children. It sometimes happens because administrators make policy decisions that require large groups of students to be moved from one program to another, not realizing the time it will take to reevaluate the children involved. Whatever the source of the pressure, people in the regular program do not understand or value the school psychologists' consultative services as much as their administrative services. The psychologists become marginal to the extent they capitulate and expand their testing role.

I use this language of defeat because their entire job structure changes when the volume of testing carried out by psychologists increases. As the volume of testing increases, there is not only less time available for consultation, the very process of testing also changes. The correlation between the number of tests a psychologist performs each year and the hours devoted to each child study is $-.38$, well beyond the .001 level of significance (see Table 2). As psychologists do more child studies per year, the time devoted to each child study becomes shorter and the process becomes more automatic and formal.

This relationship is easy to understand. When psychologists test at a relatively low rate, each child study is given in about the same amount of time—six hours—for reasons I will explain in Chapter Two.

TABLE 2. **Correlations between Testing Rates and Measures of Race and Class in Psychologists' School Districts**

	Number of Child Studies Psychologists Conduct per Year	Number of Hours Psychologists Devote to Each Child Study
Number of child studies per year	1.00 (200)	−.38*** (199)
Percentage of student body, black	.38*** (200)	−.31*** (199)
Percentage of parents, professionals	.26*** (189)	−.32*** (188)
Percentage of parents, unemployed	−.33*** (192)	.32*** (191)

*** = p < .001

This time will be somewhat longer in difficult cases and somewhat shorter when tests are finished quickly. Low-functioning children, for example, may complete fewer items than higher-functioning children, and so the test may take less time. Meanwhile, a certain amount of time must be spent traveling, in meetings, and conducting other necessary business. There must be some point at which the number of tests one gives fills up all of one's remaining time.

Because the average psychologist in my sample spends a bit under one-half of his or her time testing, three to four test sessions per week is a practical limit on the number of child studies that can be carried out at six hours per child study. Having reached this limit and continuing to receive demands for testing, psychologists can only increase their volume of work by shortening the test session or spending less time consulting with parents or other school officials. Among high-volume testers, the mean time devoted to each child study not infrequently drops to three hours or less per session.

The ratchet effect that increases the volume of testing and lowers the amount of time devoted to each test has destructive effects. As they have less free time, psychologists feel less in control of their work and more controlled by administrative pressures. Because the role of the school psychologist is so powerfully and symbolically associated with testing, it is testing that takes over when a psychologist becomes passive. This passivity is not innocent—test scores are the most powerful variable predicting whether a referred child will be placed in a special education class.[11] The increase in the amount of testing means psychologists are giving less attention to the time-consuming business of talking to the child, his parents, and his teachers to learn how the current problems came to pass. More and more, the psychologist depends on the test and its objective norms to make decisions about a child's fate.

Brusque testing is unfortunate for any child. It is especially troublesome in my sample because the psychologists with both the highest volume and rate of testing worked in those school districts that had the largest fraction of minority and low-income students (see Table 2). As the percentage of black students rises in psychologists' school districts, the number of child studies rises dramatically ($r = .44$, $p < .001$) and the time devoted to each child study drops ($r = -.29$, $p < .001$). There is a similarly powerful relationship between measures of parents' social class [How many parents in the district are professionals? How many are unemployed?] and measures of the rate and volume of testing. These correlations are enormous for sociological research where correlations of .20 are usually about the strongest relationships one will find.

Testing is most controversial with minority students because there is fear that tests are culturally biased against them and because minority students typically test poorly even under laboratory conditions.[12] These are the children who need to be most carefully studied by school psychologists. That they receive such hurried testing is a straightforward demonstration of the institutional racism that continues to be built into special education despite the elaborate due process reforms of PL 94-142, The Education for All Handicapped Children Act. That law was explicitly formulated to prevent the misclassification of minority children, a problem Mercer and others found to be epidemic in the special education classes of the 1950s and 1960s.[13] My data suggest that an important effect of the new federal law was to make people think the problem of racial overrepresentation in special education classes had been solved when in fact there had been little change in the treatment of minority students.

Two Special Education Systems: Urban and Nonurban

How could these enormous racial differences in special education classification procedures continue despite a decade of public outcry, legislative reform, and litigation aimed at preventing the use of culturally biased tests on minorities for purposes of special class placement? The main reason is that prior to the 1960s, there was no special education to speak of outside of the major cities. Special education meant classes for the educable (or mildly) mentally retarded, which primarily enrolled low income and black children, who lived in cities. Special education enrollments exploded between 1960 and 1980. This happened in two ways. First, classes for the learning disabled were created, allowing children to be placed in special education without suffering the stigma attached to the more global label, "mentally retarded." Second, special education classes were added in districts that did not have them before—districts that enrolled higher proportions of white children and children from wealthier homes. As these children were included in special education classes, aggregate statistics that showed racial overrepresentation changed, showing a more equitable pattern of special education enrollment. Because many large cities (like Chicago) have a large number of minority students, it is understandable that special education classes there would be heavily colonized by minority children.

Most of the race differences in the number of tests psychologists conduct and the amount of time they devote to each test session are explained by the contrast between urban and nonurban education. Compare the data in Table 3 with those in Table 2, where correlations among the same variables were given without controlling for whether psychologists had urban or nonurban work settings. In Table 3, with the control in place, there is no longer a significant correlation between race and either measure of testing practice. Social class, as measured by the proportion of parents holding professional jobs in a psycholo-

TABLE 3. *Correlations between Measures of Race and Class in Psychologists' School Districts, Controlling for Whether Psychologists Work in Urban or Nonurban School Districts*

	Number of Child Studies Psychologists Conduct per Year	Number of Hours Psychologists Devote to Each Child Study
Number of child studies per year	1.00	−.15*
Percentage of student body, black	−.01	−.08
Percentage of parents, professionals	.03	.14*
Percentage of parents, unemployed	−.01 (192)	−.11 (191)

* = p < .05

gist's school district, remains significant, but is not significantly related if we measure it by considering the proportion of parents who are unemployed.

Why does school psychology vary between urban and nonurban areas? There may be a different administrative structure in Chicago than prevails outside of the city and that city psychologists are forced to test quickly. If this is the case, it is not picked up in my survey, shown in Figure 1, which reflects no difference in the structure of supervision reported by psychologists in Chicago and elsewhere. Neither group of psychologists reports close supervision either by administrators in the special education system or by those who oversee their services in the regular program. Psychologists in Chicago were slightly more likely to work alone, answering to no one in either a special or regular school hierarchy, which suggests that they are not closely controlled by an elaborate administrative system that mandates a particular rate of testing.

My interviews suggested that psychologists share a similar formal administrative situation in Chicago and elsewhere in the state. The differences between urban and nonurban areas are due 1) to the kinds of people who are recruited to school psychology and 2) to differences in the occupational cultures that prevail in the two areas.

These differences are the subject of Chapters Five and Six, and so I will not discuss them at length here. Briefly, there are two distinct segments or orientations among school psychologists. Members of the profession-oriented segment, concentrated in the suburbs, view themselves as clinical or community psychologists and view everyone in schools—students, teachers, and administrators—as their clients. Members of the the school-oriented segment, concentrated in Chicago, view themselves as educators, probably because many once worked as teachers and have been promoted up through the ranks to become school psychologists.

Members of the school-oriented segment tend to think that their primary job is to provide support to the regular educational system. This means that if they are asked to do a particular job—test x number of students, for example—they ought to carry out that task supportively and cooperatively. Their attitude of cooperation and acceptance leads them to accept the administrative structure of the schools as fixed and bureaucratically partitioned. Consequently, they see other, more powerful people in the system as the main decision makers, deciding what people should do at work. Because they are part of a large, complex organizational system, they see others—their invisible supervisors?—as primarily responsible for whatever consequences result from

Amount of Supervision by Regular Program Supervisor

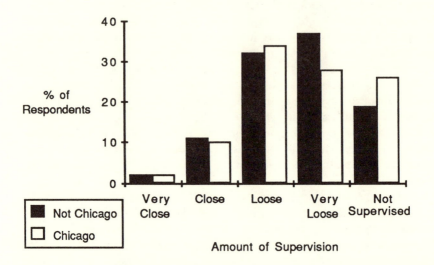

Amount of Supervision by Special Education Supervisor

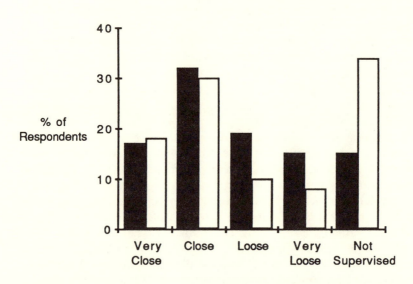

school psychologists' work. Theirs is essentially a bureaucratic job responsible for carrying out certain elaborate administrative procedures. Although they examine students, these children are somewhat distant, impersonal figures for psychologists. Objectivity is an important value that guides their child studies. Often these psychologists do not want to know too much about the students they see or the situations that lead to referrals for fear that this context-based knowledge would bias their test results.

Profession-oriented psychologists are more inclined to believe that student problems in schools are products of conflictual interactional situations. These may be rooted in a child's family, and they may result in personality disorders. They may also, however, be products of school conflicts that are sometimes quite removed from the child in question. These conflicts may arise from the way a teacher relates to a class; to disruption in a school caused by conflicts among groups of students or between principals and teachers; or even to district-wide, disruptive policy decisions. Children are sometimes scapegoats in these conflicts, and special education referrals can be a consequence. Sometimes the problems teachers complain about represent students' efforts to defend themselves in situations where they feel powerless. Other times family conflicts and school hostilities interact, leading a child to act out hurt and anger or fail in school. The point is that "objective" tests cannot tell why a child is failing in school. Only more complete knowledge about the situation of his or her failure can show the roots of the problem and what kinds of intervention are appropriate. Sometimes the appropriate intervention is for a psychologist to work with a teacher on his or her problems or to intervene with higher administrators when an employee is causing difficulty for others in the school system.

These two perspectives are radically different, and they have radically different implications for the evolution of school psychologists' roles. One reason for this is self-evident. The two ideologies suggest that school psychologists should be engaged in sharply different activities. The school-oriented psychologist tends to accept educators as *the* experts in instruction. Teachers and regular program administrators should call the tune and decide what the special education diagnostic team ought to do. School psychologists gain their authority from being experts in objective psychometric measurement, and that is what they should spend their time doing. Indeed, that is what people from this orientation do.

Psychologists from the profession-oriented segment test to the extent regular educators require that they do so. But for many of these psychologists, testing is in part an impediment to the real business of talking to people and helping them with their school problems. Although they may be a bit cynical about testing, most members of this group that I interviewed also acknowledge that testing is their bread and butter, the basis of their legitimacy to act in schools. Psychologists also are powerless within schools—they are marginal. Consequently, a major part of their time is spent struggling to reduce the load of testing they do, expand their access to the social life of their schools, gain acceptance for a more diverse menu of psychological services, and increase the amount of time they spend with children and teachers.

The main argument of this book is that these work orientations are responsible for the different testing patterns we see in school psychologists between those who serve black children and white children or between those working in urban and nonurban schools. Urban school psychologists allow their work to be defined by their regular school colleagues. A consequence is that their testing load slowly climbs, and the speed of each test session increases. Their administrative passivity is an important reason for this acceleration of testing. Profession-oriented psychologists avoid this acceleration only to constantly struggle to broaden their tasks, to affect interactional patterns, and to limit the power of the regular system. The marginal status of the occupation means that only if practitioners see schools as malleable environments and their work as political or strategic can they hope to prevent testing from taking over and squeezing out a more child-centered approach to the work.

This argument of mine is one other observers of school psychology have suggested in the past.[14] That the profession orientation might be widespread among school psychologists, however, is an assertion that many professional psychologists greet with disbelief. Because skepticism about school psychology is so widespread and the methods of what Sarason calls a transactional approach—a conception that sees cognitive handicaps as inextricably tied to the contexts in which they are identified as problems—are so poorly understood I will devote many of the coming pages to a meticulous description of it.[15]

The main theme in the remainder of this book is that recruitment patterns, organizational strategies, and occupational culture work are the main variables determining the relationship between organizational marginality and task effectiveness. People in peripheral roles often feel threatened and at risk of being punished by those in core roles. To some extent, these fears are realistic. As I showed in an earlier study, regular educators can deny special educators meaningful control over the preselection of candidates for special classes by limiting their access to regular classrooms, and they can make it difficult to reintegrate children into the main stream.[16] These fears also reflect the isolation and loneliness felt by people whose work others do not understand or value. Conforming to stereotypes held by people in the core of what one ought to be doing, or performing services to make the lives of core members easier is one way of feeling comfortable at work. We wish to understand how school psychologists come to feel comfortable in their differentness, as well as what follows when they try to be "one of the educators."

CHAPTER 2

One Psychologist's Day

Psychometric testing has a mystique. In our technological society, advanced education is one of the signposts of success, and people believe that to become a doctor or a lawyer or a university professor, one needs to have a high IQ. Conversely, one of the profound stigmata in our society is that of stupidity.[1] Schoolchildren caricature stupidity by aping the abnormalities of those whose mental retardation is coupled with severe motor difficulties. We pretend mental retardation is clearly visible as a physical sign. The vast majority of cognitive handicaps are invisible and can be disguised with greater or lesser effort by their victims.[2] Indeed, the modern concepts of mental retardation and learning disabilities are artifacts of psychometric tests. We know that there is a distribution of intelligence and a low tail to that distribution only because we have intelligence tests.[3] Thus when we speak of people being stupid, we are referring to behavior that is concretized by the judgments school people have made and objectively legitimized, thanks to scientific testing.

That mystique presents a problem for this book. One audience for this research is certain to be people who make their living working either as school psychologists or as professional psychologists—teaching, doing research, or conducting psychotherapy. Those people are used to thinking about testing as a process carefully hemmed in by guidelines about procedure, norms that govern the interpretation of results, and knowledge that has been built with meticulous attention to the canons of the experimental method and scientific objectivity.

Readers who are not trained as psychologists may well have a different experience of treating tests as carefully constructed measurement instruments, yielding precise results that can be used for complex statistical studies. I refer here to members of my own discipline, sociology, who use test results to study the effects of education or who attack the methodology of tests, trying to demonstrate ways that they are biased against minorities.

In this book, I will generally downplay or even ignore these traditions of rigor. I treat intelligence testing as behavior. That is, I am most interested in what school psychologists do at work, how they justify their work—I want to know what motivates them—and what interpretations they place on events and on the results of their test sessions. To some extent, I intentionally exaggerate my role as a naive observer so that I can convey to readers, knowledgeable and uninformed ones alike, what it is like to be a school psychologist.

The more important reason that I downplay the tradition of rigor in psychometrics is because trying to judge the methodological quality of what school psychologists do at work falls into one of the classic traps plaguing social engineers. Those of us who try to precisely understand and explain social phenomena tend to think that abstract plans and technical procedures carried out in the sterility of a laboratory setting will or ought to be applied in practice exactly as they were designed in the lab. Lindblom and Cohen, along with any number of other chroniclers of social policy experiments, have shown that technical plans almost never are carried out in conformity with the dreams of researchers.[4] Practitioners rarely use technical procedures because they want to be good scientists; rather, they want to get things done. What they want to accomplish with a technical procedure may depart sharply and surprisingly from what designers of those procedures had in mind. Kitchen knives and forks are used for all manner of tasks other than eating—that is why they are so often bent out of shape. The same is true of a technical procedure like intelligence testing. One is foolish to think that those giving intelligence tests in schools will or ought to administer those tests to produce the most careful, finely calibrated measurements of individual characteristics possible.

If we are worried that intelligence testing is misused in schools and that minority children, among others, are targets of inappropriate and cynical administrative procedures, we must begin by asking what we mean by testing and what kinds of procedures are a problem. We will see in the coming pages that school psychologists routinely mangle those finely tuned procedures written into test manuals. But not infrequently that mangling is carried out for child-centered reasons. I will argue that giving slavish attention to the instructions one receives with a testing kit is a sure way to produce results unfair to children. Readers will miss the point if they dismiss what those I interviewed do or say, concluding that they are psychologically unsophisticated or incompetent simply because they present details of the testing process in a way that is incorrect, given the understandings that rule in research settings. True, these people may not deserve to pass a Ph.D. oral exam if they think their techniques are methodologically proper. But they have direct knowledge about why children are perceived as problems in schools, how children go about failing, and what they, as relatively detached observers, can do to make the situation better. Sometimes helping out means using intelligence tests as weapons in some sort of administrative struggle. At other times, helping out means minimizing the wasted time and bureaucratic clutter meticulous psychometric examinations produce.

A look at testing as it is done in schools, and jettisoning rigid procedural controls, will eventually present us with the problem of how we possibly can protect against abuses of testing. An advantage of psychometric rigor is that it constrains testers to practice in a manner prescribed by thoughtful, experienced professionals situated outside of schools. Once we throw away these guidelines, how can we tell whether an instance of unconventional testing represents concern or callousness?

Developing the capacity to make such distinctions is one of the main tasks of this book. We cannot tell whether a school psychologist is doing a good or bad job by looking at the content of his or her work. Someone who is methodologically careful can be a person attuned to the interaction of cognitive and emotional problems and skilled at communicating to educators how school programs might be adjusted to help a child. Or such a careful person can be fascinated with procedures and indifferent to the violence schools can inflict on children referred to special classes and labeled incompetent. We can evaluate school psychology only indirectly.

I shall use indirect measures of two kinds in this book. The first kind involves what Stinchcombe, studying steel plant engineers in Third World countries, calls time budgets.[5] Steel plant engineers are effective at increasing production only if they have time free to work creatively on finding ways to prevent equipment breakdowns. This time creativity is limited by committee meetings and bureaucratic chores. To compare the productivity of engineers in different settings, Stinchcombe observes engineers at work, determines how long it takes to do different tasks, and then uses surveys to learn how much time engineers spend carrying out each task in various factories. Those engineers who have the most time available for creative problem-solving tasks also work at the most productive steel plants. Notice that Stinchcombe has no idea whether specific engineers are actually doing creative work or whether they are particularly good at problem solving. What he knows is that engineers at plants who have little time for this kind of activity are not working creatively.

I use the same approach with school psychologists. This chapter is mostly devoted to describing what a psychologist does during a child study—a process that includes testing, scoring the products of a test session, and holding discussions with parents and school officials where results are explained. The description of tasks that follows allows us to create a time budget for school psychologists, distinguishing those who have time to pay attention to the politics of student referrals from those who do not. As we saw in Chapter One, time differences vary significantly among psychologists serving many black and white children. This and Chapters Three and Four show why that finding is important.

The second measure I will use to evaluate school psychologists focuses on the power of socialization and organizational structure to shape psychologists' work behavior. We saw in Chapter One that urban and nonurban psychologists test in sharply different ways. Yet that this difference could not be accounted for administratively. Urban psychologists, like their nonurban counterparts, are loosely supervised and left free to set their own schedule. If they test rapidly, it looks as though they are choosing to do so. This oversimplifies the psychological situations urban psychologists face. We will see that there are differences in personal work history, in career advancement patterns, and in constraints and risks that psychologists may face in their school assignments that sharply distinguish urban from nonurban psychologists.

In the remainder of this chapter, I present the field notes I wrote as I travelled with Sam Osterweis, the psychologist in a suburban school district outside of Chicago. I occasionally depart from my daily log to provide background, to offer comments and interpretations necessary to show how Osterweis's behavior illustrates some general feature of the role of the school psychologist, or to comment on what would be lost if some part of the child study process were eliminated to save time. I chose Osterweis because, in contrast to most of the other ACORN psychologists we shall meet in coming chapters, he believes that psychometric tests are truly objective measures. He tries to follow strict methodological guidelines as much as a large school caseload will allow.

His example is important because, as we shall see in Chapters Five and Six, an ideological dispute about how to practice divides school psychologists into two segments or orientations. One group is concentrated in urban settings and asserts that tests are and should be treated as objective measures that stand on their own. Members of this group prefer to insulate themselves somewhat from the ongoing interaction of schools they serve, partly to ensure against biasing their results.

Members of the other group tend to be more cynical about the accuracy and value of tests. They find reason to doubt their accuracy, think they are overvalued by educators and that they distract attention from the more important fact that many student problems grow out of conflicts and other disturbances at home or in the organizational life of the schools.

Of the people I interviewed who took the objectivist position. Osterweis is the person whose work assignment gave him the most free time to decide exactly what should be included in a child study session. His choices and interpretations are not necessarily a proxy vote for everyone who shares his ideological position. At the same time, however, the actual tasks that go into a child study do not change much from one school psychologist to another. Among the thirty-three people I observed at work representing both persuasions, there was little variation in terms of the intelligence, achievement, and projective tests they used in child study sessions. Similarly, state and federal law mandates that the results of a child study must be reported to parents and shared with an interdisciplinary team, and that the psychologist must participate in creating an Individualized Educational Plan (IEP) for each student. In this chapter, readers should pay attention to the apparent inflexibility of the time requirements built into each task.

What I call Osterweis's perspective mostly refers to the attitude he and most of the urban school psychologists I interviewed bring to the child study process. The attitude includes a desire to be objective and precise in one's work, somewhat restrained in one's warmth in relating to subjects, and disengaged from the social complexities of the schools one serves. The psychologist must be friendly and supportive to subjects to build sufficient rapport for the student to be comfortable in the test setting. But Osterweis also believes one must maintain a certain distance so that one's perceptions of the children will not be colored by one's desire to have the child study produce some foreordained outcome. Being too involved emotionally with one's subjects or with educators who are seeking some outcome from the evaluation process might bias one's judgment. Osterweis seeks to be an objective, uninvolved observer. Tests are essential tools for him in maintaining his disengagement.

A Sample Child Evaluation Session

Sam Osterweis is the school psychologist for the small, white, working-class community of Richmond. Many of the families in the school district have recently migrated from Appalachia to this area, and few parents have received a high school education. Many families are fundamentalist Christians and they tend to be suspicious of the schools. This, coupled with frequent conflicts at the area high school between local children and black students from the next town has led the alliance between parents and schools to be uneasy at best. In this setting, Osterweis's brisk, clear-cut, technical way of acting the role of school psychologist serves local interests perfectly.

Osterweis worked for a number of years as the psychometrician on a large research project on neurological handicaps at a local university, and from this he became fully convinced of the accuracy of tests and the important contribution testing can make in understanding psychological problems. He tries to hold as constant as he can the many qualities of the setting in which he observes children. This includes the kind of room in which he tests, the neutrality of his interaction with the subject, and the content and order of tests he uses. He finds that observing children in exactly the same setting in which he has observed hundreds of others makes the unique qualities of each child stand out. He thinks this makes it easier for him to thread together clues gained from different test items and to form a theory about the structure of a subject's personality and the interpersonal strains the subject is now facing.

This emphasis on the value of a standard test setting and absolute neutrality in the manner in which one interacts with subjects is widely shared among psychologists I interviewed. Other psychologists—I only found this among people working in Chicago—so value the standard setting that they refuse to test children anywhere but in their office. It seemed to me that it would be uncomfortable and rather formal for a child to have to travel to a central office to be tested. My respondents explained that it allows the psychologist more freedom to use the test session as an opportunity to observe. They also said that it is particularly important to them to be nondirective as they interact with subjects, and a standard setting makes this easier to achieve. Osterweis's concern with standardizing the setting and the technique by which he administered the various test batteries gave me a sense of mechanical precision in his interview technique, a quality he shared with others I observed, and a sense that each moment of the interview is carefully and unchangeably scheduled.

This day, Osterweis was interviewing Ann, a 13½-year-old girl referred to him by the junior high school counselor. As he looked over the case referral, Sam expressed frustration because no reason was given for the referral. He would not know what to look for nor would he know how his report might affect her educational program until he could talk to the principal and other members of the staffing committee that makes decisions about special educational placements for that school. That committee would be meeting in the afternoon following the test and would immediately precede a conference with parents about their daughter.

Not knowing anything about the origins of cases referred to them is a common problem for psychologists. They generally serve many schools and often are busy with meetings and other administrative work during those days when they do visit a particular building. Psychologists, consequently, often cannot keep up with the gossip that circulates in the schools they serve nor can they easily maintain informal contacts with teachers, principals, and school counselors. There is a lot of paperwork that goes along with referring students for a child study and arranging to have them placed in special education classes. Many school officials play a role in processing all of these forms, and sometimes the different stages of the paperwork process become uncoordinated. It often happens that a request for an examination by the psychologist will be sent before he or she has a chance to hear from local school personnel their perception of a given child's problems and what their agenda is for testing and special education referral.

Though it may be common for them to lack information about children they are asked to examine, psychologists I interviewed did not find that this routine neglect became less frustrating with repetition. This was especially the case for those who, unlike Osterweis, especially look for interactional origins of student problems. One may learn about a child's cognitive style or discover some general themes of his or her personality structure from testing alone, but one cannot put this information into a context or use it as part of a broader effort to construct a picture of how school problems emerged from a student's life situation. Deprived of information about the reasons for a referral, testing becomes little more than an intellectual game or a bit of detective work with few clues to start off with.

Psychologists generally have a consulting relationship with the schools they serve. Both they and officials in these schools think of the psychologist as someone who is brought in to help resolve a difficult case. The psychologist is expected to test and may be criticized sharply for refusing to do so. Thus, even with inadequate background information, my respondents would plunge on, trying to learn what they could about a strange child living in an unknown world. They hope that with careful technique and imaginative interpretations, they could piece together enough about a given child's life to talk intelligently later with the parents and other social officials. Perhaps believing strongly in the objective techniques of testing helped these people become less frustrated with the limitations of their situations in schools. However, embracing pure technique can make the psychologist even more withdrawn from the child and less attuned to the social and emotional crises that often are at the heart of referrals.

Osterweis brought me to the interviewing room and assured me that as long as I said nothing, just watched and took notes, my presence during the testing session would cause no problems. He then left for a moment, returning with Ann.

They came into the testing room and sat down at 9:15. Osterweis was very cheerful in talking to her as he led Ann in and introduced her to me. Trying to make her feel more comfortable, he said that the tests would be like games and that they would be fun. Ann appeared upset during this time and looked to me as though she had been crying. Osterweis's cheerfulness seemed artificial to me and his comment about the tests being games was hollow. Ann knew that being tested was no innocent affair. She was unhappy because she was being tested. I was not sure that portraying the tests as games rather than work would help much, since they were similar to those activities she had not been successful with in class. He told her that I was watching him, not her, and so she should not worry. He said this in a way that suggested he too was being examined, and she took it, appreciatively, as a sympathetic joke. She seemed to relax and resign herself to going through the battery of tests.

Later, when we spoke with her mother, we learned that Ann had tried to refuse the test and that she was upset about being forced to take it. Along with being anxious about its outcome, she worried out loud as the testing period proceeded that one teacher would be angry that she was missing class and that another would be angry that she would be late. She seemed to relate the testing to whatever problems she had been having with her teachers.

Osterweis's bland good humor in the face of Ann's disturbance was striking. That he seemed so unconcerned bothered me, since she appeared so upset about leaving a conflict-filled classroom to come into the test setting. I gathered she did not think her best interests could be served by an agent of the school like Osterweis. Maybe she was right. It looked to me as though Osterweis was in a hurry to get through his testing procedures. Being responsive to her distress might bog him down in a long conversation and throw him off schedule. He had only three hours to finish the examination and could not afford to spend much of that time providing emotional support.

When I talked with Osterweis after school, and later with other psychologists, I found that the issue of whether to react and be sympathetic to students is a subject of hot debate and some concern. Osterweis asserted that he had in fact been aware of Ann's fear and anger. He acknowledged that wanting to remain neutral and trying to move the test session along were among the reasons he does not reach out much in these situations.

He asserted that more important reasons have to do with the logic of psychometric evaluation and the necessary limitations of his role. One of his main concerns is to see how students work under stress and, by using the tests as a medium of observation, to learn why they are angry. He wants to see how disturbances distort a subject's performance on different tests. Osterweis would not respond to Ann's disturbance for a more controversial reason—he did not want to enter a therapeutic relationship with the child.

Like other psychologists I interviewed, he felt it is important to sharply limit one's involvement in emotional crises, especially since for psychological diagnosticians, they are almost commonplace. Because others in schools tend to view psychologists as experts in emotional disturbance, the school psychologist may be the first person to be called when parents seem violent or when a student threatens suicide. One of my respondents observed that she probably was, in fact, better equipped than the other educators to handle such situations because she dealt with disturbed people in her therapeutic practice. She really was skilled at calming people. Still, most of the psychologists I interviewed asserted that becoming heavily involved with students in a concerned, supportive, interactive way is dangerous. They worried that this invites a dependency psychologists cannot afford. They do not want to risk becoming a key figure in a child's school life and then be unavailable during a crisis should they be immersed in meetings they cannot leave or stranded in a school across town. More realistically, perhaps, few school psychologists have much training in therapy and they do not want to take on more than they are sure they can handle.

When I have discussed this issue with psychologists working outside of schools, some have been sharply critical of this point of view. It suggests to them, not responsibility and concern for children, but rather a desire to avoid human contact and a reluctance to be supportive, concerned, or involved. A psychologist who avoids the heat of emotional upset and social conflict misses the point of the whole enterprise. Indeed, these critics suggest, perhaps this is the reason people become school psychologists. Given the demands of the role, those who are uncomfortable making close emotional contacts with clients can remain cold and formal. This is the flaw in the whole notion that psychological diagnosis in schools is useful, they would argue.

A response to this criticism makes up the heart of Chapters Three and Five, and thus it is not a debate I wish to join here. I shall argue that although it probably is true that some psychologists, and perhaps Osterweis is one of them, do use the pressures of the role to avoid meaningful relations with students, there are reasons psychologists might avoid intense involvements with the students they test that sounded legitimate to me. The administrative process that leads to a child study and the test sessions themselves simply are not conducive to the psychologist playing an interventionist role. A certain amount of sympathy and concern is important during a test session to develop rapport with a subject. There are better ways, however, for psychologists to learn about the emotional lives of children than to become involved with them in a concerned, therapeutic way. My respondents seemed to be saying that it is strategic to remain uninvolved during the test session and to save one's limited energy for other times and other settings. It is best to use the test session as a time to gather data and to accept that during this time one must discharge certain administrative responsibilities as efficiently as possible.

Osterweis began the actual examination by giving Ann a Bender Gestalt test. This involves copying a set of ten standard geometric pictures. With younger children, he later explained, this is a fairly good test of visual-motor coordination. At more advanced ages, with subjects like Ann, he believes it tells the psychometrician something about the subject's sexual identity and acts as a kind of projective test. The ways in which geometric forms are distorted or sizes are misrepresented indicate problems with sexual identity or with subjects' relations with parents or with other strong sexual identification objects like teachers.

I was a bit skeptical about this, but I had recently been involved in several seminars on projective testing and had heard stranger things. Another psychologist later commented, "Gee, Freudian school psychologists are very unusual." They were not so rare in my interview group. Both in ACORN and elsewhere my respondents used projective tests liberally and enjoyed proposing elaborate interpretations of their subjects' responses.

As we talked about the testing session later, Osterweis noted that on the Bender, Ann did a lot of counting of dots as she copied some of the pictures. This had immediately suggested to him that she is compulsive. From one of the dot-copying exercises, Osterweis also surmised that Ann has had trouble accepting a female sexual identity. She recopied a half circle of dots with a line of dots running diagonally away from it,[6] normally a feminine image, as two straight lines of dots coming together to form a vertical line of dots, as shown in Figure 2. Osterweis reported that

FIGURE 2. ***Bender Gestalt Figure 5 Compared to Ann's Drawing***

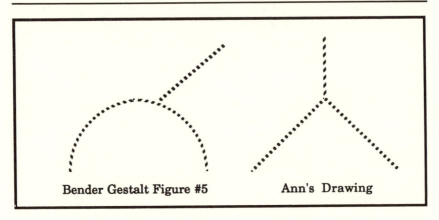

Bender Gestalt Figure #5   Ann's Drawing

in the tradition of Bender-Gestalt analysis, this is a phallic response. The arrow-like image Ann drew is also interpreted as an aggressive one. Osterweis pointed out in another picture where she was asked to copy a truly arrow-shaped figure, Ann had made a very blunt end. This suggests to him that when aggression is suggested directly by someone else, as in the test arrow, Ann has trouble facing it and expressing her own. At the same time, the drawing in Figure 2 shows she has many hidden, aggressive feelings.

To someone like myself, inexperienced in projective testing and unfamiliar with either the stimuli used or with the logic of interpretation, all of this seemed like an overinterpretation and overgeneralization of some simple, direct behaviors—something like palm reading. Osterweis pointed out later, however, that these interpretations are not just readings of Ann's behavior. He has seen the variability of subjects' responses to tests that a naive observer like myself has not been exposed to. Furthermore, his Bender interpretations are not final conclusions or objective results. Rather, Ann's responses set the tone of the testing session. By watching her responses, he tries to form hypotheses about her style of working, about the structure of her personality, and about her interactional problems. These initial interpretations alert him to things he should attend to later on. Other testing instruments can be used to validate and expand upon these preliminary hypotheses.

Perhaps one reason Osterweis is withdrawn during the session and inattentive to Ann's being upset is that while he is carrying out the elaborate, precise activities required in test-giving he is constantly on the lookout for clues that he should follow later in the session. His interpretations of the Bender drawing may seem ambitious, but they are less so when added to his observations of her performance on the Rorschach and other tests.

Ann seemed immediately to enjoy the Bender test and worked on her copying with vigor. Meanwhile, Osterweis timed her progress. She finished the ten pictures by 9:20. By that time, the distress she had brought into the session seemed to have dissipated, and she was interested in trying out other test tasks.

Returning again to Osterweis's refusal to respond to Ann's being upset when she entered the test room, one wonders again whether his indifference was not calculated. Here only minutes after the test session has begun, she seems involved, interested, and eager to please. Perhaps Osterweis had put the Bender first knowing that children like the test, do not find it threatening, and that it helps them think of the tests as games that are fun to do and intriguing to work at.

I suppose the discomfort I felt at first has more to do with my ideas of how a psychologist should behave than any failing of Osterweis's. Watching how involved Ann became, I am reminded of a strategy I often have seen teachers use to distract children or to defuse an increasingly disruptive situation. Rather than confronting a problem or becoming empathetically involved in a child's upset, teachers will often try to distract the student's attention. The children then become interested in some intellectual project or involved in group-oriented activities that are easier for the leader to control and to direct.[7]

Next Osterweis began giving Ann the Revised Wechsler Intelligence Test for Children (WISC-R).[8] This is a standard intelligence test used by most of the school psychologists I observed. Administering it takes up the largest portion of time in the test session. As she watched Osterweis open his two attaché cases and arrange the many pieces of paper, the booklets, the packets of materials, and the blocks, Ann seemed a bit nervous about the complexity of what was to come.

Nonetheless, she willingly answered his questions. He began asking various information questions: How many pennies are in a nickel? What are the four seasons? Who discovered America? She made her first mistake on the question, "In which direction does the sun set?" She also did not know from which country America became independent. She said oil floats on water because it is light. She thought the countries bordering on the United States were Iowa and Missouri, the states bordering Illinois. Ann knew she was getting answers wrong and began to get upset. After a certain number of mistakes, Osterweis switched to another task. By now it was 9:23.

After the information questions, Osterweis moved on to asking how two words or concepts were similar. At 9:28 he began the next section, which required that as she looked at the pictures in a small book of cards, she find what is missing in each. Osterweis timed her. At 9:32, he began a subtest which required that she put four pictures which tell a story in an order. This lasted until 9:38.

As I watched, the most striking thing about the testing was how mechanized or structured it is. The activities are complicated and require many different skills of the subject. They are offered in such a rapid-fire fashion that it would seem hard for a respondent to see much of a pattern in the activities. One also can understand once again why Osterweis might ignore Ann's disturbance about taking the tests. Just getting through the test requires briskness and goal orientation. Knowing that he will have no long-term contact with Ann, Osterweis seems to feel that he can much better spend his time with the girl gathering information that is useful to him, encouraging her to enjoy the activities, than to spend much of the testing session letting her talk about her problems. It is as though he views the temptation to do therapy as a trap.

Osterweis also seems to enjoy his system for managing the testing process and keeping the sequence of events flowing with minimal confusion. He had, for example, a pencil box (like the kind second graders buy at dime stores) sitting in front of an open attaché filled with seven or eight sharpened pencils. As he wrote and arranged new parts of the test, he accidentally knocked the pencil he was using on the floor, and without breaking pace took a new one out of the box and continued writing.

As Ann worked on one test segment, he took cards for the next out of the case, sorted them and stacked them ready for the next stage. He did this as one of several activities carried on simultaneously. Going through a subtest with eight cards, he flipped to a new card when she finished one; sorted the next task for a moment; jotted down on a ready pad of paper observations made out of the corner of his eye; noted the time spent on this card; and then, since Ann had just finished a task, flipped to the next card, at which point the process started over.

As I mentioned before, Osterweis had two attaché cases. One had materials for the WISC-R; it sat on a student-type desk to his right. To his left, the other case was opened on a chair he carefully had positioned before bringing Ann into the room. The WISC-R question book was opened and propped up on this second case, but positioned so Ann could not see it. This way he could prepare another of the tests or write answers and notes without having to hold or shift the book. Meanwhile, he held a clipboard with the WISC-R answer form on it, on which he recorded answers. His stopwatch was propped within easy reach on the desk at which Ann sat. Watching him work was a bit like watching a one-man band in full swing. The rapid-fire sequence of activities in the WISC-R continued in two- to five-minute segments until 10:11.

After the WISC was completed, Osterweis started Ann on the Wide Range Achievement Test (WRAT).[9] This test is less involved than the intelligence test since it is more like conventional school work. Paper, pencils, and a test workbook are all that is required. However, both Ann and Osterweis seemed to have become increasingly restless and uncomfortable. Ann began to have trouble with the WISC-R tasks toward the end and now was clearly uncomfortable with the schoollike tasks required by the WRAT. She worked more and more slowly and showed frustration, looking around occasionally, and her mind seemed to wander. Osterweis, with no bustling around or cleaning up to do, seemed restless. As she worked, he stared off into space and drummed his fingers on the table top.

After the WRAT was completed, Osterweis asked Ann if she would like to stretch and relax for a moment. As I watched, it was apparent that he was trying to change the tone and pace of the session. He was about to administer the Rorschach Test.[10] Ann, for her part, was not very receptive to his efforts. The WRAT was uncomfortable for her, reminding her, I suppose, of her anxiety about school. She began talking about how she ought to get back to class because her teacher would be angry. Osterweis for the first time became sharp in responding to her.

He said, "Well, this is a little more important. You go to class every day, and he won't mind your being gone."

When I walked with Osterweis later, he reported being frustrated with Ann at this point in the session because she had not become involved in the test process. She was hurried, had not paid close attention, and, despite his best efforts, was not sufficiently interested in the test tasks to do them well. Because of her uninvolvement, the process was moving along much more quickly than it usually does. Perhaps this was one reason the session appeared so mechanical and impersonal to me. Osterweis was concerned because a subject's uninvolvement produces little material to think about and to draw upon later when he tries to analyze the test results.

Osterweis used the break between the WRAT and the Rorschach for one final effort to encourage Ann to relax and to feel more comfortable in the test setting. The Rorschach was especially important to Osterweis because it is the most extensive projective test he uses.

Although Osterweis's outburst did nothing to calm Ann, it is hard to be critical of his transgression. The tests he must administer are strikingly different in the kinds of work they demand of a subject and in how subjects are likely to respond to content. The Bender seemed interesting to Ann because it was simple and straightforward, but the WRAT was alienating—it reminds a poor student of school and failure. Now suddenly very different demands are made. The subject is supposed to relax, open up, and reveal deep personality features by talking in imaginative ways about the ambiguous pictures of the Rorschach. It is hard to imagine Ann recovering so fast from that upsetting confrontation she had with vocabulary and arithmetic on the Wide Range Achievement Test. At the same time, as Osterweis pointed out at the beginning of the session, a key part of this whole exercise is to see how Ann would work under pressure and to learn what causes her stress. I squirmed a bit, seeing that pressure applied.

Osterweis then showed Ann the ten Rorschach cards. Having sat in on a number of Rorschach scoring seminars at ACORN, it was immediately apparent to me that this would be a rather painful session for him. Ann simply refused to react in more than monosyllables. By this time, she seemed uncomfortable with the whole testing process and resistant to Osterweis because of his refusal to worry about her tardiness.

When he showed her the first card, Ann did not respond for about thirty seconds. Finally she said, "It is a moth."

"Anything else?" he asked.

"No." Then she said, "Holes."

"Holes in the moth or in the picture?" he asked.

"In the picture."

He went on to the next card. His approach is to go through a whole set of cards to get some response and then to come back around to ask more probing questions.

When Osterweis showed Ann the second card, she responded with consternation. She picked it up, turned it around, looked on the back, and then announced that she did not know what it is. He said, "Take your time. Go ahead, try." She still did not know. He encouraged her to try again. She just stared at the picture hopelessly as though to say, "What does this guy want from me?" There was a long silence. After perhaps two minutes of trying, he said, "We'll save it, OK?" With the third card, Ann's previous reaction was repeated, but this time without even the initial curiosity. Ann stared for two or three minutes and again he said, "We'll set this one aside."

After Osterweis showed Ann Card Four for ten seconds or so, she announced that it was a crab, after which she turned it over and placed it on the stack of the first three cards. He picked it up again and asked

FIGURE 3. **Rorschach Inkblots**

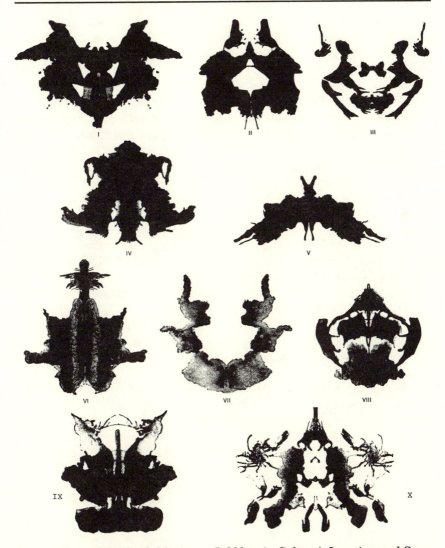

Source: From *Rorschach Miniature Inkblots in Color: A Location and Summary Form*. Copyright © 1986 by Western Psychological Services. Copyright © the Rorschach Ink Blots 1921 (renewed 1984) by Verlag Hans Huber, Bern, Switzerland. Reprinted by permission of the publisher, Western Psychological Services, 12031 Wilshire Boulevard, Los Angeles, California 90025.

her if she saw anything else. She said no. She just seemed to want to finish working with the cards.

With Card Five, however, Ann seemed to begin to warm up to the challenge of interpreting the pictures that she first accepted with Card Four. After looking at the card for a moment, Ann said, "That's a butterfly." Osterweis said, "OK. That's all you see?" "No—a bat." He seemed relieved with this answer.

Each of the Rorschach cards have standard responses for which many people will give so-called "popular" responses. The popular responses on Card Five are obvious to most people and quick responses are the norm. A subject who does not react to the black, winged-animal-shaped blob taking up most of the page either is thought to be out of touch with reality or completely resistant to the situation. Being satisfied now that she could give a response, Ann was ready to work harder on other cards. This was what Osterweis seemed to have been waiting for.

Later, as we talked about the testing session, I recalled Ann's discomfort, recalcitrance, and anger at this point. Rather than a problem of rapport, Osterweis was inclined to see it as a product of her general psychological style. It is socially uncomfortable to sit silently, as she had with the first few cards. Had answers been easy for her to make, as they were on Card Five, she probably would have spoken up. Perhaps she was uncomfortable at first, he argued, but the way she expressed her discomfort was consistent with her style of responding to challenges up to that point.

Based on the earlier Bender results, Osterweis had come to see Ann as someone who is rather compulsive and defensive about dealing with authority figures, particularly with males. She is uncertain about her sexual identity, and she is restrained in the nonverbal aspects of her behavior. All of this suggests to Osterweis that she is somewhat anal, dependent, and afraid to show her emotions. He said her developmental problems are those that must be mastered in the second year of life. He wondered whether her dependence does not date from that time.

Osterweis's suspicions were supported by her Rorschach performance. When people are slow to respond imaginatively to the ambiguous splotches of ink, analysts claim this indicates discomfort with showing emotions and with openly fantasizing. He saw Ann as a defensive child who takes some comfort in compulsively following directions from authority figures while investing little of her own cares or her own imagination in activities. Osterweis explained that anyone with Ann's profile, upon being asked to respond to patently ambiguous stimuli, would be upset, as was Ann. After she left at around 11:00, Osterweis described her reluctance to respond as "shock." He believes she used her intellect to suppress her emotions. When she becomes intellectually confused, she does not know how to react.

Osterweis's interpretation of Ann's behavior during the test session may seem forced and unnatural to us. I think discomfort with this kind of thinking, however, has less to do with the assertions that are made than with our habit of not assigning meaning to the small, trivial behaviors that litter each of our lives and all of our social relationships. How could we attach significance to the particular choices of metaphor someone else uses while talking or to every instance in which someone else drifts off and does not pay attention? Not only do we not have time for this, but all of our relationships would be frozen in a mass of doubt and suspicion.

Yet it is precisely by taking these minute events as significant that psychoanalysts, social psychologists, and ethnographers have made some of their greatest contributions. We think of Freud's analyses of slips of the tongue.[11] Social psychologists also have trained their microscopes on the interaction process in interview and small group situations in a way that gives equal significance to each utterance of every participant.[12] Similarly, a sociologist like Goffman certainly gives as much weight to the language of gestures as does Sam Osterweis.[13]

I listened as Osterweis speculated about why Ann fails in school, although we did not yet know whether she actually was failing. Although I might find his unwillingness to be supportive, friendly, fatherly, and encouraging a sign of coldness and a tendency on Osterweis's part to substitute intellectualism for caring, I would not be surprised to learn that the resistance Ann showed to him is like that which she shows to her teachers. What is failure in school but an unwillingness or an inability to perform intellectual and creative tasks when they are requested or demanded in an impersonal way by a stranger? Sympathetic as I might be to Ann and to her reluctance to answer test questions, Osterweis is equally justified in asking what it is that makes it so hard for this particular child to succeed in this situation where so many other children succeed. By reacting to his desire to impose complex psychodynamic interpretations on her behavior, I am saying that there is nothing to talk about in Ann's behavior that is problematic. But given her classroom performance, Osterweis's speculative interpretations become justifiable. We may disagree with the way he gathers data or with the interpretations he offers, but the general activity of detailed psychological evaluation becomes legitimate.

Though he had received no specific explanation for Ann's referral for testing, Osterweis launched into an explanation of what her school problems were likely to be. He said that she is the sort of student whose educational problems cannot be resolved until her emotional ones are addressed. He revealed that he had examined other children in her family in the past and found that they, along with their mother, have shown similar patterns of educational difficulty. The mother finished eighth grade only because she was in special education classes through most of her school years. By the time she was sixteen, she was still in eighth grade. She reads at the third grade level. She married at seventeen and was separated at twenty-three. With this story in his mind before the session started, one wonders whether Osterweis was really as dispassionate and objective during the session as he claimed to be. Did he have her pegged as just another member of the troublesome x family?

He went on to say that although Ann's achievement is between the third and fourth grade levels, which might be reason for educational concern, he suspected that her real problem at present came from having just moved on to junior high school. She is the sort of child who feels most comfortable in a highly structured setting like the elementary school, because she tends to intellectualize her fears and is uncomfortable with demands that she confront or express those anxieties. Junior high school, being more fluidly structured and peer-group oriented, presents a radical change in the kinds of emotional demands children confront. Students like Ann may react by becoming resistant and passive.

After Osterweis completed the Rorschach testing session at 10:57, he talked with Ann for a few minutes about her future plans. She said she was looking forward to high school in two years. He asked her what she would like to be when she grows up, and she answered, "A detective." Sam did not appear particularly interested in her answers at this point and seemed most interested in finishing up the session. He later said he thought her interest in becoming a detective was a bit inappropriate. He had not noticed (as I did) that two mystery books were in her jacket pockets. Her mother later said that her nose is always in one of those mysteries and that over the weekend she had read two of them. I wondered to myself how child with such an interest in reading could avoid building up her reading skills beyond the level Osterweis had found. Finally, he allowed her to hurry off to class.

When the testing session was complete, Osterweis and I drove over to the school district administration center where his office is located. By now it was lunchtime, so we picked up the district special education supervisor, John Nash, who is trained as a school psychologist, and we went out to a local restaurant. As we ate, we talked about the uses of testing in schools and about what school psychologists strive to achieve.

Osterweis explained that his primary concern is to maintain a sense of objectivity in his work. His greatest contribution is made when he helps to explain why a child fails, rather than simply showing that a child is so many points below the mean. Like other psychologists interviewed and observed for this study, he believes that most learning problems are as much emotional and interactional as cognitive. He believes that most teachers are unwilling or unable to recognize and confront these emotional dimensions of learning and that his job is to help them understand why a child is resisting instruction and to help teachers structure the classroom to accommodate the emotional needs of students.

It seemed odd to me to use an artificial environment, such as a test session, as the main setting for gathering data if one's primary interests were in discovering any emotional difficulties children have with learning, and communicating an understanding of these difficulties to teachers in a way that would make the students' classroom adjustment easier. Osterweis's response suggested that his idea of what constitutes objectivity is different from that which an experimental social psychologist might practice in the lab.

One can easily be seduced, he said, into worrying about problems as teachers define them if one becomes too involved in classroom dynamics. He is opposed to the movement toward informal classroom observation in school psychology because he does not think one can tease apart causal relationships very well when one has no control over the environment. A testing session is like a controlled experiment. In observation, the psychologist can become one of the actors, losing the capacity to analyze the setting in a detached manner. Without this detachment, he feels, it becomes difficult to distinguish what are real deficits in a child's performance and what are simply perceived as deficits by those associated with a child.

Part of Osterweis's concern is with being sure that during the process of student evaluation and classification, someone has taken the time to learn something about the child as a personality independent of the school. He does not trust educators to do this, and he is concerned about fairness to the child and about having appropriate services delivered. However, he does not see himself as a child advocate or an agent of school change. To the contrary, he envisions his role as socially uninvolved. He is not much interested in education, perhaps because he recognizes his role as peripheral and his influence as slight. He is content to offer interpretations for educators or parents, which they may or may not use as they choose. Objectivity refers to disengagement from the setting rather than to some notion of hard, impersonal measurement.

Nash added a pragmatic note to Osterweis's philosophical statement. He explained that there are a variety of actors in schools who perform counseling functions—school counselors, social workers, and even principals. All of these are people who spend most of their time in one or two schools and who know the local problems intimately. The psychologists, by contrast, are relative strangers. Their only distinction is the special skills they have in giving and interpreting psychological tests. Because other educators accept tests as authoritative, psychologists must rely heavily on testing and on the results of testing if they wish to be influential in educational decision making.

Other psychologists I interviewed, even those who are considerably less enthusiastic about tests and who are less convinced of their objectivity than were these two, agreed. One must use tests as a way of gaining influence and respect among other school actors. What sets off Osterweis and Nash as testing-oriented school psychologists is that they believe tests are an effective medium for communicating with other school actors and for educating these actors about the psychodynamic elements of educational problems.

After lunch, Osterweis and I returned to the junior high school to meet with Ann's mother, and the three of us settled in the counselor's office to discuss Ann's school problems. Osterweis still had not been told exactly what they were. It was absurd to be meeting with a parent in hopes of solving her daughter's problems with no information about what those problems are, and there was plenty of room for embarrassment should Ann's mother start pressing for information and answers. Left with little choice, and perhaps confident that he could think on his feet, Osterweis went ahead asking questions about the girl's emotional problems and making suggestions about things the mother might do to make Ann feel more secure and cooperative at home and in school.

He began informally by asking the mother how her relationship with her daughter has been going lately and what her feelings about the girl are. She compained that her daughter talks back to her all the time, and that she is very stubborn. Ann recently has found an older boyfriend, which is a relief to her mother because he seems to be helping Ann become more mature. The mother was disappointed to see Ann begin having school problems because she had not had these problems in the past and because she loves to read.

As an afterthought, Ann's mother said that perhaps all of the reading was related to her interest in detectives and that might have something to do with the mother's brother being a night watchman with a private police firm. Osterweis encouraged her to talk about her brother. He had been in the military police but, because of an injury, could no longer do regular police work. He was bitter about having to do the rather dull duties of a night watchman. She speculated that it is this frustration that causes him to be domineering and insulting to other family members. Ann fights with him, yet there is this detective interest. In contrast to Ann's relationship to her uncle, she and her mother get along well and Ann accepts with equanimity being disciplined.

The mother seemed a little bewildered when Osterweis asked her if Ann has any dreams or nightmares, so he continued on. He began to talk about things she might do, based on the test results, to make Ann feel better about school. He emphasized the importance of asking Ann to do concrete tasks and giving positive feedback after she does things successfully.

In the course of this conversation, the mother again returned to the problems she is having living with her brother. He is restless because his military injuries do not let him do as much as he would like. Because he is around the house during the day, they often fight. However, she needs his rent money since her job does not give her enough income. Osterweis sympathized with her problems and suggested that perhaps some of Ann's school problems were related to these problems at home. Because the father had left the house when Ann was two, her uncle was no doubt an important male role model to her. All of the arguments were upsetting to her. He suggested to Ann's mother that psychological counseling be sought.

They then talked over the possibility of a special education placement. Ann's mother was worried that this would stigmatize the girl. Osterweis emphasized how important it is to Ann to achieve and to see concrete rewards from her work. He also explained that Ann would probably feel more comfortable in a classroom that provided more support and structure than the regular junior high school program.

After the mother had left, Osterweis said he was pleased that the session had so smoothly become like a therapy session. This let him off the hook since he did not really know what to tell the mother about why a psychological evaluation was considered necessary. It also gave him valuable information about Ann's home situation, supporting his prior impression that the problems that had suddenly surfaced in school were more emotional than cognitive. He was able to test the impressions he gained from the psychological examination without having to commit himself about the results of the examination.

It was the prospect of having to discuss the results of the morning test session in detail, perhaps having to use those results to explain what the school's plans were, that had most worried Osterweis. The impressions he had given me about Ann's performance were off the top of his head and largely reflected his thoughts as he gave the test. They reflected choices he made about how to manage the interaction during the test session. Still, although he was not really prepared to talk to Ann's mother, he was not really nervous. This situation happens so often to him that he is adept at controlling the conversation, steering it away from subjects that might embarrass him, and using the interview to gather information that will help fill out his evaluation report on the student.

Osterweis prefers to fully analyze the test results before he gives a formal report. He believes analysis is the most important part of the testing process, though it is also the least public and the least appreciated. Interpreting the Rorschach Test is the most creative and difficult. The other tests are not nearly as complicated, but they too must be analyzed in terms of dimensions other than the simple performance scores they yield. The WISC-R and the Bender may both be used, as Osterweis indicated, as projective tests, like the Rorschach.

Analyzing the ways subjects make mistakes helps the psychologist find evidence of learning disabilities. These often manifest themselves in substandard performance on one segment of an intelligence test or through particular kinds of errors in copying the Bender pictures. Interpreting test results for evidence of a specific disability is a difficult analytic activity.

In general, it takes Osterweis as long to analyze test results as it does to give the test. In most cases, he will go back to school in the afternoon, as we did, to talk with parents. Then from 2:30 to 4:00 or 5:00, he will work on his testing analysis. This is not usually sufficient time to finish, so he must complete the analysis another day.

The Testing Process

There are two important things to learn from this account of Sam Osterweis's day. The first has to do with the rhythm of testing activities and the lack of slack in a psychologist's day. The second has to do with a constant tension between the psychologist's responsibility to carry out certain observations in a detached manner and the child's need for support and assurance.

The Time Structure of Testing

Looking back over this sample day, one can see that a child study takes a fixed amount of time. The day is summarized in Table 4. The pattern is widely shared among school psychologists, though in some districts, like Chicago, psychologists may give fewer test batteries in a session so that they can squeeze two children into a morning, or they may schedule their parent interview sessions so that they do four or five rapid-fire interviews in a single afternoon. If a psychologist follows the broad outlines of Osterweis's pattern, it is difficult to complete a child study—the sequence of testing, interviewing, scoring, and in-school observation or interviewing with teachers—in fewer than six hours, or one complete day. Osterweis finds it generally is difficult to complete a child study in one day, and so he must finish up later. Were he to test every day, he would simply fall further and further behind in writing his reports.

TABLE 4. *Time Requirements of a Child Study Session*

Time of Day	Activity
8:30– 9:00	Pick up test materials, administrative forms, work assignments at central office; travel to test site.
9:00–11:00	Administer standard test batteries: Bender Gestalt, WISC-R, or Standford Binet, WRAT, Rorschach.
11:00– 1:00	Travel and lunch. Often includes meeting informally with teachers or other special educators over lunch or in the teachers' room.
1:00– 2:00	Meet with parents to discuss test results (required by law).
2:00– 3:00	Meet with school special education screening committee to discuss cases (often several cases will be discussed during such sessions).
3:00– 5:00	Score tests and write reports. (One to two additional hours usually will be required to finish scoring and report writing.)

The time usually required for this sequence is six to seven hours.

Analysis and Empathy

Intelligence testing and the fixed set of activities that surround testing are central to the work of school psychologists. They spend most of their time huddled with one child at a time in book rooms, nurses' examining rooms, or assistant principals' offices going step-by-step through a series of tasks that make up the three or four most commonly given intelligence, achievement, and projective tests. After examining each child, a psychologist meets with the principal, the child's teacher, and perhaps other specialists assigned to the school—a learning disabilities teacher or a speech therapist. Later, the psychologist may meet with the child's parents individually or with other educators. Then at home or in his or her office, he or she returns to the child's test materials and spends several hours scoring them and writing a report.

These activities are required in part by law and in part by state or local school district policies. They vary somewhat from school district to school district. However, their overall pattern remains the same from case to case, month to month, school to school, and year to year. Psychologists repeat this pattern from eighty to two hundred times each year. Gradually, the process of testing becomes automatic, routine, and in some cases ritualistic.

Because of the tremendous amount of time they spend giving tests, analyzing results and writing reports, and explaining the implications to parents and to school personnel, many psychologists are detached from the testing activities. For some, this ritual has become so automatic that the substance of actual test activities loses its importance. The test becomes a stage upon which to observe a child at work and in interaction. For others, testing is primarily a required or legitimating activity. These psychologists may put most of their energy into a few free hours per week when they can talk with teachers or parents or observe children in class. Such psychologists may be profoundly ambivalent about testing and about their role as mass screeners and diagnosticians in schools.

In this chapter, I explored the manner in which one psychologist conducted a child study. My detailed description shows the administration of a tightly structured test battery with the psychologist as observer. The process of testing is not easily compressed; a fixed length of time is required to move through all of the activities associated with a child study. This understanding is essential to the argument that will follow in later chapters of this book.

At the same time I show how important is the fabric of time in school psychology, I also want to alert the reader to the profound discomfort I believe most observers, not themselves committed to the enterprise, would feel about the activity of testing in schools. The man I describe, Sam Osterweis, is not the most admirable character one might have found. He loves to test, and he is not particularly concerned about the discomfort of the student he examined. He believes deeply in the significance of projective tests and in the validity of interpreting their results liberally. He is committed to the idea that intelligence tests accurately measure student characteristics, and he is cautious about violating the methodological guidelines that psychometricians have established to govern the process of test administration.

Though Osterweis is perhaps a psychometric extremist, much of what we observed in this chapter represents not his zealotry but the consequences of the school psychologists' situation. Osterweis works for a school district that allows him to extend the amount of time he has to devote to each child study as he sees fit. Most psychologists are not so lucky. If Osterweis was callous in his treatment of Ann, others might have trouble being more sympathetic to the student being tested because there is no time to develop a relationship. Psychologists have only two or three hours with a child and they must forge ahead.

Similarly, although an observer may be profoundly uncomfortable with Osterweis's enthusiasm at interpreting test performances in elaborate, fanciful ways on the basis of seemingly flimsy evidence, some of our discomfort comes from being unfamiliar with the strategy of investigation represented by tests and testing. Tests are by design elaborately artificial. They are intended to define normality with great precision. Yet normality is a relative concept that must be seen in reference to a specific context and set of norms. Intellectual normality historically has been defined by comparing test results with school performance, because school performance provides an independent measure of performance that is stable and quantifiable.[14] With this stable measure in hand, psychometricians and experimental psychologists have proceeded to explore a variety of subtle implications of different test strategies and results. Because practitioners handle these artifacts of the testing culture with confidence and the conviction that their techniques are valid and valuable, they seem strange to an outsider just as they seem fully worked out and meaningful to an insider.

One of the tensions inherent in testing is that the elaborate attention to precision and to systematic analysis of test results that we observed with Sam Osterweis is coupled with uncertainty about what the immediate significance of an observation or interpretation might be. Osterweis's desire to interpret a child's failure to duplicate a curved line of dots as a sign that she has difficulty relating to male authority figures may seem eccentric to an observer. However, many of the psychologists (both in and outside of school work) I talked with during this project would not fault Osterweis for this attempt to find symbolic meaning in the child's performance. What criticisms they might offer would focus on the way in which he used those interpretations to learn about the child's life, how supportively he worked with the child to help her learn about and solve her psychological problems, and whether he intervened constructively on her behalf with the school.

The reader should see in this chapter a conflict between the psychologist's need to be an analytic observer and the need of the child to find help and sympathy. Perhaps one of the shortcomings of testing in schools is that psychologists cannot give adequate time to both. The need to finish testing in a fixed length of time, to answer the questions of teachers and parents, and to meet the paperwork requirements built into the law leaves little time for listening to the child.

Disturbing as this is, the unpleasant reality of life in schools is that no actor is free to pay attention just to the problems and needs of the children. The tests of the psychologist are impersonal and have an air of cold precision about time. We shall see in later chapters that they also are the strongest source of legitimacy available to psychologists within schools. It is their precision and impersonality that makes them an object of respect by other educators.

Other school psychologists might be warmer and more sympathetic as they test than is Sam Osterweis. However, in my experience psychologists never escape the dilemma inherent in testing that the instrumental use of tests to understand student problems or to influence the way educators think about a child interferes with their ability to make human contact with the students they visit. This tension is like the tension of the primary medical practitioner who must approach each case as an intellectual problem just as the clients who visit them are feeling scared and threatened by the prospect of illness.[15] To do their job as it is structured in schools today, psychologists usually must be brisk, formal, and impersonal during the testing session. I shall argue that the measure of a good school psychologist is whether he or she builds on the impersonal observations of a testing session by seeking out cases in which he or she may make an impact and then becoming more involved in those cases.

CHAPTER 3

Activism versus Formalism in School Psychology

According to my survey, about two-thirds of school psychologists are primarily diagnosticians. These people spend most of their time managing the process of placing children in special education classes, returning them to regular school programs, and monitoring them after placement. The activities described in Chapter Two—testing, interviewing, writing reports, and attending meetings to discuss cases—take up most of their time. Carrying out the specific, mandated rules and directions involved in these activities engages between 60 percent and 80 percent of their time. This happens even though psychologists are generally left unsupervised and are allowed to set their own schedules. The content and the tempo of their work makes supervision unnecessary, at least as a way of controlling how they spend their time. Despite being free from the kind of close regulation of time that governs classroom teaching, for example, school psychologists see their work as busy and highly structured.

The way that activities like the testing session come to dominate their work lives is important to understand. One can see from Chapter Two how testing can easily become rushed and dominated by routine. Not only are the tasks tightly structured but, to the extent psychologists are asked to evaluate children in the absence of a meaningful description of what the problem is, psychologists are expected to provide informed recommendations to parents and to educators, often in tense situations, with tests providing most of the information they have to share. Rather than focusing primarily on what students are feeling and on what clues the tests give that might help one know why children make the mistakes they do, psychologists seem often to be most concerned with having the child study session run quickly and efficiently.[1] Although Osterweis justified the emotional neutrality and mechanical character of his testing style in philosophical and scientific terms, it is a small jump from his position to one that says testing is important for itself, a position voiced during some of my interviews with Chicago psychologists.

Psychologists deal with many pressures—they often lack information about why they are testing, they are embedded in traditions that emphasize emotional distance and objectivity, and they face school officials who, seem to worry that psychologists will practice some sort of psychotherapeutic witchcraft on them. An impersonal, precise, socially withdrawn style of evaluation helps them to cope with stresses built into their role.

Unfortunately, it is then only a small step for testing to become a routinized activity. In routine activities, the process of carrying out the activity becomes automatic, and its repetitiveness allows the actor to practice without thinking creatively, innovatively, or critically. In school psychology, this means being inflexible about testing: letting hard, empirical results from the tests, rather than soft, interpretative material, determine the contents of one's reports, and not critically examining what contribution teachers, principals, and the school setting might be making to the supposed problems of children.

Although Chapter Two shows that some psychologists *do* become narrow, test-centered, and rule-bound in their work, the central questions of the chapters to come are *why* and *how often* this happens. Some school psychologists fall into a bureaucratized role, dominated by the routine aspects of testing, even though they are largely free of direct supervision. Others resist apparent coercion and gain support for playing an independent, creative role in their work.

Asking why testing becomes routine is important for two reasons. First, testing is most questionable technically and morally when it is conducted in a hurried, automatic fashion. We have evidence that IQ testing done routinely artificially lowers scores, because examiners do not establish sufficient rapport with their subjects.[2] Further, as the administration of test batteries becomes more routine, the less likely it is that the data they produce will be combined with or used to guide the collection of interactional data. As I stated in the Introduction, combining test and interactional data allows an examiner so inclined to make allowances for inherent cultural biases built into tests. When there is no time to collect interactional data, tests must stand on their own merits. Then cultural biases are more likely to influence test results in important ways. Automatic testing raises serious ethical issues about the appropriateness of school psychology.

Second, given their lack of supervision, it is important to understand why school psychologists take on a routinized, bureaucratic role. It is important to see that they *choose* this role. One might overlook the fact that psychologists have a lot of control over the manner in which they work because, as we saw in Chapter One, there are sharp differences between the testing styles of psychologists working in large city school systems and those working elsewhere. One might argue that psychologists in the urban school systems test more routinely because large systems are more bureaucratic than small ones. Although it is certainly true that most urban psychologists work in more complex organizational settings than do those working in small school districts, it is not obvious how the greater "bureaucracy" (whatever we mean by that) of an urban school system translates into routinized work.

Contrary to laymen's perceptions of schools, sociologists have generally argued that they are not strongly bureaucratic organizations and that the means of control that typically operate in bureaucracies are weak in schools. In the tradition of Max Weber and administrative science, we say that bureaucratic organizational structures produce explicitly formulated work rules and routinized jobs because such organizations are sharply hierarchical with centralized decision-making arrangements.[3] Top-level administrators define the content of jobs explicitly for their subordinates, and lower-level administrators supervise workers to make sure that tasks are completed as specified.[4] In such organizations, a clearly defined technical system and close control by supervisors give subordinates few choices about how they may do their work and encourage repetitiveness and routinization as they carry out their assigned tasks.

In these terms, organizational theorists tell us, schools are not bureaucratic organizations. They have a flat administrative structure (not steeply hierarchical), and they have a "loosely-coupled" decision-making apparatus, both of which limit the amount of control supervisors can have over subordinates.[5] The lowest levels of the organization have substantial autonomy to make their own decisions about scheduling, work content, and the methodology of practice. While studying school psychologists, Weatherley and Lipsky coined the term "street level bureaucrat" to emphasize the bottom-up decision-making structure that prevails in many public service organizations.[6] Given this autonomy, why do school psychologists (whether in the city or country) allow their work to become routinized and bureaucratic? Blaming the oppressiveness of urban school systems is not enough. We want to know how that oppressiveness penetrates to shape work.

In this and the following chapter, I shall discuss in detail the differences between an automatic style of testing and the more eclectic version. I disapprove of routinized testing, and find many good points in the alternative style of school psychology I describe. At the same time, it is important for readers to understand that the examples I offer are not necessarily typical of the way school psychology is practiced if psychologists are not hurried. There is no guarantee that more leisurely school psychology will produce the personal sensitivity or the awareness of organizational politics we will observe in coming chapters. I offer exemplars only to illustrate possibilities of the school psychologist role and to show that reasonable people might use tests in ways that diverge from the norms of practice laid down in research settings.

Although I gave examples of what school psychologists have done that were insightful; sensitive to the needs of children, teachers, principals, and even superintendents; and effective at solving problems, my arguments about the ultimate goodness or badness of the occupation are mainly negative. I can make strong arguments about what is "bad" school psychology, but I cannot make equally strong arguments about what is "good" school psychology. Consequently, I cannot say how often people do what I like and describe in the following pages or whether those activities make much difference in schools.

This is not a failure of my methodology. Rather, it has to do with the intrinsic difficulties of telling what makes for good practice in any profession. It is not much easier to define good medicine than it is to define good school psychology.[7] Meanwhile, everyone in these professions will agree that certain failures or mistakes represent bad practice. This is because, as Bosk explains, mistakes tend to represent failures of attitude or professional morality about which there is consensus within the profession. Good practice, on the other hand, is creative and creativity breeds diversity. With this diversity, it is hard for people who focus on different ways of working to agree on the best ways to practice. Good practice is varied, bad practice is less so.[8]

Two School Psychologists

In the remaining pages of this chapter I will contrast psychologists who allow their role to become automatic with those who attempt to broaden their role despite a heavy testing load. The former I call "administratively oriented psychologists" and the latter, "activist psychologists." To develop this distinction, I will describe the way two psychologists approach their work. Violet Hoffritz and Arnold Cohen are both older, experienced people who were among the smartest, most competent, and dedicated people I interviewed. They work in very different kinds of school districts, Hoffritz in a middle-class black area of Chicago and Cohen in a working-class white suburb. Ms. Hoffritz, able though she is, has been overtaken by the difficulties of carrying out broad-gauged psychology in an urban educational system. Mr. Cohen, in contrast, uses great ingenuity to inform staff members and parents in a conservative district how psychology might be used to good effect in their schools.

Violet Hoffritz: A Testing Machine

Violet Hoffritz is proud of her ability to produce a high volume of testing. By the time I spoke to her in May, she had already conducted 170 tests during the school year. She works eleven months per year and averages 1.3 testing sessions per day. This volume is possible because she has worked out a variety of ways to make her work more efficient. If possible, she will only test children or visit parents at her office, which is located in one of the elementary schools. It is convenient to most people living in the decentralized school district she serves in Chicago. This reduces the amount of time she must spend traveling, and allows her to be more flexible in choosing the tests she will use in a child study. Having all of her test kits available allows her to fit instruments to the characteristics she sees in children; gives her more freedom to use various tests as screening devices that are intended only to pick up gross disabilities or problems if they exist; and saves time because she does not have to conduct full, detailed examinations when she does not feel they are needed to describe some dimension of student functioning.

Ms. Hoffritz and I talked at length about whether she can test intensively without shortchanging children or limiting her effectiveness as a psychologist. She was emphatic in believing that, working quickly, she is able to understand what problems led a child to be referred for examination. She has worked in this part of Chicago for twenty years and knows well the schools, the teachers, and many of the families. She knows what problems the schools have, and often is more concerned that her knowledge about a teacher or a family will bias her test results than that she will misinterpret data for lack of information on the setting from which a child is referred.

Ms. Hoffritz is confident of her ability because she feels she has solid clinical training. Although she does not have a Ph.D., she is a fellow of the American Psychological Association; has been in private practice for years; and, until they were discontinued, participated regularly in sessions conducted by her supervisor at the Bureau of Child Study of the Chicago Public Schools to train school psychologists in the techniques of administering and interpreting projective tests. Using tests as an adjunct to therapy and being well schooled in the clinical uses and interpretation of tests make her feel well equipped to recognize underlying patterns in test performances.

She also argued that although a strong clinical background may or may not allow her to test accurately in the manner she prefers, one also must take into account the context in which she works. First, she believes that most children are referred to special education programs in good faith. She does not think school officials refer children to get rid of them or because they are discipline problems. She is alert for the personality conflicts that sometimes occur between teachers and children. As the psychologist, she does not want to be a policeman, charged to oversee the legality of referrals.[9]

Second, she is keenly aware of her limitations as an educator. Most children are referred to special education classes because they are not learning in class. Ms. Hoffritz is not a teacher, however, and feels she would be out of place to suggest that a child was failing because a teacher ran her classroom poorly. This would suggest that she knows more about how to teach than the teachers do.

Third, even if she thought she ought to be continually doubtful about why children have been referred for a child study and always ready to believe that something other than an intransigent cognitive or emotional problem was leading a child to fail, it would be dangerous for her to be too outspoken. Teachers are likely to resent her telling them how to run their classrooms, and they would become less cooperative with her rather than more so. Principals come to see psychologists as intruders, partly because psychologists work only part time in any one school, so they are outsiders, in some sense. She also said that educators tend to be somewhat afraid of tests and psychology. They worry that psychologists will reveal some sort of deep secret about them and so they are suspicious. An aggressive psychologist can cause a principal to make it difficult for him or her to work in a school.

Finally, Ms. Hoffritz is the senior psychologist in her district and feels responsible for the quality of work she and her colleagues turn out. Some of the other psychologists are slow workers and others, she frankly admits, are badly trained. They do not want to work to improve their clinical skills, and they do not understand the intellectual basis of testing technique. She takes on more work herself in part because, however bad her products may be, she feels always more competent than these colleagues.

Although being assertive that her way of working is justified, Ms. Hoffritz also admits that she has become more test oriented and more insulated from school activities over time. She is getting older and does not have the energy to sell new ideas and programs to people in regular programs that would allow her to use more of her psychological skills around the schools. She no longer drives, which makes it difficult for her to travel around the district. She has found her private practice more and more satisfying and feels no need to make schools the site of her main clinical work any longer. She also feels a general pressure to fill up the special education classes now that programs are expanding.

At the same time, Ms. Hoffritz believes that a psychologist might want to become involved in the day-to-day life of schools for personal reasons. She sees absolutely no demand for this involvement on the part of other educators. If anyone approached her, she would be glad to start a therapy group, provide in-service training, or meet with parents. For several years, she had a weekly group therapy session with several boys at one of the high schools, which was very successful. However, once those boys graduated, the staff made no effort to have her continue with new students.

Although there is no demand for broader psychological services, Ms. Hoffritz also sees no impediment should she desire to organize groups or to meet with teachers or do just about any kind of psychological work she might choose. Partly, she admits, this is because many people are a little afraid of her. She has been around a long time, and she speaks her mind. However, there is also no one to supervise or direct her. To do more therapy in her schools she would have to sell her ideas to teachers and principals. At present they believe she best serves them by giving tests. She could probably change their minds and convince them to accept other kinds of services.

Despite feeling she has this autonomy, Ms. Hoffritz also acknowledges that it was more difficult for psychologists to make their voices heard at the time of our interview than it was in the early 1970s. At that time, psychologists still worked out of a central office at the Bureau of Child Study. There were three supervisors for each of the major regions of Chicago, and psychologists' regional directors provided intellectual leadership and constant supervision. School psychologists around the city saw each other often, meeting in the central office to do their paperwork; there was much more of an occupational subculture then.

That subculture was an important force for convincing psychologists to improve testing techniques and to try out new services in schools they served. Now that the Chicago Public Schools are broken up into twenty-seven small districts, psychologists see each other less often. They are more dominated by regular educators and by the way particular superintendents play the politics of the citywide school district. Ms. Hoffritz and some friends have tried to keep the occupational culture alive by organizing the Chicago Association of School Psychologists and conducting monthly in-service and social meetings. But this does not attract the younger psychologists who, she feels, have much less of a commitment to psychology as an intellectual discipline and as a personal avocation.

Her practice of intensive testing is in part an accommodation to these changes. When she was younger, and she and her psychologist friends around the city met often to share their excitement about their work, she tried to influence people more around schools. It is too much trouble now. She receives sufficient gratification from her work outside school. She will be retiring soon, she is content to work quietly in a way that satisfies other people in her school district.

Arnold Cohen: An Experimentalist

Arnold Cohen at fifty-three years old is one of the oldest psychologists working in the ACORN cooperative. He has been working there for only two years after having spent twenty years working as a school psychologist in two other districts, one a large city and the other a small rural district. Being older, with no aspiration to work outside of schools and with low seniority in ACORN, Mr. Cohen has been assigned to two of the least desirable districts the cooperative serves, Freedom and Corsica. He also spends one day per week at ACORN's School for the Trainable Mentally Retarded (TMR). The districts he serves are both small towns on the edge of the Chicago Metropolitan Area; each has two elementary schools and one junior high. The residents of both towns are primarily white migrants from Appalachia, much like those who live in the district Sam Osterweis serves. Like the people they serve, those who run the Freedom and Corsica school districts are conservative and somewhat suspicious of experts like the school psychologist.

Mr. Cohen finds it difficult to do anything but diagnosis—testing and the attendent work of a child study—in these districts. A policy of the ACORN cooperative, intended to help expand the psychologists' role, seems to have backfired for Cohen and is partly responsible for his restricted work situation. Instead of psychologists being assigned to work only in particular districts, ACORN insists that individuals be employed by the cooperative and that school districts contract for specific services. It is as though the cooperative is running a temporary help employment agency, even though most psychologists spend most of their time working in their districts and are likely to keep a successful assignment for years. The ACORN supervisors I interviewed said that they insist on this arrangement to force district administrators to think through why they want a school psychologist and what their expectations are. The supervisors hope the psychologists and educators will be able to talk more frankly and easily about the role of psychology in the school. For Mr. Cohen, to his profound frustration, the arrangement drives a wedge of formality between him and the teachers in his district. It becomes easier for district leaders to control his work than it would be if his status were less well defined, because they can say they only want to buy particular services.

The school district is somewhat stingy about the number of his hours it buys, and beyond this number, the superintendent and principals do not want him to "hang around the school" doing nothing in particular. The lack of extra time in the schools denies him opportunities to get to work with the teachers and to sell a more diverse package of services to them. ACORN also encourages client school districts to think of his time in terms of units. Because the only thing his districts want to buy is testing and because they can calculate how much time it takes him to conduct a child study, his supervisors tend to set up his schedule so that he has no free time. He is protected by other ACORN rules that allow him to spend a long time on each child study—he may only conduct three child studies per week and must spend Friday in the ACORN central office—but he still cannot do much other than test. He reports conducting about one hundred child studies per year, spending five and one-half hours on each.

Although Cohen feels respected in his two school districts, he finds this esteem both embarrassing and limiting. People respect him because he has esoteric knowledge, but this also means they want and expect him to exercise that knowledge. They feel uncomfortable if he is not testing or trying to explain the mysteries of test results. For his part, Cohen finds testing extremely dull, made worse by the social distance that is imposed on him. He would be happier with a more humble role in which people thought of him as equal to teachers so that he could work on projects informally with them.

When he launches an initiative in the schools he serves, Cohen is eclectic in the kinds of projects he undertakes since he has no particular specialty. When he worked in the large city district he, like Violet Hoffritz, found it generally difficult to find people who were interested in having him invent new kinds of psychological services. However, after looking for some time in his urban district, he found a junior high school principal who encouraged him to experiment with different projects in his school. For several years, he ran therapeutic groups with adolescent boys.

Cohen enjoys his work at ACORN's TMR school because there his main job is inventing ways of applying psychology to problems in the school. I visited him there once and watched as he spent an hour with two boys from the high school classes at the school. He explained that he must keep close watch on them because they are sometimes violent. He thought that this seemed normal enough with trainable retarded children. They probably feel frustrated because they cannot do things, he said, that are easy for their more able friends and relatives. Not infrequently they also have troubled home lives and emotional problems. Such children are not as easily controlled by the verbal commands and implicit contracts that are important to maintaining order in high schools for normal students. The safety of women teachers, who are much smaller than some of their students, is occasionally in jeopardy. A frightening example occurred earlier in the year when, during an angry outburst, one of the boys hit a teacher and shoved her across the room. Cohen was asked to help after this event.

After discussing the problem with the teacher and observing the class for some time, Cohen created a solution that has practically eliminated the problem of classroom violence. Violence was nearly always preceded by disagreements of small outbursts that gradually spread to include more students or that became progressively more intense. He suggested that the students learn a technique called progressive relaxation, which requires that people lie down and consciously tell each muscle group in their body to relax. Once the class was trained in the technique, the teacher could immediately stop all activity and have the students do progressive relaxation when someone began to get upset. This not only helped calm the students, it also forced them to focus on and become involved in a group activity, and has helped to create collective pressure to control people who are acting out against the group.

Cohen imagines that problems not very different from this one at the TMR school also crop up in his school districts, and he would like to work with teachers to develop similar solutions. To do so, however, requires that one be able to talk informally and in a relaxed way with teachers on a routine basis. One needs to gain their trust and to demystify one's work as psychologist. Having done so, Cohen finds that teachers become more inclined to seek him out when they are upset about something. Alternatively, in the course of a conversation or seeing something happen in a school, Cohen may have an idea he can suggest to teachers or others.

He is not optimistic about being able to sell people in the Freedom and Corsica school systems on the value of his experimental interventions, but he has set out to do this, nonetheless. After working in the districts a short time, he discovered that the amount of vandalism that occurred around the schools was a problem concerning many. There also was much teenage fighting and general violence. As he talked with parents during child studies, he found that many of them were upset that their children often were disobedient and hard to control.

In response, Cohen last year began offering weekly parent group meetings to talk about how to discipline and control teenage children. His classes were immediately oversubscribed, and they have continued through this year. The Corsica district superintendent has encouraged him to continue that work.

Although he conducts these parent group meetings in his free time and the support he receives is for a particular activity rather than for general experimenting with programs, Cohen believes he is making progress. Eventually, he hopes to start other projects that do not interfere with the assigned time he must spend on diagnosis. As people recognize that he is effective at spotting and responding to problems, he hopes that administrators will become more flexible about how he uses his time and that teachers will begin to seek him out on a continuing basis to talk about their classroom problems. In the meantime, Cohen feels he must be very circumspect about his efforts, because his clientele is so easily frightened by the thought a psychologist might try to take over their school or use his mysterious knowledge to lay bare deep personal secrets of the people he works with.

Passive and Active Conceptions of Role

Both Violet Hoffritz and Arnold Cohen spend most of their time conducting child studies, and in this their day-to-day work is similar. They have different production levels; consequently, Hoffritz's work is more narrowly occupied with testing. She faces considerable pressure to test because she works in a large urban school system, but the bigger reason her volume of testing is greater than Cohen's is that the two psychologists have a different sort of commitment to school psychology. Hoffritz has an administrative orientation, whereas Cohen is an activist. The difference between the two work orientations lies in what social psychologists call the locus of control.[10]

Hoffritz is content to allow the social system of the organization to define her work for her. She does actively take on more cases than necessary, but has self-consciously chosen to allow her work to be structured by formal rules about what her responsibilities are and what the relationship of her organizational position should be to other ones in the public school system; the time structure inherent in child studies; and expectations people occupying adjacent organizational positions—principals, teachers, and special teachers—have about how she and they should interrelate. In important respects, she is passive in the definition of her life at work, and she allows these three factors to intrude upon her and to interact with each other. Together, they create for her a stable pattern of work and interdependence with others. The locus of control in her work is outside herself.

Cohen, in contrast, tries to take command of his own life at work. Like Hoffritz, he faces pressures from the same three organizational factors, but he is not willing to accept a closed, static definition of his work. He adds a fourth factor, his conception of what a school psychologist ideally ought to be doing in a school system. Hoffritz is primarily reactive, trying to balance external, sometimes contradictory, forces; Cohen is an actor. He sees the organization in which he works as material to be formed and rearranged as he constructs a role for himself.[11] His locus of control is internal.

The difference in the locus of control for these two psychologists parallels two radically different ideas social scientists have developed about the nature of roles in organizations. One role theory traces its history to the anthropologist Linton, who distinguished between status and role.[12] A status is a position or a node in a social matrix or system. It may be a level in a hierarchy, or it may represent a stable pole in a set of continuing exchange relationships. Each status is defined by its position within the social network or system and by obligations and exchanges that relate it to other statuses. Roles refer to the behaviors carried out by those who belong to those statuses.

This distinction between status and role has been elaborated by a group of organizational social psychologists who have treated role behavior as a dependent variable. They focus on how a variety of discomforts in organizational life interferes with the performance of workers. Conflicting definitions by members of other positions of what one's status position is or should be—role conflict—and insufficiently defined status positions—role ambiguity—are two common sorts of problems. Implicit in this view, however, is that the causal arrows go only in one direction. Status relations cause role behavior. Each role is associated with one and only one status, even though there is no reason in principle that the same set of work behaviors could not be associated with several different statuses.[13] The substance of role behavior is also determined by the values, demands, and structural patterns of a particular organization. All of this is consistent with the way Violet Hoffritz works as a school psychologist.

The contrasting view of role structure is offered by sociologists in the symbolic interactionist tradition. I take some liberties in calling this tradition symbolic interactionist since I wish to include people whom sociologists tend to place in two different traditions. One group is made up of structural functionalists like Robert K. Merton and Philip Selznick. The other is composed of "real" symbolic interactionists like Everett Hughes and his students.[14] These two groups emphasize somewhat different views when they study organizations, as I shall explain shortly.

I group them together here because they all study people in occupations who are creative and semiautonomous in their work. Generally, the focus is on people working in organizations, though an important branch of this work lies in the study of professions and professionals. A focus in all of the work is how people occupying structural positions create and enforce norms by and for themselves.

Organizational structure plays an important role in the evolution of norms, but structure has a dual role. It is not only a source of formal rules and assigned responsibilities, it also buffers, governs, directs, and provides opportunities by which actors can escape or overcome the demands of people in other positions. Roles are not defined only in terms of particular organizations. They generally are also influenced by broad values, systems of laws or formal rules that compete with the organization for authority over the worker, and by value systems—like a professional value system—that are independent. One must examine a role or occupation in the context of a complex of organizations, value systems, and interest groups that together form an institutional sector. This tradition in sociology is called institutional analysis.

Structural Functionalism

The structural functional branch of institutional analysis is built on a conception of roles like that of social psychological role theory. The structure of roles is a product of functions the system must perform, hence the name *structural functional*. Roles are described as products of conflicting expectations imposed by the social systems in which a status is located. Confronted with the stress of these value conflicts, groups of people collectively define what responses are appropriate and defensible. These are the norms that define role-appropriate behavior and that shape the contours of social structure.

The difference between this conception of roles and the conception described earlier is that for structural functionalists, role conflicts do not immobilize workers or lead them passively to allow others to define the character of their work life. These are disabilities organizational social psychologists see rooted in role strain.[15] Structural functionalists use role conflicts to explain activism and independence. Generally, important role conflicts are not the demands specific people in other positions make. This is closer to the way social psychologists view role conflict. Rather, the role conflicts structural functionalists pay attention to are overarching value conflicts produced as abstract organizational purposes are played out in the particular activities assigned to people in their jobs.

The conflicts produce central dilemmas in occupations whose members recognize each other as members of meaningful primary groups. Those groups form as workers confront and resolve basic contradictions inherent in their work. Police must balance the need to maintain order in a community against their responsibility to obey the rule of law in their treatment of suspects.[16] Physicians must balance the need to be caring and sympathetic as they treat patients with the impersonality necessary to analyze and solve problems.[17] These dilemmas gain symbolic power as the need to resolve them is recognized collectively by members of an occupation and seen as related to the sort of expertise they must develop. The dilemmas also become foci of informal occupational organizations, training programs, and claims for professional autonomy.

Symbolic Interactionism

The other branch of institutional analysis, the Chicago tradition of Hughes and his followers, such as Howard Becker, Elliot Freidson, Anselm Strauss, Dan Lortie, and Rue Bucher, focuses more on the permeability of organizational boundaries than on struggles within an organization that cause structure to be created. The content of any role is only partly defined by the organizations within which that role is located. Laws, public expectations, and professional values all compete with organizational rules and interdependencies to define an ideal of a role. To understand how roles within organizations are structured, we must consider the interaction between symbol systems and different audiences or constituencies of organizations.

Chicago institutional analysts also emphasize a tension within people. On one hand, they are individuals whose personalities are evolving. On the other, they are people who are enacting prescribed roles. All of the descriptions of school psychologists I have offered thus far focus on how they have structured their lives at one point in time. However, I could also interpret the behavior of the three people I have talked about in terms of positions in an occupational life cycle. Violet Hoffritz is passive in part because she is going to retire soon. Her organizational situation contributes to her general feeling that she has fought long enough and that she wants an unambiguous, conflict-free job for now. From a life-cycle point of view, roles must be interpreted not just in terms of what forces now come to bear on people but also in terms of what the career pattern of a role is. Are people at one or another stage of career development selected for a job? What differences might it make for the way a role is structured if people spend only a few years in one organization before moving onto another for the next stage in their career development?

The activism Arnold Cohen brings to his work suggests that an analysis of his institution is needed to understand why he behaves as he does. Certainly he is neither constrained or encouraged by his organizational situation to tilt at windmills as he does. To understand him better, we would need to examine why he is so influenced by the ideas and the world view of psychology. We would need to know more about how he has come at his age to find himself in this backwater school district with so little that nourishes his personal desires. We would need to know whether ACORN or some other organizational or social forces influence his relationships with the local district.

To understand how actors in a role behave, we need to know what values and expectations they embrace and which groups they define as significant others. In deciding how to act, people try to anticipate how these significant others would judge their behavior and what consequences would flow from various courses of action. Symbolic interactionism takes its name from this process of anticipating reactions since the subject is imagining interaction or interacting on a symbolic level. A role happens only when groups of people use similar reference points in conducting these symbolic interactions. Without this commonality, behavior is simple idiosyncratic. With commonality, behavior comes to represent or embody a collectivity.

What Difference a Role Orientation Makes

Neither of the two conceptions of role offered by social science, that of the organizational social psychologists and that of the institutional analysts, is ultimately correct or faulty. They are suited to de-scribe and explain different organizational situations and analytical problems. This book seeks to explain why some psychologists act more like Arnold Cohen and others act more like Violet Hoffritz.

Explaining their behavior requires that we simultaneously bring several levels of analysis to the interpretation of their actions. We have to consider how they manage relationships within their local schools, how they relate to their professional peers, what developmental stage they have achieved in their careers, how their origins influence their professional ideals, and how they identify and relate to some broader professional group—whether they identify with psychologists, with ed-ucators, or with neither. The narrow conception of roles offered by orga-nizational social psychologists will not help much in sorting through this complexity. We must adopt an institutional approach.

Why it is so important to explain how people become like these two psychologists, Hoffritz and Cohen? Creative, innovative psychology is more appealing to me than is the sort of dry, administrative work that takes up Violet Hoffritz's time. This, however, is a matter of taste. A reason for preferring an activist work orientation is that psycholo-gists' efforts to expand their roles are likely to produce, directly or as a side benefits, psychological diagnoses sensitive to the needs of children and less prone to errors of measurement. Although I did not show how his orientation affects the conduct of child studies in Cohen's case, we will see how activism broadens the child study process in Chapter Four. An active style makes a difference in the following three ways.

First, their difference in orientation leads people like Hoffritz and Cohen to seek different test loads. Accepting an administrative service role, Hoffritz seeks out child studies and looks for ways to reduce the amount of time spent on each examination. Cohen, in contrast, is con-tinually trying to do more involved child studies. Psychologists with Cohen's inclination tend to use the child study session as a way of lob-bying for a broader role. The data-gathering phase of a child study is one time psychologists may legitimately talk with teachers about their classroom problems or use test reports as an aid in teaching some psy-chology to educators.

An intentional by-product of this lobbying may be collection of a variety of nontest data. As we shall see in Chapter Four, the psycholo-gist may learn about children's relationships and about their lives, making the test findings more meaningful and problem-focused. With additional information, psychologists are more likely to learn whether some personality conflict or personal crisis in the life of a teacher con-tributed to a special education referral. Child studies that contain this information seem more likely to be free of measurement biases built into tests; to be sensitive to individual differences among children; and to be keyed to making specific, child-centered treatment recommendations. This is why the number of child studies conducted per year and the average time spent per child study are such important variables for understanding different aspects of the school psychologists' role. It is indicative of an orientation as well as a measure of the character of the child study itself.

Second, in addition to leading psychologists to gather more diverse data on children, an activist orientation leads them to fight to give fewer tests. However well they succeed, the effort alone can help reduce the demand for testing. It discourages principals or teachers from using tests in symbolic ways. When tests are used symbolically, the needs of children or the results of a child study are irrelevant because the session has been requested for some reason apart from a child's situation and problems.

One school principal I met during my earlier California research provided an example of symbolic referral. He sometimes refers twenty or thirty children at once for psychological examinations because he believes this action may help administrators in the central office realize how difficult things are in his school. He does not seriously expect all of those children to be placed in special classes, nor does he think about how such a test load will tie up the psychologist's time. The psychologist in this school was primarily oriented toward diagnosis, and the principal was unaware of the pressures the psychologist faced. She was overwhelmed by testing demands but too passive to fight against the principal's ill-considered effort to communicate his problems to the central administrative offices of the district.[18] By repeatedly confronting such a principal with alternative activities and by sometimes opposing his suggestions, an activist psychologist may make others more cautious about increasing the work load.

Third, an activist psychologist is more likely than an administratively oriented one to remain interested in the discipline of psychology and to believe it is important to continually learn about the field. Hoffritz was an exception to this pattern, but other administratively oriented psychologists I met were often professionally inactive.

Ongoing training is important, not just because it might improve knowledge and skills that will make psychologists more expert or proficient in their diagnostic work. It keeps them interested in the psychology in their work and helps them think creatively during interviews. Remaining focused on ideas and the abstract implications of what they see is hard to do in the face of their unending routine. During interviews, some psychologists reported that without frequent contact with other psychologists they begin to feel stale and bored with testing.

If they meet with others, and particularly if they have intense discussions of testing technique or with other technical areas, however, they are more likely to look for and find psychologically compelling insights in test results. This is not just a matter of proper technique in testing. If one takes the psychological perspective seriously and if one accepts the need to treat each child as a unique individual, then one also must consider the need to be an advocate for that child. Advocacy might mean fighting for the student's rights in the decision-making process involved in making special education assignments. It might just as well mean working in unconventional, innovative ways with educators to make the school more responsive to a child's needs.

As we talk about ACORN later, we will see that peers also may be critical of colleagues whom they think test in too mechanical a fashion. Although there is nothing to guarantee that a group of school psychologists will define acceptable practice in line with some ideal of clinical practice, peer pressure encourages psychologists to look for the broader implications of their day-to-day work in schools. The pressure of completing requests for child studies and the discomfort of being an outsider in the schools encourage psychologists to try to be accepted as good, conscientious members of their school staffs.

This can lead them to make professional compromises, like conducting more tests than they can comfortably complete in the time available, which makes it difficult to be careful about their psychology. Peer pressure from other psychologists encourages people to be cautious about making compromises. It is not that psychologists slavishly follow a formal code of ethics or that they are afraid of their colleagues. The caution helps psychologists avoid constructing a role that is based on expediency and comfort in one's day-to-day work life.

An activist role is preferable to an administrative one because it is built on idealism. It is difficult for psychologists to create new ways of applying their academic knowledge to the existing situations in schools. It is dangerous for them to challenge established ideas of what a school psychologist should do or to seem critical or not trusting of other school staff members. To be activists in the face of opposition, they must be committed. An image of psychology that requires involvement in and an understanding of the whole setting in which they work often provides the fuel for this commitment.

Activist psychology will not grossly change or improve schools. Rather, the psychologist who uses this approach will have a self-interest in being somewhat distant from and critical of the core enterprise of schools—regular classroom instruction. Only with this distance can they see problems and find the freedom to innovate. This in turn leads them to serve children more completely and in a way that is more attentive to both the students and of the educators who serve them.

Perhaps it would be too much to call these psychologists in-house advocates for children, but when psychologists are activists, they are likely to be on the lookout for conflicts, organizational problems, and emotional problems involving everyone in the schools. They are more likely to recognize instances where such problems lead to special education referrals. They also are likely to have ideas about how to intervene on those problems. Although they behave as child advocates as they intervene in the school, they are not advocates per se. Rather, advocacy acts as a catalyst, giving them opportunities to help themselves and broaden their role as school psychologists.

CHAPTER 4

The Strategy of School Psychology

Up to this point, the distinction between activist and administration-oriented psychologists might be taken as equivalent to a distinction between psychologists who serve children and those who serve school staffs. I have asserted that a tendency exists among school psychologists to allow testing children to crowd out activities that might be therapeutic for children. This tendency, coupled with the desire of regular educators for psychologists to devote their hours to psychometrics, might make it seem that any psychologist who takes seriously the responsibility to serve school system needs must capitulate to "hyper-testing syndrome." Although we shall see in Chapter Five that there is a strong relationship between an administrative orientation and rapid testing, the causal factor is passivity, not a desire to help other educators do their jobs well. There is a sharp division in the ranks of school psychologists based on occupational background and professional orientation that is linked to activism or passivity.

It is important that we explore in more detail what potential exists in school psychology for activism or role creation. We will focus on the potential for strategic thinking in organizational action. This chapter will outline the realms of strategy in which the psychologists whom I observed operate. Again, the distinction between activist- and administration-oriented psychologists is important to keep in mind. The latter take the organizational structure of the school system as externally defined and static. In fact, this might be a pragmatic, reasonable attitude to adopt in certain situations. With that attitude, however, one sees roles as sharply defined and functions as clearly separated. There are clear hierarchies of authority. One has superiors who define the

scope of one's task responsibilities and, most importantly, who take responsibility for outcomes.

Activists treat organizational structure as malleable material.
Formal administrative responsibilities present real constraints that
limit the scope of action. But those responsibilities also legitimate one's
presence in an organization, provide one with an area of authority that
others tend not to challenge, and establish routine settings for interacting and exchanging services with others. Formal structure is limiting, but it also provides means for performing activities not anticipated
in any organizational plan. For activists, organizational structure is one
of the tools available for advancing one's interests or for carrying out
goals that may or may not be publicly known.

Organizational activists tend to move outside the formal confines
of their defined organizational status, seeking to become involved in
defining and solving problems in an eclectic manner. Some do this because they have an entrepreneurial attitude toward their work. They
are interested in expanding their realm of activities, forming bonds
with influential people, and being influential in organizational affairs.
Others want to work on problems they find interesting rather than simply on those tasks assigned them by a formal organizational chart. Still
others try to expand their role as necessary "foreign relations." To avoid
having others define their role in narrow terms, they must educate
teachers, principals, specialists, parents, and special office administrators about the range of functions a psychologist may perform. Education
becomes possible when one builds strong, informal relationships with
people elsewhere in the school system. It also becomes possible if one
can design new functions that illustrate the power and usefulness of a
psychological approach to educational problems.

The overt purpose of this chapter is to show how strategic thinking can enter into all aspects of school psychologists' work. We will see
that it applies as much to routine role activities and mandated cooperative relationships as it does to intrigues that break the mold of standard
operating procedures.

There is a troubling, analytically difficult side to this presentation
as well. As we look at different modes of strategic thinking, we will repeatedly see psychologists bending the rules, hiding their real purposes
as they interact with others, and flirting with dishonesty in other ways.
Up to now, I have argued that psychologists who rush testing violate
test norms and risk improper evaluations of minority children. The best
defense against rushed testing is an aggressive, creative, activist approach to work. Now as we explore what this approach involves, we will
see that an activist orientation, like the administrative one, also entails

violating test norms and engaging in other activities one might say violate professional ethics. I can explain why I think it is all right for activists to break the rules but not right for their more passive colleagues to do so. If we wish to objectively distinguish "good" from "bad" school psychology—something one might do for policy reasons or to carry out survey research—we are likely to have trouble. Chapter Five is devoted to overcoming this analytic problem.

Sources of Influence for School Psychologists

As just suggested, strategic activities by psychologists may grow either from unconventional, entrepreneurial relationships formed with other school personnel—out-of-role behavior—or from the evaluation-related activities that most characterize school psychologists' work—in-role behavior. Their strategic activities also vary in terms of the organizational level or unit that provides the setting for their intervention: psychologists may engage in small scale, relatively private projects involving one or two other staff members; they may operate in small groups made up of other special or regular staff members; or they may intervene at the level of formal administration. As Figure 4 shows, psychologists may operate in or out of role at all three levels. There are six types of strategic action for us to examine: test giving, team work, test score reporting, informal extensions, alliances, and program developers.

Test Giving

In their role as diagnosticians, psychologists are generally given a choice either to approve or veto the placement of children in special education classes. This is a negative power since a veto does not encourage involvement in the process of selecting children for referral. By the time psychologists are called on, educators already have decided which children have learning problems requiring special attention. Mercer shows that educators typically will have referred students as learning problems for several years before they ask for a psychological evaluation.[1] Before trying special education, teachers and principals often will have switched children to different classes, given them special instruction, and held them back a grade. Desirable as these adjustive efforts might be, a consequence is that by the time children are called to the attention of school psychologists, their status as school failures has long been established. They are referred to special education as a last-ditch effort.[2]

FIGURE 4. **Types of Strategic Intervention by School Psychologists**

ORGANIZATIONAL LEVEL

	INDIVIDUAL SERVICE	INTER-STATUS RELATIONS	ORGANIZATIONAL INTERVENTION
IN ROLE: TESTING RELATED	TEST GIVING 1	TEAM WORK 2	TEST SCORE REPORTING 3
OUT OF ROLE: NOT TESTING RELATED	4 DIAGNOSTIC EXTENSIONS	5 ALLIANCES	6 PROGRAM DEVELOPMENT

Psychologists, having been uninvolved during the years of frustration when teachers and principals worked with children who had problems, find it difficult to veto many of the children that have been referred. They know neither the teachers nor the children very well in most cases. Just as they had little involvement with the pupils prior to referral, they will have little contact after a decision is made. They will not suffer whatever costs educators might anticipate should difficult children be returned to the regular classroom. Given their peripheral position in schools and a desire to become more involved and valued in school life, most psychologists are reluctant to veto referrals.

Intelligence tests provide psychologists with a convincing, legitimate tool for reinforcing their decision when they feel it is necessary to refuse a child entrance to special education classes. Because educators so respect test scores, the strongest move a psychologist can make to change minds is to test a child and report definitive results that support his or her point of view on the case at hand. Such a report is generally accepted without question.

Despite the power of test scores, psychologists are reluctant to use them to veto cases. Besides wishing not to confront the regular educators, test results are not completely under psychologists' control. They are behavioral measures, and as such often provide ambiguous information. Results could support special class placement or be used to argue for retention in the mainstream, perhaps with support from reading or speech therapy, parent tutoring, or some other sort of extra help. Children referred for special classes, after all, generally have not been doing a satisfactory job of completing cognitive tasks. In larger cities, those children are also likely to be poor, minorities, or both. Since tests are normed against school performance and minorities and poor children consistently score below the mean, most of those children referred to psychologists will perform subnormally whether or not they are educationally handicapped in the purest sense. It is easiest for psychologists to go along with a referral rather than point out the ambiguity of test results.

There are cases about which psychologists form strong opinions. This may happen because of facts that appear during their child study. More commonly, one of the educators a psychologist has come to know well will consult with him or her about particular children before a referral is made. Having worked out a treatment program, the psychologist then may approach the child study and decision process with strong ideas about how the case should be resolved. Under those circumstances, test results can be a powerful weapon for influencing the decision process. Regular educators usually do not understand the logic of testing or how tests may be used to build a diagnostic argument. Consequently, they are rarely equipped to challenge the way psychologists use the ambiguities of test results to build their case. Taking test results as objective, invariate measures, regular educators tend to accept interpretations of test results as unavoidable, "hard" results. Psychologists can capitalize on this misunderstanding of test results to affect the outcome of a case as in the following example.

Betty Sue Wheeler: Advocate. Betty Sue Wheeler was assigned to the Severely Learning Disabled Program (SLDP) of the ACORN Special Education Cooperative as well as to the Barnard-Thompson High School District (BTHS) at the time of my interview/observation. She was in her first year as a full-status psychologist after having served a one-year internship at ACORN. Wheeler, like other first-year psychologists at ACORN, found herself working in a school district with which other more experienced members of the ACORN psychological staff had encountered problems. Since ACORN provides psychological services to fourteen small suburban school districts, the senior psychologists gradually move into the more interesting and accepting school settings. Most openings for new psychologists are in districts that provide few opportunities for diverse applications of one's psychological skills or in ones in which psychologists have previously found themselves unsuccessfully embroiled in political battles within the local school system administration. Some of the younger psychologists had prospered in such difficult settings, but Wheeler found her present assignment to BTHS stifling.

The SLDP was much more interesting to her. She is more comfortable working with younger children, and this is a new program. It is still establishing itself and is still seeking a niche within the system of regular and special education programs ACORN serves. Because most of the member school districts run their own learning disability programs, the SLDP has had some difficulties establishing a need for its services. ACORN runs the SLDP with its own staff independently of any local school district, hoping to serve children with low incidence problems. A number of administrators from ACORN's member districts doubted the need for the SLDP when it was proposed, even though their superintendents, serving as members of ACORN's board of directors, had voted to create the program.

There were continual problems with parents, school principals, and district administrators who questioned whether particular children really needed to be assigned to a self-contained classroom so far from their neighborhood schools. Much of Wheeler's time was given to answering these complaints, and she responded energetically. Not only was she concerned with protecting the SLDP teachers and their classes from the disruption such complaints threatened, she hoped that if the program were well established and accepted it would become a full-time assignment for her.

On the day I observed, Wheeler had received queries about two students in the SLDP, one from a parent and one from a regular school principal. Both asked whether the students really needed to be in the program. The students had already been screened, evaluated, and classified according to normal special education referral procedures, yet dissatisfaction continued.

The legal status of special education programs is such that their directors may stand by a student placement in either a special or a regular class if that placement has been established as the most appropriate one for the child. Thus, Wheeler was in a position to simply deny that the LD students should be transferred to some other setting. She was convinced that they needed to be in the SLD class.

At the same time, a new program like this one can be easily threatened. Dissatisfied parents or school administrators can cause the superintendents to later withdraw their support for the program. Also, special education programs depend for their success on parents, regular teachers, and principals to suggest that the right kinds of students be referred to them and to cooperate with special teachers, supporting their operations.

Wheeler thus felt obligated to go through the motions of evaluating the students in question. Because she felt convinced about the outcome ahead of time, having worked in class with the special teacher, Wheeler did not feel compelled to give each child a complete child study of the kind described with Sam Osterweis in Chapter Two. All she needed to gain was sufficient data to support the case she wanted to make before the principal and before the parents. The tests she gave were brief and disorganized.

In the morning, Wheeler concentrated in getting proper test results from Billy, the first of the two students. We began by looking for prior test records that had been removed from the ACORN central office by Mrs. Wright, a teacher from one of his special classes. Mrs. Wright spent the morning at a school other than the one in which Billy's SLD class was located, so we drove for half an hour looking for her, hoping to retrieve Billy's old records. We then spent forty-five minutes talking with Mrs. Wright about the dissatisfactions of teaching in the special programs of ACORN. Then we drove twenty minutes to Billy's school to find him. Once we arrived in his class, his teacher, Mrs. Hansen, asked Wheeler if she would also have time to test another student, Mary, whom the two women had previously discussed. Wheeler agreed, and took both students at once for testing.

The testing session was chaotic. We went off to the school's book room, a large closet that contained several small desks and tables reserved for the psychologist's use. Neither of the students seemed ready to concentrate. Each was given a paper and pencil test to work on—a Wide Range Achievement Test (WRAT)—but they spent most of the next half hour fooling around, joking, and fighting with each other. Finally, Wheeler decided she had enough of a result from Billy's test and took the two back to class. She felt it was hopeless to try to test Mary today and put off her testing session until later. Meanwhile, Billy's test results should be sufficient to convince the principal that he needed to continue in the SLD class.

We went on to find Sammy, our other testing candidate. In his school, we ran into more disruption and housekeeping chores. Eventually, we took him to the book room for his session with the WRAT. Sammy was no more interested than Billy and Mary had been. He completed one or two sections of the test and then announced he would do no more. It was late in the afternoon, and by now both Sammy and the psychologist were tired. Wheeler decided she had enough material to make her case and did not fight him any longer. She took him back to class.

Despite these unsatisfactory testing sessions, Wheeler was unconcerned. She does not like extended testing sessions and was glad she did not have to wrestle with all of the different subtests one must manage in a complete test session. She also enjoyed the informality of the session and the opportunity it afforded her to chat informally with the kids. She wants to do more of this.

Essentially, this sort of testing is a formality as far as she is concerned. Wheeler and the SLD teachers knew Billy and Sammy had not gained much in their time in the LD class and that returning them to a regular class or to a higher level LD class was unwarranted. What she needed was some concrete evidence of their performance to show the parents and school officials that would convince them her position was correct. Because of this, she implied, it was not necessary for her to give the students complete work-ups or even to be very careful about how the test sessions were conducted. She only had to have evidence that she had tested them and that the test results confirmed her suspicions about their inadequacies.

Teamwork

The Education for All Handicapped Children Act mandates that school psychologists work as part of an interdisciplinary team that evaluates children referred by regular school personnel as candidates for special education classes. Teams seem like a logical approach. Made up of a social worker, a nurse, a speech teacher, and a special class teacher, in addition to the psychologist, these groups possess a combination of skills that can address the reality that student problems are often multidimensional. When experts operate within their particular disciplines, they may miss problems that are outside their area of interest. Combining knowledge with other professionals allows more thorough evaluations—one would expect that it is less likely that important information will be overlooked in team evaluations—and facilitates creating deeper and richer knowledge among the diagnosticians.

Although this interdisciplinary team idea sounds terrific, in practice it is hard to find teams that work well together. My overall impression was that their teams were, at best, irrelevant for most of the psychologists I met. Typically, none of the team members would have great influence in the schools they served, so team meetings would be an exercise in futility if they sought to have a meaningful impact on those schools. Furthermore, teams tended to suffer from overwork and poor coordination. Not all members of a team served the same schools. Each team member received individual requests for services from their host schools; as a result, they would not be working with the same child at the same time. In some cases, team members would compete with each other for influence with local school officials. I visited one school where the social worker sought to be the only one working closely on the interactional problems of teachers and principals and competed relentlessly with the school psychologist who, ultimately, was relegated to a narrow testing role. All of these factors conspire to make interdisciplinary teams little more than a bureaucratic fiction for many psychologists.

There were occasions, however, when I found teams working together closely and effectively. These teams generally did not follow the idealized model of interdisciplinary coordination I described earlier that justifies this structural arrangement. Members of the various diciplines shared information with each other, but the cohesion the teams enjoyed did not come from a simple love of knowledge and a desire just to produce a fully rounded picture of each child. Teams become effective when their members agree on some collective goal. Even though teams are mandated, it is difficult for their members to find the time to meet regularly. There also may be subtle conflicts of interest that must be overcome before close cooperation is possible. Effective teams do not just happen. They happen for reasons. We see this with Maria Higgins's team.

Maria Higgins: Voice of La Raza. Despite her Anglo name, Maria Higgins was born in Mexico City and is fully bilingual in Spanish and English. She works in several schools that have heavy Hispanic enrollments in Chicago and is the leader of the most effective interdisciplinary team I have ever observed. All of the team members are bilingual; this makes them an unusually effective lobbying group working on behalf of Hispanic children as those students encounter difficulties in the public schools. Although the Chicago School System has a large number of minority group members on its staff, my observation occurred during the time when integration of local school staffs was a primary concern for educational policymakers. Shortly after I left the field, the board of education ordered that all local schools must have equally integrated staffs. This meant that minority group members who had been working in their communities might be sent to the predominantly white northwest side. A consequence in Maria Higgins's schools was that many of the Hispanic children were being taught by Anglos with little knowledge of Spanish and little capacity for understanding why children were failing.

The interdisciplinary team Higgins led played an important role by helping the regular educators distinguish children who needed the help of a learning disability class from those who mostly needed to be placed in a bilingual class. Some of this was a straightforward matter of informing the regular educators what ought to be done. Unfortunately, the team sometimes had to be more forceful in its lobbying efforts. Some bilingual classes were taught primarily in English, for example. Children with language deficiencies would not benefit from such a class, and so team members might have to argue forcefully that the child ought to be placed in a learning disability class with a bilingual teacher, even though the child was not learning disabled.

My impression was that the team gained much of its collective influence from Higgins's leadership. She was a force. Maria Higgins came to school psychology with a Ph.D. in counseling psychology and a master's degree in comparative literature. In contrast to many of the other Chicago school psychologists I interviewed, she had never taught. Rather, she came to her job via a series of research projects involving bilingual education. When she was an undergraduate in one of the local colleges, she had been hired to work on a curriculum development project because she was bilingual. One project led to another, and she found this a convenient way to support herself as she did her graduate work in literature. Eventually, however, she was convinced to switch over to psychology as she worked on her Ph.D.

With her degree in hand, Higgins began teaching part-time at a local college. Part-time work and evening classes were convenient for her at first as she married and began raising a family. She continued to be involved in bilingual educational research, which she also did at night. Some of this work was done cooperatively with the Chicago Public Schools, and she developed a close working relationship with the head of bilingual education for the Chicago schools. He urged her to take a full-time job with the board of education and to begin working as a school psychologist since there were very few bilingual psychologists in the system. She decided to take this job because the hours were regular, the pay was good, and her alternatives mostly involved university teaching jobs that would require moving to another city.

Higgins joined the Bureau of Child Study with a clear personal agenda. She had an extensive background in the problems of bilingual education and was familiar with the difficulties the Chicago schools were having serving Spanish-speaking children. Although she and her other team member were quite positive about their relationships with others in their host schools, they saw their task as that of shaping school programs and intervening on behalf of children whose problems of bilingualism were not fully understood by school officials.

I spent a morning observing the team at work and talking to its members. They met once a week as a group, and each member did his or her paperwork on the cases they were assigned. They explained that it is suprisingly awkward for the team actually to coordinate its work. They all are assigned the same cases, but the rate at which they can collect data is different and the demands of the work days are different. Because all of the team members have a special interest in bilingual children, however, they have insisted on meeting together each week just to do paperwork. Their meetings have no agenda. They simply sit around a large table, fill out forms, think out loud as they work up a particular case, and allow group discussions to spring from this parallel paperwork.

The process is surprisingly effective at focusing attention on troublesome cases. In discussing one student, Jorge, with whom Mary Bailey, who teaches the mildly learning disabled (LD), works on a part-time basis, it was revealed that Jorge is in a bilingual class. Conversation followed about whether it was legitimate to test him in English if he requires a Spanish language class. This led to a discussion of his bilingual teacher and the collective observation that, as far as they have been able to see, little Spanish is spoken in the class. The boy has made no progress in that class even though he has done well with the LD teacher.

The social worker commented that since the bilingual teacher does not seem very good for Jorge, perhaps they should recommend him for a full-time LD placement, a class taught by an LD teacher other than Bailey. This led to a general discussion about the inconsistency of bilingual programs in the schools the team members served and their frustration in helping students like Jorge. They began discussing special education alternatives, but rejected the idea of placing him in a severe LD class since there was no way that label could be justified. They asked Bailey if she had space in her full-time class but she, somewhat horrified at more overcrowding, said no. Eventually, frustrated at their lack of alternatives, the group put the case aside to be taken up later.

The conversation was a rambling one that took perhaps twenty minutes and showed how this collective paper processing allowed people to informally share ideas about a particular case. The conversation seemed quite different from those in the other interdisciplinary groups I observed when they met to make decisions about children. The discussions in Higgins's team meetings were unfocused, filling in details on children and schools so that people could better understand the intractability of problems. Most due process meetings I have attended seem hemmed in by formality, the need to make a decision, and by the limitations of mandated rules.

In this team meeting, members saw their task as that of honestly assessing the shortcomings of the schools they served, the resources that were available, and the needs of the children they were working with. Their job is to find the best fit between services and students' needs, even if the rules are broken and a stubborn regular educator must be insulted. Although it perhaps seems obvious that a team would do this to serve the interests of children, members of this group clearly saw their efforts at coordination as a struggle to maintain and as a procedure that was unusual. My impression was that they made this effort because they shared a strong sense of purpose focused on bilingual education problems.

Some of that sense of collective mission no doubt came from the backgrounds of individuals and from the experiences they had had with children. I had little doubt, however, that Maria Higgins was the main source of commitment and energy for this group. She was clearly a respected leader. Group members liked her, but more importantly she was enormously competent, deeply informed about issues in bilingual education, and clearly tied into a city-wide coalition of educators seeking to improve the school experiences of Hispanic children. She joined the "big" politics of this city-wide coalition with the "little" politics of her interdisciplinary team.

Test Score Reporting

The special education classification process culminates in meetings that include members of the special education team—school psychologist, social worker, school nurse, speech pathologist, and special teacher—the school principal, regular class teacher of a child, and, perhaps, parents. Specialists' findings from their child studies are reported, and this data forms the foundation for a group decision about how to resolve the case. Of all the data collected, Berk, Bridges, and Shih report, IQ test scores tend to be most predictive of the final result.[3] At the same time, as I suggested earlier, psychologists tend to feel that they cannot easily counter the wishes of regular educators, whatever they may be.

There is an irony in this juxtaposition. The tests carry the authority of objectivity, but the people who administer the tests often are denied similar legitimacy. Organizationally marginal and politically weak, psychologists risk being further excluded from regular school activities if they too often and too vigorously oppose regular educators. At the same time, the authority of tests is based on frequent misunderstandings by educators of what these devices are and how they are used in psychological evaluation. Educators tend to view them as objective measures of student abilities. Although test socres are based on behavioral measures, the results a psychologist reports are an interpretation. The psychologist must explain what the behavioral results mean to the uninitiated and with this responsibility goes considerable editorial freedom. One can dramatically change the meaning of test results by emphasizing different aspects of the data. Because test results are respected but their opinions are not, psychologists tend to make their points covertly. Rather than saying, "I think . . ." they are likely to say, "The subject's shock at encountering this symbol in the Rorschach test means he has this sort of problem and needs that sort of treatment."

One incentive for psychologists to act covertly is the intractability of educators' ignorance. Test theory is statistical, subtle, and often counterintuitive. Most educators at best have only an introductory knowledge of it. Psychologists have neither the time nor the authority to instruct principals and teachers on test theory, so there is little they can do to correct the misperceptions. Misunderstandings of their work and of its products seem to be an unavoidable and permanent problem.

Faced with this knowledge, psychologists have a choice. They may fool themselves and decide that test scores really are objective and accurate measures of student psychological characteristics and that educators, being responsible people, will not or could not misuse them. Alternatively, being concerned that test socres will be taken as more consequential and more culture-fair and revealing than they are, psychologists may decide it is more important that educators come away from a test session with an understanding of the children involved than that they come away with test results that are calculated in a scrupulously correct manner. Psychologists may alter the way tests are given or they may add information to a report not gained from a test session to enhance the effect of important results even though these alterations may be improper from the standpoint of test methodology. These alterations of standard technical practice to produce a stronger or more authoritative effect is what I mean by covert action. They take advantage of the mystification of testing to build their organizational influence.

Psychologists may be convinced that regular educators do not fully understand why many of the children who are referred for diagnosis and special class placements are having problems, but they do not often give the extraordinary effort required by collection of diverse information and careful staging of their report. They hold back for several reasons. Some children are referred for instructional problems psychologists do not feel competent to address. Others are referred for acting out in school, and the main problem is how to contain them. These and other children are referred for problems that may have little to do with the definition of learning disabilities or other educational handicaps, but since the schools lack resources to handle those children in other ways, psychologists may go along with placing them in special education classes.

The most important reason psychologists do not take special pains with each case, however, is that they cannot. However competent, interested, or concerned a psychologist may be, he or she is still likely to face a production pressure to complete child studies. There is not time enough to become immersed in each case, so psychologists must engage in triage. They will select some cases because they are interesting, others because a special injustice seems to have been done, others because staff members are involved of whom they have learned to be suspicious, and still others because staff members they are close to want a particular outcome that is different from that desired by someone else. Whatever the reason for choosing a case, those that are selected must appear infrequently. Most cases, however troubling they may be, must be treated as routine approvals to which one devotes a minimum of energy.

In some respects, it is the infrequency of their greater efforts that allows the psychologist to be effective. Other educators expect psychologists to be formal, perhaps terse, and to present somewhat abstract and esoteric findings that confirm what everyone else thinks already. This contributes both to educators' misunderstanding of tests and to their feeling that the psychologist is a useless bureaucratic appendage to the schools and a narrow, technical specialist. When the psychologist plays a more active role, introducing data collected in a more eclectic, humanistic manner, educators are not likely to notice the change.

To them, the psychologist remains in role. Suddenly in this case the measures and the esoterica come alive. By acting as though diverse information is test data, psychologists can play on the respect educators have for scientific gadgetry and the expertise of the technician to have their recommendations accepted. By managing an image and choosing cases carefully, psychologists can wield influence out of proportion to their marginal role in the whole enterprise, as we see in the following example.

Al Simmons: Salesman and Politician. Dr. Al Simmons, one of the leaders of ACORN's psychologists, works in two high schools, Marsh North and Marsh South. Both schools draw black and white students from low-income and working-class towns, and the schools have a history of student rebelliousness and racial conflict. He has considerable autonomy in deciding how he wants to spend his time, although he is primarily engaged with in testing or in talking with students. During the time I observed at ACORN, he repeatedly said that he believes the psychologist must be a salesman and a politician in the school. Younger psychologists in ACORN valued Simmons's insistance on the importance of recognizing that their relations among school staff, not objective qualities of their work, would determine how effective and successful they were at helping children in schools. Despite this attitude, he does not involve himself in the politics that swirl among school staff members, nor does he try to influence the way his schools are run. He contents himself with learning as much as he can about the students and using this information to influence the outcomes of specific cases.

Simmons emphasizes that his job is to let teachers know he is there, that he is willing to talk, and that he is interested in their problems with students. So that he does not have to go out and drum up interest in his services, he believes it is important to take advantage of certain aspects of his role that allow him to get information not available to others. This not only includes the standard data psychologists alone are competent to gather, it also includes taking advantage of the scheduling flexibility one has as a psychologist and the freedom one has to move from place to place within schools, between schools, and around the neighborhood. These advantages allow Simmons often to provide teachers with straightforward facts about what is going on in the lives of their students that the teachers otherwise would not be aware of. Most important to him in talking with teachers or reporting his findings in a classification meeting is presentation of his data so they are understandable and compelling and offering them in a way that seems insightful to the teachers and to other members of the education staff.

To this end, Simmons has developed a network of contacts around his schools of people who are not normally included in school decision making. The day I observed him, he spent perhaps forty-five minutes in the teachers' lounge talking to the school security officer, Joe Malchuk. They discussed three or four students who had been referred to Simmons. Malchuk was a former local football star who had gone on to play with the Chicago Bears, had been hurt, and now was back home working for the school. He combines great familiarity with local families, whom he has known for years, with popularity and admiration among young people in town. These attributes allow him to learn about the local adolescent subculture and about the background to disruptive incidents involving students. Simmons goes out of his way to talk to all of the school security guards because, although other educators tend not to respect them, they often have useful information about students.

As Simmons talked to Malchuk, there was no sense that this was a formal interview or that Simmons was gracing the security guard by including him in the psychodiagnostic process. The psychologist maintained a studied chattiness appropriate to the coffee room and to a time when two people who happen to work together and enjoy each others' company take a rest from their labors. During the conversation, the focus was on events that had happened in school, like last week's football game, or disturbances that had occurred recently. When a student's name came up, Malchuk would usually make some comment about how he had had to quiet the student down or how there had been trouble in his or her family. Simmons might then ask a specific question, coupled with a bit of information he had to trade. Malchuk would continue and Simmons might follow with a comment, mentioning that he had interviewed the student and that he had the impression that he had trouble relating to older males or was having trouble with the opposite sex. During my interview, Simmons said most of his speculations are based on interpretations of projective test results. Joe Malchuk, however, then would offer his comments on Simmons's observations, filling in with concrete details. Later, this information becomes part of Simmons's psychological report on the students.

However well integrated you are into the informal network of the school, Simmons told me, the most important thing is that you be competent in your work. Competence is a hard quality to define. For him it means being able to give answers during staffings (e.g., classification meetings) to teachers' questions about students. A danger in volunteering answers, however, is that people turn to you, the psychologist, as someone who can explain causes of erratic behavior or of learning failures. It is tempting to give elaborate explanations whether or not you really understand the case. This is deadly. You have to be candid, he says, and acknowledge your ignorance about certain techniques or admit that you do not have ideas about a particular student.

Teachers have to become confident in the psychologist and in what he or she says, because the psychologist is a consultant who can be used or discarded. Anyone who believes that the way to be a good psychologist is to give the correct test and to provide careful, objective reports about students is asking to be ignored. Teachers must become convinced that they should believe the school psychologist because he or she is likely to think of constructive things that they may miss.

Although Simmons also tries to broaden his psychologist role by seeking out new projects, the focus of his efforts to make his presence valuable to the schools he serves is on classification hearings and teachers' conferences. To build support for a fuller role, he counts on being able to demonstrate in these meetings that he is better than other staff members at observing students and school life and at gathering data. Not only does he try to present information others do not have, he emphasizes that his investigations are done in a short period of time and involve students others know much better than he does.

To create this effect, Simmons presents his information as a summary of his formal data gathering. He does not let it be known that he is rehashing the security guard's gossip. Malchuk's information, rather, becomes part of his child study. The information is presented to enhance the prestige and influence of psychological knowledge and of Simmons as the local psychology expert.

When we speak of test score reporting as a source of influence, it is precisely in this sense that reporting provides opportunities for building respect as an expert and a specialist. This is the institutionalized time at which the psychologist is invited to contribute to the management of difficult students. As Simmons recognizes, his role as expert depends heavily on the expectation that he will be a consultant, someone who 1) is relatively uninvolved in the daily problems of schooling and 2) who has some special skills that provide useful insights. Creating and preserving this image demands that in his actual work he not be an isolated, technology-bound expert. Rather, he must be continually in touch with what is going on in school, seeking out concrete, mundane information about students referred to him for evaluation. This allows him to capitalize upon the expectation of educators that he spend most of his time doing routine testing and the insights he reports seem primarily to be products of that work.

Informal Extensions

The psychologists I wish to characterize in this section seek out informal extensions of their role and see these as essential or core elements of their school work. We saw Arnold Cohen in an earlier chapter establishing parent groups in the evenings to discuss problems controlling adolescent children. He did this in part simply because a need existed, but Cohen also saw the program as a device for educating parents and regular school personnel about the possible services he might provide beyond testing. These therapeutic services are the kind of work he thinks he ought to spend most of his time engaged in. Because his school district is conservative, these activities are not readily accepted, and he is left either to develop programs in his spare time to or to work only with receptive individuals whom he can help without being obvious about spending substantial amounts of time counseling and advising.

Although some psychologists achieve informal extensions of their diagnostic role as Cohen did, by self-consciously creating programs to educate or convince other educators about the value of psychology, others expand their role in response to specific problems that crop up as they conduct child studies. Where teachers or principals seem chronically implicated in contributing to student failure experiences, a psychologist might feel obliged to learn more about the personal or social problems of school officials that seem to be involved. Finding receptive school people, a psychologist might work closely with a group of teachers or with a principal for a year or more providing support, advice, and administrative assistance during a stressful period. In such a relationship one can really "do" psychology. It also can provide the foundation for further broadening of one's role. An example of such involvement is provided by June Allen.

June Allen: Teacher Counselor. June Allen is one of the younger psychologists working in the ACORN cooperative, having been there only three years. She works in the Pond Lily School System, which consists four elementary schools, all of which she services each week. Pond Lily is a town that has existed as a community for some time, in contrast to the newer bedroom communities that have sprung up around it in the last twenty years. Only recently has it been infiltrated by suburban migrants, and so there is a strong sense of local tradition and identity among local families and in the school system. One manifestation of this feeling is concern that blacks, who have progressively been moving into nearby towns, will come into Pond Lily. The political activism racial concerns have spawned has spilled over into school politics, resulting in a conservative movement on the school board. Dr. Henry Jones, the superintendent, has consequently emphasized economizing in programs and district autonomy from school district unification efforts advocated by organizations like ACORN. Regional programs generally require that local districts make financial contributions for new programs and that they accept some supervision of their programs by an outside authority. Resisting these, Dr. Jones has been seeking ways of withdrawing from ACORN.

With such a district, it did not surprise Allen to find a large testing backlog when she began working in Pond Lily and that people expected her only to work as a diagnostician. She claims that though this restricted her for a year or two, she has recently had less difficulty with test pressure and has been able to direct more of her energy to helping teachers resolve frustrations and anxieties that arise in relations with their principals or as a natural by-product of teaching. She was able to do this quickly, in part, by being assertive about what she wanted to do and about how she thought her skills could best be used. She also has come to be accepted by a core group of teachers who talk with her often and involve her in helping to resolve their school program difficulties.

According to Allen, whittling down one's testing load and reducing the demand for child studies is primarily a matter of knowing your own mind and not being afraid to insist on work arrangements that allow you to work most effectively. At the same time, she has a keen awareness that demands superintendents, principals, and teachers make upon school psychologists can originate in conflicts they are having or insecurities they feel. She also believes certain teachers and principals regularly contribute to and exacerbate problems children have concerning learning and getting along in their classes. She is not very optimistic about being able to solve the continuing problems these instructors present in a school, but she tries hard to "clean up the mess" such people create. In addition to being assertive, one must be attentive to the politics of the local school and seek to make constructive contributions to the resolution of conflicts if one wishes to expand one's role.

The clearest example of a problem person in one of Allen's schools is the principal of the Elm Elementary School. She describes him as a fellow who professes to run an open school, but whom she finds to be a "dictator." There is no structure, she explains, except when he needs it to achieve a goal of his own. There are no ways for teachers to formally express their needs and to have them met. Teachers also feel that there are ever-shifting expectations for performance, which make them uncertain about how to organize their classes, how experimental projects will be viewed by the principal, and what the consequences will be should their classes become disrupted for a time by student misbehavior.

The teachers react with frustration and sometimes with anger to the ambiguities the principal creates. He does not react much to their outbursts or to their discomfort. Because he retreats when teachers make demands for help or support but is insistent that they help when he wants to complete some project or meet some deadline, it appears to teachers that he wants to take all of the power in the school and use it to further his own purposes.

Teachers have reacted by becoming passive and by appearing weak. They let him run things and try not to interfere with his efforts to achieve goals. Unfortunately, a consequence is that if teachers find children in their classes who persistently cause them problems, they do not get help from the principal. They must try to find some way within the limits of the classroom to manage or to control the children. There is a further danger that they will act out some of their anger at the principal with these difficult children.

Allen became alerted to these difficulties as she was working her way through the testing backlog that greeted her arrival in the district. Gradually, she got to know the teachers in the school during child study sessions and found that several of them were looking for someone to talk to about their anger with the principal. Over time, they also came to talk about new problems they were having with students. Today Allen has come to spend most of her time talking with teachers and helping them solve problems the principal ignores. She sees herself virtually as a surrogate principal and as a lightning rod for teacher anger. Because she is there to talk to, and knowing that other teachers work closely with her, teachers in the school have come to work more closely with each other. Where the principal's hostility tended to make individuals defensive and reluctant to talk openly about their problems, Allen provides them with a bridge because the teachers have learned who they can talk to safely about their problems. As the teacher group builds in intensity and confidence, it becomes less essential that Allen be the one who solves everyone's problems. The principal, meanwhile, seems to recognize Allen's effectiveness, and even though the teachers see him as controlling and power oriented, he leaves her alone to do pretty much what she pleases.

Effective as Allen has been at Elm Elementary, one of her most striking qualities is cynicism about her role. She sees her efforts as a necessary but ultimately insufficient stopgap to the organizational chaos that prevails in the Pond Lily School System. She believes that student problems often have organizational origins like those we have seen at Elm. But she also believes that as school psychologist her influence is so limited that her only practical course is to work with teachers who want help and stay away from those who reject her. She has to accept that many social problems will go on in the schools, either playing themselves out eventually or becoming permanent negative features of the schools.

With this limited view of her role, Allen sees her involvement in problem solving as sporadic and ad hoc rather than programmatic. She has no analysis of what the schools' problem is and how she, as a heroine psychologist, can save children and her colleagues from their bumbling. Rather she is a gadfly, jumping from problem to problem as it comes up and being content with what the system gives her to work on.

With this outlook, child study sessions seem useful to Allen because they give her access to new cases and situations. If she saw her task as one of trying to systematically attack one kind of problem—say, trying to work continually with teachers at Elm—a consequence might be that she would not learn of new problems that have come up in other schools. She would not meet new people who might be receptive to working with her, and she would not learn about new opportunities for working with people who previously had rejected her efforts. Child studies are frustrating because the decision process tears her diagnostic work out of its context. She should have a long-term relationship with teachers and children, working to define and resolve problems, but instead has only a snapshot exposure to their situations. But that very ad hoc quality keeps one from defining the role of psychologist too narrowly or falling into the rut of believing that one approach to school psychology is the right one.

Alliances

Alliances with people outside special education—principals, pupil personnel directors, superintendents, or parents, for example—are another way psychologists can use overt action in the child study process to increase job automony. A psychologist who develops a personal base of support or a constituency may become so influential that he or she may dictate how school psychology will be practiced in the district. With strong support, one can smother opposition from teachers, social workers, or others who have a contrasting view of a school psychologist's role.

In practice, alliance building may lead to behavior not very different from program development. When psychologists use alliances to back up resistance to test pressure, they usually seek to support construction of a role that includes more general psychology. Forging alliances with important people in their school districts does not mean that psychologists need have poor relations with lower-level school personnel.The latter may value relations with an influential psychologist who has the ear of high-level administrators. Alliances thus are not important just because they allow psychologists to win conflicts, they may enable psychologists to become valued and respected members of a school system.

What distinguishes psychologists who form alliances from those who focus more on program development is that the former are more likely to give advice to the decision makers and, in smaller towns, to be included in the policy formation process at the district level. Some of the reasons they can become important are the same ones that normally marginalize psychologists. Because they are not part of the direct line of command from superintendent to regular classroom teacher, psychologists can give help in a variety of administratively unconventional ways.

More importantly, the relative position of the school psychologists in the administrative hierarchy of the public schools often is not well worked out. Their testing is done upon request from principals, which indicates that they are subordinate to this chief officer in neighborhood schools, but other aspects of the role make this subordination unclear. They cannot usually be given orders by any one principal, because they work simultaneously for four or five schools. They must work out an agreeable way to allocate their time to several principals at once. This presents problems like those faced by people who supervise (rather than who are supervised by) principals. Psychologists also tend to be well trained compared with other school personnel. Not only can they pull academic rank on school administrators who are less well trained, many psychologists have extensive experience outside of schools. They are experienced at organizational in-fighting, and they are skilled at casting immediate organizational conflicts into the broader perspective of the professional administrator.

Depending on how talented and ambitious they are, psychologists may tie into the regular educational hierarchy at nearly any level they choose. They may be content as service personnel to teachers, allowing their time to be structured by instructors' demands. Alternatively, they may become personal advisors to higher level administrators—anyone from the superintendent to the assistant superindent for special education. Dr. Allen O'Rourke illustrates this approach.

Dr. Allen O'Rourke: Administrative Consultant. Dr. O'Rourke is the head psychologist of the ACORN cooperative. He spends half of his time working as an administrator and supervisor of other psychologists at ACORN and half working in Watertown, the town in which the cooperative has its offices. Despite his administrative position at ACORN, O'Rourke has the usual responsibilities when he works in his district. On the day I interviewed and observed him, he spent most of the day in classification hearings with other district special education personnel. They were reviewing cases of children placed in private schools for the handicapped. With the expansion of special education programs, these children had to be transferred from the private schools to public programs in a regional center for children with low incidence handicaps. O'Rourke had done child studies of each student.

O'Rourke has worked at ACORN longer than any of its other staff members and has been instrumental in establishing and preserving the strong orientation toward professional psychology that prevails among the psychologists working there. Although most of his work experience has been in schools, he has a long-standing interest in clinical work. He has started a private clinical practice with Dr. Simmons and a former ACORN psychologist and spends most of his spare time working there. Yet he likes working in schools and does not expect to leave school work even when his private practice becomes large enough to allow him to work in it full time. He enjoys teaching and supervising other psychologists and seems genuinely interested in finding ways of injecting a clinical psychology orientation into the standard operating procedures of school systems ACORN serves.

O'Rourke's role in the Watertown School System is strongly colored, on one hand, by his continuing interest in being a clinical psychologist doing private, individual psychotherapy, who happens to work in schools and, on the other, by his experiences in ACORN as it has developed organizationally. When he first came to the cooperative in the mid-1960s, it functioned mainly as a psychological consultation service to the suburbs in the area. Special education programs at that time were small, and relatively few children were referred for evaluations. So psychologists typically served not just several schools but two or three districts. Psychologists had considerable personal autonomy and were encouraged to think of themselves as consulting professionals providing services, rather than as school employees. It was almost as though they were on a fee-for-service arrangement.

As special education programs expanded during the 1970s with the passage of the Education of All Handicapped Children Act (PL 94-142) and demand for child studies increased, local district administrators objected to the autonomy psychologists enjoyed. Other school staff members are so constrained by the physical arrangements of school buildings that most of their time must be spent in particular places doing particular things. Teachers, principals, and administrators all came to be suspicious that the ACORN psychologists were not working as hard as they might. Since the cooperative is controlled by a board of district supervisors, pressure soon began to mount. Mrs. Ethel Johnson was eventually hired by ACORN at the request of its board of member superintendents to straighten out the psychologists.

She, however, made an agreement with O'Rourke and the other psychologists that she would support the importance of in-service training and high professional quality in psychological services as long as the psychologists would let local districts decide what services ought to be provided. Psychologists would have strong support in challenging local district policies if they could argue that those policies interfered with maintaining a high standard of psychological practice. This meant that the psychologists as a group would have considerable power to protect any member who wished to challenge a local district supervisor. The catch was that individual psychologists had to convince the other psychologists that the issue they were embroiled in was important enough for the whole group to risk incurring the anger of a superintendent. That superintendent, in turn, might convince other superintendents to adopt more restrictive policies.

Conflict with local district administrators, coupled with the strong professional orientation O'Rourke and other ACORN psychologists bring to their work, led to creation of an organization in which training, supervision of psychological practice in schools, and a special view of the school psychologist's role became central. ACORN in some respects functions like a graduate school department with elaborate apprenticeship arrangements and strong pressure on participating psychologists to continue to develop intellectually and professionally. All psychologists must work in ACORN's central office on Fridays and all participate in biweekly seminars on a variety of subjects, ranging from neuropsychology to evaluation of Rorschach test protocols. O'Rourke is the director of this program.

Although the activities of the ACORN psychology department are focused on matters of psychological practice, an important side effect is that the psychologists are encouraged to think of themselves as autonomous workers within schools rather than as part of the administrative hierarchy in local districts. O'Rourke is particularly outspoken about this. Psychologists need to be autonomous, he says, because they must believe that their job is to decide what action is called for in a given situation on the basis of their private professional judgment. Autonomy is important if one is to be a *psychologist* in the schools. Equally important, however, O'Rourke believes that the psychologist ought to be a person who can mediate between people in different roles and between educators and various nonschool people—parents, physicians, and professionals in other social service institutions.

This mediating role presents psychologists with both organizational and professional challenges. To be an active but relatively impartial intermediary between all parties who might be involved in a special education case, the psychologist must be relatively free to set his or her own schedule and respected enough to feel comfortable giving advice to the superintendent in the same manner as it would be given to a teacher. To work with all of these different groups intelligently requires that a psychologist also receive eclectic training. Psychologists must understand test and measurement issues to meet the demands of teachers and principals. But they must also be comfortable in a clinical setting to understand and manage emotionally charged situations, and they must have some knowledge of neuropsychology so that they can interpret the meaning of medical findings to educators.

To carry out the mediating role, psychologists must gain the support of people at all school levels for their having an undefined administrative position. O'Rourke works to gain and maintain this support during his school work by talking regularly with people at all organizational levels. He spends about half of his time doing this. He is as likely to listen to the superintendent complain about difficult parents as he is to listen to principals talk about teachers with whom they do not get along. He tries to be sympathetic and nondirective and occasionally helps to cool down conflicts or helps people with personal problems.

Although O'Rourke spends half of his time doing conventional school psychological work, testing children, and attending screening sessions, one has the sense that he is most interested in people from the level of principal on up in the district. As I walked around the Watertown district with him, he exchanged friendly banter with an assistant superintendent. During classification sessions, the director of pupil personnel (the special education director for the district) deferred to his judgment or encouraged him to answer objections to school recommendations raised by parents. One feels that O'Rourke writes his own ticket and that most of the people in the school district are reluctant to oppose him either in matters of professional judgment or in the way he spends time in the schools. He is helpful and informed. He also is a bit too big a fish for them to tangle with.

Some of O'Rourke's authority is a by-product of his position in ACORN, but a good part of it comes from his self-confidence and the self-assurance that he radiates while in schools. He is intelligent and informed on a wide range of subjects. He knows powerful people and expects to be respected. Because he projects such an image, other educators seem willing to let him do pretty much what he wants.

Program Developers

June Allen's case was striking not just because she has so adroitly escaped the limitations of the diagnostician's role but also because she sees a certain peripheralness and disorganization as inherent to the position of the school psychologist. Her strength comes from capitalizing upon her irreverence to the powers that be in Pond Lily. It is a short step from the autonomy she attained, however, to a school psychology role that is not so peripheral and where in fact the practitioner becomes recognized as an important problem solver or troubleshooter for the school system.

What distinguishes such psychologists from people like Allen, whose role comes from a broadening of their diagnostic and consulting function, is that among the former their specialty as diagnostician has largely fallen away. For people assigned to regular school districts, this happens in most cases because a psychologist has moved aggressively to show that he or she can do something other than test that educators value. Sometimes by escaping the diagnostic role a psychologist becomes free to attack just about any problem he or she sees in a school system, as we see in the case of Donna Blackman.

Donna Blackman: Master Teacher. Donna Blackman stood out among all of the psychologists I interviewed as a person who thought of herself primarily as a professional psychologist—rather than as an educator—but who spent virtually all of her time working in classrooms with teachers. She helped develop new instructional programs and helped foster communication and cooperation between teachers, parents, and the children. She was involved in and committed to the educational process in schools and was critical of the aloofness characteristic of many profession-oriented school psychologists. Yet she would not take existing school practices as given. She continually translated abstract psychological ideas or narrow research findings and techniques into practical educational applications. Thus, she was both education oriented and creative in the way a research scholar would be in her work, an unusual combination.

Blackman is a middle-aged woman who came to psychology rather late. She began work on the B.A. at a prestigious local university, but married before she finished her degree and quit school to go with her husband when he was transferred to another city. She reared a family, then when her children got older, returned to college. She earned a B.A. and an M.A. in clinical psychology. She worked as a research assistant and as a clinical psychologist in a state mental health facility. After one year, her husband was transferred back to the Chicago area.

Having only an M.A., Blackman found it difficult to get back into clinical work in Illinois where a Ph.D. is required for clinical psychologists, and for three years she did not work. She considered going back to school for further training but decided she did not want to do the work required for a Ph.D. Instead, she took a job with ACORN. At first, she served several school districts, traveling from place to place giving tests and providing other psychological services. One of the districts she served was the Edgewood Elementary School District; after two years she began working full time in that district. Although she came to Edgewood as one of ACORN's traveling psychologists, she ultimately resigned from ACORN and became a regular employee of the school district. This was an unusual arrangement among the people I interviewed, since ACORN was the state-mandated enforcement agency for PL 94-142. ACORN administrators argued that school psychologists had to be accountable to them, even if they were employed by school districts. Blackman's desertion was not appreciated. She had worked full time in Edgewood for five years when I interviewed her, however, so apparently the tension between her and the ACORN supervisors was managable.

Edgewood is a middle-class community with many professionals who commute to Chicago for work. The schools have an excellent reputation and the administration puts a premium on staff having a "professional attitude." Perhaps this is the reason the administration was so eager to employ Blackman full time rather than as a staff member rented from ACORN. Her present supervisor, James Allen, director of Pupil Personnel Services for Edgewood, is a man trained in conventional education who has become especially interested in mainstreaming and in tailoring special education programs so that they interface smoothly with regular school programs. Although he and Blackman do not agree on all issues, it is easy to see that her sort of psychology might be important in a district pursuing an aggressive mainstreaming program. They work very hard *not* to refer children for special education and in fact have successfully kept some seriously handicapped children in regular programs.

Even though Edgewood as a district is committed to mainstreaming children and to deemphasizing the labeling that goes along with special education, district administrators recognize the need for some testing. Blackman did all of that testing when she first began as an ACORN cooperative staff member serving the district. She has virtually stopped doing any for the district now, however, and a new ACORN psychologist has been assigned part-time duty in Edgewood to handle the diagnostic case work.

Blackman works as a sort of master teacher. I use that term advisedly since she is not trained as a teacher. This has sometimes caused problems according to Allen. He claims she does not have the "behavioral" orientation instructors have because she lacks classroom experience. She has had conflicts in the last several years with a reading specialist employed by the district who was a former teacher and who has a strong behavior modification orientation. The reading specialist has been sought out by some teachers because she can produce clearly observable results. The children perform better after working with her. Blackman is more interested in personality dynamics and in psychotherapy. Her focus on emotional problems and developmental processes does not usually produce the same sort of striking changes in the school performance of children. Her helpfulness is most evident when she explains how children develop or works through problems with parents. Her methods are indirect, and she tends to focus on noninstructional issues that might be causing a student to fail. Because she is more concerned with helping people feel effective and happy than with being sure they carry out some specific educational task, Blackman's approach does not always fit comfortably with the achievement orientation of many educators. Because of this conflict it is not quite correct to call her a master teacher.

At the same time, Blackman does work directly with instructors, trying to solve particular problems that arise in planning their programs or working with their students. She is most interested in solving educational problems by thinking of an innovative way to bring psychological knowledge to bear on them. She is an advisor or a consultant to teachers. She is eclectic and her program development efforts are ad hoc. She moves from classroom to classroom and school to school as people request her services. This means that she has no long-term involvement in any one kind of program, although she has begun recently to specialize in early childhood programs.

Blackman's time is divided between helping to resolve emergencies that involve individuals and program planning. I observed her the day she visited two schools to help resolve parent problems. She described the first to me. It involved a kindergarten student with a growth problem. Though he was an intellectually normal five-year-old, he was the size of a two-year-old, and people tended to treat him like a baby. She had become worried about the possibility that over time the boy would become overly concerned with his small stature and that this would interfere with his personal and school life. She asked his father to come in for a talk.

The father is an English teacher whom she characterized as someone who avoids talking directly about difficult issues by deflecting conversation to his concerns with the precise use of language. She would say, "I am concerned about whether your son will continue to succeed in school," and he would respond, "Well, success has many meanings." She could agree with this but felt that he did not really want to confront his son's problem.

She suggested that the boy might visit a doctor so that they could learn whether some sort of hormone therapy might correct his condition. The father objected, saying he did not believe that hormones should be given to people. He felt instead that everyone has to confront and deal with the fact that as humans we have limitations. His son's limitation was his small size. Blackman spent an hour talking with the father before she could convince him to have the boy visit a doctor.

During my conversation with Blackman, she mentioned perhaps five other cases in which she is currently trying to smooth relations between schools and parents. This keeps her traveling between the five schools of the district. Between parent consultations, she does long-term work with teachers.

On the day I visited, she was working with a speech teacher to develop a demonstration project on how children come to recognize words. This is part of her work in the Early Childhood Program, and the demonstration project was going to be part of the district's introduction to school for parents. In addition to providing service to handicapped children who are not yet school-aged, Blackman and the others in the Edgewood Early Childhood Program hope to socialize parents so that they understand and accept what the schools try to do with their children. By involving parents in school life before their children begin and by introducing them to staff members in an unpressured way, those in the program hope to make later school-parent relations easier.

Blackman showed me some of the other things she has worked on. She described a learning disabilities screening technique she and the speech teacher developed. She had noticed that children with learning disabilities could often recognize objects but could not think of words to describe them. She had studied the psychological literature and found this to be commonly noted, so she created an inventory of common objects that could be shown to children. Some of the learning disabled children, when they have trouble finding the correct word, can then be examined more carefully. She said she had been unable to find a psychological test based on this principle but found that it worked well as a screening tool.

Blackman also showed me a chart she had compiled that summarized information about children's development. The chart combined descriptions of Piagetian stages of development, specific tasks children ought to be able to accomplish at different ages, and behavioral styles that characterize different ages. Parents often are interested in this sort of information. Having the information available in one place helps them recognize problems if their children are slow to develop in some way. Thus, such a chart is an aid to the early identification and management of learning handicaps. At the time of our interview, there was apparently no similar compact compendium available for school use.

These are both good examples of what Donna Blackman tried to do in her program development work. In both cases, she recognized a school problem that she could solve simply by pulling together a variety of information routinely available to psychologists and putting it in a useful format. She saw these and most of her other projects as original scholarly work, since few other psychologists go to the trouble of presenting their knowledge in a way that is accessible to educators and parents. She is not particularly interested in marketing her ideas to a broader audience; she simply sees her job in schools as that of being a source of information and knowledge to be applied in fortuitous ways as problems arise.

Strategy, Race, and Morality

With an official status in the public schools, defined and reinforced by state and federal legislation, school psychologists work within a set of constraints that both limits and directs them and provides opportunities to create roles that integrate personal interests, professional responsiblities, organizational needs, and policy requirements.[4] The six strategies illustrated above show some of the tools available to psychologists for role creation in school districts that are open to this sort of innovation. I have offered them as concrete examples for the abstractions I laid out in the opening pages of this chapter.

Also, these examples challenge the effectiveness of codification as an approach to implementing educational policy. I suggested in the Introduction that the scientific guidelines laid down by those who have created, normed, and used psychometric tests for research purposes do not always apply to the school context. This chapter suggested a variety of reasons that psychologists might bend or otherwise torture scientific norms of test administration. Psychologists might want to use test results primarily to make a point with parents or regular educators, as Betty Sue Wheeler did. Or, like Dr. Simmons, they might use the reporting of test results as a medium for presenting common sense information about a child. Either practice probably violates a narrow definition of testing norms. Yet I find myself sympathetic.

PL 94-142 is another attempt to codify behavior deemed proper in government's attempt to guarantee student due process and to be sure that special education placements will not produce racial disproportions and unduly restrictive placements for handicapped students. Chapter One showed us that meticulous obedience to procedural detail traps psychologists in a narrow testing role that tends to burden them with a large diagnostic load and to result in a gradual speed-up of testing as it is practiced. A consequence is that psychologists working in large cities, the people who most often test minority children, usually move inexorably toward a bureaucratic style of testing that elminates the sort of empathetic, detailed knowledge about the whole child and the context in which educational difficulties have occurred that psychologists have long insisted is essential for accurate assessment. The strategies psychologists in this chapter used to add diversity and automony to their role seem necessary if children are to receive relaxed, child-centered assessments.

Yet those strategies can also be seen as self-conscious efforts to avoid the strictures imposed by paperwork and formal administrative definitions of their work responsibilities. One might argue that the pattern of institutional racism and exclusion of the handicapped from school that characterized school psychology and special education prior to passage of PL 94-142 occurred precisely because psychologists had great freedom and used it irresponsibly. Clearly defined rules, strict enforcement, and maintenance of high standards of scientific precision could be seen as a way of controlling this misuse of discretion.

The main thrust of this book is to show that, at least where school psychology is concerned, this literal, coercive approach to correcting abuses in special education does not work. If psychologists become passively obedient, carrying out explicitly defined procedures in detail, the result is bureaucracy, not psychology. This chapter suggests that the most effective psychologists may achieve their success by engaging in covert action, spreading what some might call misinformation, and engaging in hidden political scheming. If we imagine a continuum of rectitude, with meticulous obedience to legalism at one end, my favorite psychologists all seemed to be grouped at the other end, sharing more in common with spies and confidence men than with representatives of the legion of decency.

Of course, putting it this way might make school psychologists seem as though they are amoral people. I do not mean to say that at all. To my mind, this covert activity often exemplifies humanism in organizational work, showing concern for the best interests of children and of their teachers. The nature of the organizational situation school psychologists confront requires that they use indirect means to achive the proper ends of their work.

The reality is that school psychologists have to publicly acknowledge that the distinctive goals of their role are secondary in importance to those of the regular school program. That is not to say that school psychologists must carry out illegal acts if they are ordered to. But it does mean that the agenda is set by regular educators. This is true in the overt sense that special education is defined in terms of the needs, goals, and aspirations of those who run the regular program. It also is true symbolically. School psychologists cannot be obviously political or oriented to building personal power.

School psychologists I interviewed were emphatic in saying that they must *seem* to be uninvolved and uninterested in school politics, even though many in the next breath said that, of course, being clever in managing the politics of one's situation was a key to successful school psychology. The image of their role requires that school psychologists seem distant, disengaged, and organizationally weak. If one wants to address school situations that are psychologically disruptive to children and other school workers, appearing interested in power would invite attack. Because psychologists are in such a weak position organizationally, it is hard to defend oneself and to justify aggressive interventions into school problems. It is easy for powerful regular educators to make life so uncomfortable for a psychologist that resignation or reassignment are the only reasonable choices that person has.

Thus, there are two realms of action for psychologists. Their overt, manifest responsibilities are those in-role activities that go along with assessment or with formal assignment to some special education program. Meanwhile, psychologists also operate in a world of face management and impression construction that is reminiscent of Goffman's theatrical analysis of everyday interaction styles.[5] In Goffman's view, covert action, feigning, and deceit are omnipresent and necessary aspects of all human behavior. Following the theoretical ideas of social philosopher George Herbert Mead, he argued that all behavior represents a dialogue between the "I," one's core self-image or one's instincts about who and what one is, and the "me," the image recognized and defined by those with whom one interacts—one's significant others.[6]

Various situations either allow these two aspects of the self to be mutually reinforcing and similar or sharply distinct. Where there are great differences in power between one and the significant others one relates to, the chances of there being a gap between the I and one's public image is increased. When that gap is great, an individual may have the feeling of being an actor, assuming a role quite different from what one really is like. If powerful significant others are promoting a stigmatizing or negative image of oneself, promoting a role acceptable to one's private self-image can be difficult and stressful. Ultimately, that pressure can cause one's private image to be dismantled and restructured to fit the image imposed by the more powerful people in one's environment.[7] In less extreme situations, the images held and projected by powerful significant others can be managed, directed, challenged, and perhaps changed. Actors in such situations tend to feel at risk, however, fearing that their real selves will be exposed. They also tend to have a keen sense that they are manipulating a persona as they interact.

Although a certain amount of emotional stress or discomfort accompanies this sort of play acting, Goffman would deny that there is anything inherently wrong with trying to manage one's public face or with using the resources one has available to enhance one's power and prestige in a situation. Everyone is likely to be doing the same thing. Social life is multilayered and complex. People always have hidden agendas, engage in subtle power struggles, and express their desires in indirect, symbolic ways. People in powerful positions probably are less painfully aware of this aspect of interaction than are people in weak or marginal social positions. Translated into an organizational setting like that found in schools, certain people enjoy power because of their formal administrative assignment, but that power does not mean they control all dimensions of behavior. Having power, they are likely to be less attentive to the subtleties of interactional dynamics that flow around them. This leaves people in less powerful positions with many opportunities to advance their occupational or personal agendas. They can capitalize on the fact that powerful people often do not keep track of what is happening in the "underlife" of an institution. Building strong but hidden alliances, somebody holding a formally weak position can build enormous influence within the informal life of an organization.

It is this process of influence building that I have described in this chapter. For school psychologists to successfully attend to social psychological crises that are brewed in schools and for them to attend to the emotional needs of school participants at all levels, they must seem overtly conformist while covertly they seek useful functions to perform and try to build a base of support. Ideally, school psychologists can be open about their efforts. Most of the psychologists I described in this chapter had been able to tell their regular program supervisors about where they put their real efforts. Even with this frankness, most of them also would acknowledge that they have to be reticent about telling those they work with in schools on a day-to-day basis exactly what they wish to accomplish. Most educators want to know how one's work will relate to teaching. They have the power to ignore a person if that person's work seems irrelevant. Thus, it only makes sense to downplay the latent goals one brings to school psychology.

The trouble with this argument is that it seems to militate against the external evaluation and control of school psychologists. Psychologists give way before demands of regular educators that they may not judge legitimate while they pursue agendas invisible to all who are not intimately familiar with their work situations. They often seem to act improperly, but in reality the actions that seem questionable may provide the basis for the most effective interventions. It is difficult to determine whether any given psychologist is engaging in this redeeming covert action or whether the routine testing and bureaucratic referral of students we see is all there is. Regulation seems impossible.

Weatherley and Lipsky suggest this is inherently the case in the work of "street level bureaucrats," of whom school psychologists were one of their primary examples. To the extent service providers work in organizational settings where work is loosely monitored and they have little choice but to create ad hoc roles for themselves, Weatherley and Lipsky are probably correct. Street-level bureaucrats are pointed in the general direction of a social problem and left to their own devices.[8]

Most of the school psychologists I met did not work in this sort of power vacuum. Although their work was not directed and they had considerable autonomy to schedule their time, they usually felt caught in a cross fire of conflicting interests between their professional ideals and the two administrative units they served, the regular and special education hierarchies. Rather than risk being a target of attack by a powerful administrator, many psychologists prefer to retreat to the safety of formalism in a narrow diagnostic role. Those who resist formalism tend to be people who identify strongly with the profession of psychology.

Among the people I interviewed, professional identification not only provided an idealized image of practice and of the norms that might govern it, it also held the potential for collective organization, monitoring and control of practice, and resistance to control by the regular school organization. This professional organization, informal though it may be, laid the basis for a covert psychologist role to be systematized and made the standard of practice. For these people, the professional community was a moral community not unlike the community Parsons and Hughes envisioned three or four decades ago.[9] Chapter 5 has two tasks: 1) to show the importance of a professional orientation and of the professional community to school psychology practice, and 2) to explore whether professionalism can be a meaningful force to promote responsible psychology practice in a complex organizational system like the schools.

Work Orientation and Testing Patterns

This book has made two major points so far. First, the amount of time psychologists devote to each child study is a variable of broad significance. In particular, when psychologists test rapidly it is likely that they produce less accurate results than when they test slowly. We have seen that psychologists who serve many black children conduct child studies much more quickly than do those who serve many white children. This is partly a function of the time dynamics of practitioners' work in cities where most black children are located. As psychologists give more tests, which they do in Chicago, they spend less time on each one for reasons that have to do with hidden time requirements of test scoring and reporting. We have seen that testing is a highly structured activity with fixed time demands. Rapid testing means that sections of the standard test battery must be left out and that less time will be devoted to building rapport with subjects. Less time also will be devoted to gaining nontest data about a subject's classroom performance and personal life, and there will be less time available for discussion of cases that include parents and other school professionals with an interest in the outcome of a case.

One of the main reasons black children receive such rapid testing is that they are concentrated in the Chicago public schools. This school district has a longstanding tradition of rapid testing. Chicago schools do not seem to treat black children any differently from white children. The problem is that this district has an overwhelmingly higher concentration of children at risk of receiving inaccurate testing than children in smaller, wealthier nonurban school districts.

Although rapid testing may be the style of psychologists in Chicago whatever the color of their subjects, the concentration of black students in the city makes this a matter of special concern. There is a long history that intelligence tests produce much lower scores for blacks, Chicanos, and members of certain other low-income, minority groups. There is wide-spread suspicion that the tests are culturally biased against members of these minority groups and that this bias accounts for the low scores. It also is clear that giving tests when rapport is poorly established and when test data is not integrated with information about a subject's social and personal life produces less accurate results. Because research shows the difficulty of establishing rapport with minority children, rapid testing in school districts that have high concentrations of black children seems particularly ill-advised. Since the policy debate leading up to passage of the Education for All Handicapped Children Act was motivated in part by a concern that low-income, minority children were being misclassified and improperly placed in stigmatizing classes for the mentally retarded and learning disabled, Chicago testing practices, though guided in part by it, seems to conflict with the intent of PL 94-142.[1]

The second point is the distinction made between psychologists who take an activist approach to their work and those who view themselves as functionaries in a bureaucracy. The former see their work in active terms and tend to assign an important role in their work to organizational politics. The latter, in contrast, tend to see their role at work as sharply defined, determined by superiors, and controlled by others who have responsibility for how the school system runs. Such people define themselves as support personnel, responsive to the needs and demands of others, rather than as independent actors who must set their own agendas and define their own work tasks.

I have suggested that there is inexorable pressure bearing down on psychologists to become bureaucratic functionaries. To escape, psychologists must recognize and capitalize upon certain strategic opportunities that are built into their organizational role. Because school psychologists are organizationally marginal and thus weak in the formal organizational structure, most of the strategic options I described emphasize informal alliances with regular school staff and covert styles of interaction.

Urgent covert action as an approach to effective organizational action poses problems if we wish to discover a policy that would promote successful school psychology. Covert action is by definition hidden action. It is hard for those outside the immediate setting to know whether it exists. Even people on the scene may be deceived if the covert actors think they must hide their activities from locally powerful officials.

Covert action usually requires bending or breaking rules. Following Goffman, I suggest in Chapter Seven that many rules are made to be broken. Psychological diagnosis has two purposes: 1) to use standardized measures to gain insight into subjects' problems of living and performing in the school setting and 2) to organize a therapeutic method or milieu that will help subjects overcome those problems. Rapid testing blocks the first goal, and exclusion of psychologists from serious program development in schools prevents the second. Whatever psychologists do in such situations, they are going to break the rules. If they follow the administrative norms of schools, they break the rules of professional psychology. If they follow the rules of professional psychology, they must violate the norms and expectations held by many school officials. If we approve rule breaking, however, there is danger that we will not be able to distinguish destructive rule breaking—deviance or incompetence—from that which goes along with imaginative role creation.

This chapter and the following one discuss organizational mechanisms that facilitate responsible rule breaking. Among the psychologists I observed, professionalism was the central factor that distinguished activist from administratively oriented practices. In the context of education, urging professionalism can be an explosive recommendation, since often it becomes polluted with an emphasis on credentials and credentialism. The professionalism I have in mind reflects an attitude on the part of individuals and refers to an organizational structure rooted in voluntary (as opposed to formal) relationships among practitioners.

This chapter has three sections. First, I suggest that the administrative and activist styles described in chapter 3 actually represent something deeper than the accidental inclinations of individual practitioners. They embody ideologies of practice that are sharply different from and in conflict with each other. One ideology is primarily oriented to the profession of psychology, whereas the other is primarily oriented to the school as an institution. Next, I will explain how career development patterns favor different orientations in urban and nonurban school systems. In the final section of the chapter we will examine statistical data from the survey that shows how these two orientations affect testing practices.

In Chapter Six I will argue that ideological differences stem not just from constrasting personal histories. Organizational settings reinforce inclinations to be administratively active or passive in different settings. I will offer an organizational case study to show how incentives for activism can be created.

Professional Orientation, School Orientation, and the Conduct of Testing

Although I have discussed the administrative and activist orientations toward school psychology only in analytic terms up too now, this is not just an empirical distinction constructed through objective, disengaged observation. I thought to measure differences in style and the impact of those differences because school psychologists I interviewed told me there was a sharp split within the occupation. They said that, on the one hand, there were people who saw themselves as professional psychologists working in the schools and, on the other hand, that there were people who saw themselves as educators or as part of the educational apparatus providing support services. I talked to people holding both orientations and each agreed with the distinction. They tended to attack the style of school psychology practiced by the other and the usefulness of that other perspective to schools.

The attacks members of the two groups launched against the other should be familiar to readers from the material I have provided in earlier chapters. Those school psychologists who emphasize the psychology part of their job title, people I will call profession-oriented, argued that they are more child-centered and that they are more prepared to be advocates for children within and, if necessary against, the schools. Profession-oriented people suggested that those who saw themselves as educators, people I will call school-oriented, tend to take the administrative hierarchy of schools as given and as authoritative. If the administration tells them to test, they test. If the administration tells them to place a child in special education, they place. It is this attitude, the profession-oriented partisans suggest, that creates the administrative passivity I described in Chapter Three. Because they accept the authority of the school administration, school-oriented psychologists become trapped in the testing role, test too rapidly, and do a poor job of serving the children.

School-oriented people complain in response that their profession-oriented colleagues set themselves up as superior to everyone else in the schools. School-oriented people point out that the main business of a school system is to educate children. The psychologist ought to work closely with other people to help alleviate the load of tension-producing and distracting tasks that makes it difficult for the front line personnel—the teachers especially—to carry out their program. Because psychologists are not intimately familiar with the technology of teaching, school-oriented psychologists feel they should not presume to tell teachers what to do. They are willing to be helpers, team members, or supporters who make the system run more smoothly. School-oriented psychologists would point out that since psychologists are of necessity peripheral to the main business of schooling, those who are profession-oriented who try to do therapy or to create innovative programs are likely to have an insignificant impact on schools and to create an impression that the occupation is fragmented and frivolous. An austerity-minded school board might well eliminate an occupation to which it could not assign a clear function.

I shall explore the implications of this segmentation in the occupation.[2] One reason for doing so is simply to trace the ethnographic contours of school psychology. A second reason is to determine whether the assertion profession-oriented psychologists make about testing practices among the school-oriented is correct. As we have seen, there are sharp differences in testing practices within the occupation, and these differences have important policy implications. Now we need to find out what causes those differences in practice. We suspect that some people who test intensively do this because the organizational situation they work in causes them to become passive and to adopt a routinized testing style. This might happen regardless of what ideology they bring to their work. It might be the case, as the profession-oriented psychologists claim, however, that the nature of the school-oriented ideology predisposes people to routinized testing regardless of what organizational setting they work in.

We wish to distinguish occupational segmentation from organizationally created passivity. If there is a deep division, it is useful to know why it exists, how it is distributed, and how it shapes the work of practitioners. Segmentation is a product of the way individuals orient themselves toward their work and of their career decisions. It is distinct from, though not unrelated to, organizational pressures that encourage one to be administratively active or passive. Donna Blackman is school-oriented but administratively active. Violet Hoffritz is profession-oriented but administratively passive. The main purpose of this chapter is to show how work orientation and organizational pressures become mutually reinforcing. That understanding is, in turn, important for showing how policy decisions can affect school psychology outcomes.

Origins of Segmentation

Segmentation occurs in school psychology because psychologists are recruited in two sharply different ways. One group, those who tend to be school-oriented, began their careers as classroom teachers. After several years in the classroom these people seek ways of becoming upwardly mobile within the school hierarchy. Becoming a school psychologist is one way of doing this. The other group of people, those who are profession-oriented, typically have little if any classroom experience. Rather, they enter school psychology as their first professional job after undergraduate and graduate school, or they enter the school system after having worked in some other context of professional psychology.

We would expect a difference in world views from people who do not share the same fund of experience, but this does not account for the sharp divergence we see in school psychology. Rather, it is due to differences in career expectations and to the efforts people put into improving their long-term prospects in the two segments. For the school-oriented, becoming a psychologist is the culmination of years of effort, voluntary work beyond the normal requirements of their job. For the profession-oriented, school work is usually a stepping stone to something higher— a Ph.D. and a private clinical practice, perhaps. Two consequences of these career patterns are 1) that school-oriented psychologists tend to be older, more highly credentialed, and more occupationally stable than those who are profession oriented and 2) that school-oriented psychologists tend to be concentrated in larger school districts and in those with older special education programs, districts like Chicago.

Recruitment to School Psychology in Chicago. Large numbers of former teachers are included among Chicago school psychologists because there has evolved over the years an institutionalized promotion pattern for teachers within the school district. My respondents explained that there is considerable competition among teachers to escape the classroom. To do this, one must take on extra projects, form alliances with administrators and other powerful people in the system, and accumulate special responsibilities in one's school. If one is fortunate, one may eventually be promoted to "adjustment teacher." Adjustment teachers are roughly equivalent to "counselors" in other school districts. That is, they help deal with problem students, arrange tracking assignments, and generally provide support to the principal. Moving out of the adjustment teacher role generally requires that one receive specialized training of some sort. One may seek to become an administrator and take education administration courses to achieve this objective. Or one may choose to expand one's role as a student adjustment specialist by training to become a school psychologist or social worker.

An important part of this development is that it all happens within one school system. From the individual's standpoint, it is easier to progress within a large system like Chicago than to leave. This is partly because large city school systems often have better pay and benefit packages than do the suburban districts.[3] Since those levels tend to be linked to seniority in the district, city employees may be reluctant to pay the costs associated with moving to another school district. It is also possible to feel more connected to a network of people who can help one find new opportunities within a large system than across system boundaries. A large system offers many different kinds of placements within its boundaries, and it is organized so that one is likely to know people throughout the system. One can informally follow several alternative placements and apply for transfers to more attractive locations without having to search very hard and without having to suffer the risks that might attend quitting one job in order to take another in a different district.

That advancement happens within a single district also is important because it produces strong traditions in support of advancement patterns. When people are promoted internally in a large system, they tend to stay put as they get older. They build a fund of experience, improve their credentials, and become increasingly well known throughout the city. These people become role models for younger people —teachers and school psychologists—who wish to advance. The older psychologists also become connecting points in the city-wide network of school psychologists. They are the ones who know about new opportunities, who pass on gossip about what is happening in the special education hierarchy, and who have the power to intervene if someone feels he is being badly treated.

All of this contributes to a gradual crystalization of advancement patterns as special education programs age. The Bureau of Child Study, Chicago's school psychology department, was begun in 1890 and has been actively evaluating children for placement in special education classes since the 1930s.[4] This contrasts with the suburban school districts I observed that all started their special education programs in the 1960s. If older psychologists do not leave the system—as they will if school psychology is a stepping-stone to something else—there will be relatively few opportunities for advancement. People at lower levels in the hierarchy wait for their chance to step up when retirement or system expansion create long anticipated openings. When those openings occur, there is considerable pressure against hiring someone from outside the system. In Chicago, just this kind of pressure has institutionalized promotion practices into school psychology so that very few people are hired directly from graduate school. Almost all new psychologists have moved up the ranks from classroom teacher.

Recruitment to School Psychology in Newer and Smaller Districts. Psychologists in suburban districts were more likely to follow the profession-oriented pattern because those districts usually hired outside people to fill school psychology positions. One reason for this is that special education has expanded so rapidly since the 1960s that openings for psychologists have outrun the supply of local talent. Training a teacher who wishes to become a psychologist takes two or three years. Openings for school psychologists come up more sporadically in small districts than in larger ones. It usually is not practical for teachers who wish to move upward within a given district to become trained applicants and claim access to new openings when they occur. A teacher who wants to become a psychologist would probably have to plan on moving to another school district. There also tends to be a tradition outside big cities for psychological services and special education to be provided by organizations that are independent of particular school districts. Teachers may also be discouraged because it is more likely that a professional orientation will hold sway in these independent organizations. If they dominate recruitment in local school districts, they may oppose hiring former teachers as psychologists, as did the ACORN cooperative.

Prior to the 1960s, special education mostly meant services for mentally retarded and severely handicapped children. Most mildly mentally retarded children then identified by the schools were low-income, minority boys.[5] Because districts were not required to have special education programs, only large cities with long histories of special education programs and heavy concentrations of students prone to mild retardation offered special education. Many smaller districts, rather than offering classes of their own, referred candidates for special education to placements outside the district, paying tuition to private schools or to other public facilities. With little programmatic interest in special education, most small districts also had no psychological assessment personnel. Rather, they used school psychologists working out of state-funded regional offices. These practitioners traveled from one school district to another across, perhaps, one quarter of the state with an entire psychometric library packed into the trunk of their cars.

Three changes that shaped special education in small districts occurred more or less at once. In the early 1960s, learning disability theories were introduced, and belief in their effectiveness became an educational fad strongly supported by middle-class parent groups across the country.[6] Many school districts in middle-class areas introduced learning disability classes in response, and a national movement grew, demanding that all handicapped children have access to appropriate education.

At the same time, civil rights groups focused attention on over-representation of black children in classes for the mildly retarded. Court suits and public attacks created pressure for school districts to provide

adequate due process protection to children excluded from school or referred for placement in special classes. PL 94-142 eventually mandated
special education classes in virtually every school district and required
that an assessment team guarantee that each child be provided with
due process protection. Outside of cities, many districts could not themselves provide all of these services. Consequently, groups of districts
joined together to form educational service centers, called cooperatives
in Illinois, that would provide special education services and oversee the
student evaluation process.

Because small districts traditionally depended on state-operated
education service centers to facilitate their special education placements, it was easy for them to let cooperatives lay the groundwork for
their new special education programs. Once this happened, the cooperatives were in a strong position to become independent advocates of special education within the districts. The main business of educational
service centers is to provide specialized services, so they usually are not
dominated by people with a regular classroom background. They foster
a culture of specialists, and so people committed to one specialty or another tend to feel more comfortable in these organizations than are people whose main commitment is to the education of average children.
Educational service centers also depend on a certain entrepreneurship
to survive. Local districts do not always enthusiastically support their
special education programs, and funding support chronically lags behind service provision. To gain more control over their resource stream
and more autonomy from local districts, these centers across the country have pursued and offered diverse educational services, from providing vocational training and research libraries to being centers for
computer training.[7]

A consequence of having strong special education centers located
outside suburban school districts has been that advancement patterns
for specialists internal to suburban regular school districts have been
further weakened. If one wishes to change jobs it usually means that he
or she has to move to a new school district. Networks that provide information about job openings and that help mobilize the personal influence
that helps one to land a potential job like those that function within the
Chicago public schools also exist in the suburbs, but there they are outside of the formal structure of school systems. Lacking a comprehensive
bureaucratic structure within which such a network may crystalize,
the voluntary associations making up the profession provide the frame-
work for job referral networks in the suburbs. Active membership in regional and state professional associations becomes an important vehicle
for school psychologists in small school districts to change jobs. Nat-

urally, the ideological and intellectual orientation of psychology are emphasized in these associations, further strengthening the profession-orientation at the expense of the school-orientation.

Although the institutional situation of special education in small school districts favors a professional orientation over a school-orientation, that advantage is likely to decay eventually. First, rapid growth in the number of positions for school psychologists has left school districts with little choice but to hire new graduates of school psychology programs. As growth slows, it will become easier for local districts to anticipate openings several years in advance and groom their own candidates for those positions. Second, the professional network depends on high turnover for its influence. If psychologists are frequently moving out of school psychology into other kinds of practice, openings are provided for new graduates of psychology programs. If, however, people with a long-standing commitment to special education move into school psychology jobs, they will clog up the structure by faithfully remaining in their positions. Although it may be that in suburban districts fewer teachers are promoted to the position of school psychologist, it is likely that they will have a greater impact on the overall structure of school psychology when they are appointed than will profession-oriented people simply because of their longevity. Over time, movement ought to decline, and as that happens active participation in the voluntary associations of their profession will be less likely to serve psychologists' career protection interests. This should favor a school-orientation.

In the short term, the combined power of educational service centers and professional voluntary associations provides great support for the profession-orientation. Not only do they have direct influence on how regular districts will set up their special education programs and on how people will get jobs, they also have a self-conscious interest in promoting psychological knowledge as the basis of school psychology. Ideas and research reports are the currency of interaction in the professional associations while the service centers grow to the extent they can market their special services to regular districts.

Emphasizing, as they do, that a competent school psychologist has an obligation to pursue lifelong learning in psychology, educational service centers and professional associations encourage people to value career advancement within the profession over advancement within the school system. This obligation fosters the view that school psychology is a stepping-stone rather than an end point. Believing this, people try to move out of school work, and when they succeed they create new openings. Viewing school psychology as a useful entry level job also means that suburban school psychologists tend to be younger than their urban counterparts and less heavily credentialed. It also means that they are likely to invest a substantial amount of energy in professional development activities that will broaden their knowledge, increase their professional contacts, and improve their chances to move on to other sorts of work. School-oriented psychologists, in contrast, are likely to see less intrinsic value in professional development work.

Work Orientation and Testing Practices

The survey of Illinois school psychologists clearly shows the presence of the two segments among respondents. In practice, we do not find a neat segregation with former teachers in one group and young, newly minted psychologists in the other. Because the segments are organized

FIGURE 5. **Years School Psychologists Worked as Teachers by Geographic Area in Which They Presently Work** (missing values are excluded from the analysis): $r = -.31$, $p < .001$; $X^2 = 59.50513$, df $= 36$, $p < .01$.

Years Spent Teaching		Chicago	Downstate	Suburbs	Total
0	% of Col	19	33	64	117
		32%	62%	59%	54%
1-2		6	7	22	35
		10%	24%	19%	16%
3-4		9	4	11	24
		15%	8%	10%	11%
5-6		2	2	8	12
		3%	4%	7%	6%
7-8		6	3	1	10
		10%	6%	1%	5%
9-10		7	2	1	10
		12%	4%	1%	5%
>10		6	2	2	10
		10%	4%	2%	5%
Total		59	53	110	218
		27%	24%	49%	

around world views, we find people like Donna Blackman who, despite a strong psychology background, conclude that a school-orientation makes more sense. The variables that most clearly segregate the two segments are 1) the number of years psychologists have spent as regular classroom teachers and 2) the number of hours per month psychologists spend in professional development activities. The latter include meeting together with their peers regularly to discuss cases or hear instructional presentations and attending meetings of professional associations.

Figures 5 and 6 show the distribution of these two variables among the survey respondents. About one-third of the respondents had taught three or more years. The proportion of former teachers is higher in the Chicago group; a higher response rate in this cohort would probably have increased the overall representation of former teachers among survey respondents. At the same time, we also see that over one-third of Chicago psychologists have no teaching experience and nearly half have no more than two years of experience. If Chicago psychologists are more school-oriented than psychologists elsewhere, factors other than

FIGURE 6. ***Numbers of Hours Psychologists Spend Each Month in Professional Development Activities by Geographic Area*** (missing values are excluded from the analysis): $r = -.32$, $p < .001$; $X^2 = 70.41198$, df $= 24$, $p < .001$.

Hours per Month in Professional Development	Chicago	Downstate	Suburbs	Total
0 % of Column	35	5	12	52
	65%	10%	14%	27%
1	10	11	16	37
	19%	23%	18%	20%
2	5	10	15	30
	9%	21%	17%	16%
3	1	4	13	30
	2%	8%	15%	10%
4	0	3	6	9
	0%	6%	7%	5%
5 or more	3	15	26	44
	6%	31%	30%	23%
Total	54	48	88	190
	28%	25%	46%	

individuals' career advancement histories must be involved. Still, the statistics show that there is a strongly significant relationship between location and psychologists' histories as teachers.

We see that about one-quarter of psychologists spend no time engaged in professional development activities. They are concentrated in Chicago where two-thirds of the respondents report never participating. Among psychologists working elsewhere, the median number of hours spent in professional development per month is between two and three, with about one-third of the psychologists spending five or more hours per month, or at least an hour a week in professional development.

Teaching experience and time spent in professional development activities have a negative correlation $(-.15, p < .03)$ with each other, as we would expect. This contrast is most marked at the extremes. Psychologists with a lot of teaching experience are twice as likely to spend no time in professional development. Conversely, psychologists with little teaching experience are twice as likely to spend five or more hours per month in these activities. Between these extremes, teaching experience has no effect on time spent in professional development.

The relative weakness of the correlation shows that neither variable absolutely determines one's orientation towards school psychology. Many psychologists have some teaching experience and spend a little time engaged in professional development activities. Perhaps their identification with one or the other orientation toward their profession is also ambiguous. The data suggest that there are, however, rather large extreme groups and that these groups are geographically segregated. About one-third of non-Chicago psychologists spend a lot of time in professional development work; few Chicago psychologists do so. About a third of Chicago psychologists taught for more than seven years before entering school psychology; outside Chicago only about 10 percent did so.

This is important because the segmentation of school psychology represents a conflict of social movements, in a sense. During my interviews, people who identified strongly with the profession-orientation tended to be outspokenly critical of school-oriented psychologists and vice versa. We might look for members of the extreme cells in Figures 5 and 6 to act as style leaders for the others. Segment membership thus affects practice in two ways. It reflects on individuals' work experience and their resulting ideas about what their role should be in schools. And it reflects attempts by other psychologists to socialize them into a particular approach to practice. Those with ambivalent feelings about their professional orientation might be swayed one way or the other depending on whether they work with strong advocates of one or the other position.

TABLE 5. **Correlation Matrix of Measures of Professionalism and Measures of the Amount of Time Psychologists Devote to Testing**

	Teacher	Inservice	Number	Hours
Number of years spent as a regular classroom teacher (TEACHER)	1.00 (218)	−.15 (183) p < .03	.28 (193) p < .001	−.21 (192) p < .001
Number of hours spent per month in professional development activities (INSERVICE)		1.00 (214)	−.26 (190) p < .001	.22 (190) p < .01
Number of child studies conducted per year (NUMBER)			1.00 (215)	−.37 (199) p < .001
Average number of hours devoted to each child study (HOURS)				1.00 (199)

Pearson Correlation Matrix: missing cases are excluded from the analysis.

Although the two variables are not so strongly correlated with each other, both are significantly correlated with our measures of testing practices and in the expected direction (see Table 5). The number of years spent as a regular teacher (TEACHER) correlates strongly with the number of child studies conducted per year (NUMBER, .28 p < .001) and with the number of hours devoted to each child study (HOURS, −.21, p < .01. Similarly, hours spent per month in professional development activities correlated −.26 with the number of child studies conducted (NUMBER, p < .001) and correlated .22 with the number of hours devoted to each child study (HOURS, p < .01).

The reader should note that although these correlations may not look very high to psychologists who are used to looking at relationships between construct variables like test results and measures of performance on criterion measures, they are unusually strong and consistent for naturalistic sociological data. Consider, for example, that studies of school effects in the tradition of the Coleman Report have trouble showing that *any* program variable explains a significant amount of educational achievement.[8] In comparison, the results I report here are booming.

There are two reasons we see this effect of segment membership on testing practices. First, membership in a segment has a socializing effect on psychologists. I suggested earlier that classroom experience is likely to make psychologists more sympathetic to regular education goals and more reluctant to challenge the dominant administrative order of the schools. People who spend time in professional development receive regular innoculations in the ideology and practices of professional psychology. To the extent the profession orientation encourages administrative activism and a strategic approach to organizations in one's work, one would expect those involved in professional development to have a more critical, cynical, and child-centered attitude towards their work.

Second, membership is associated with participation in a career tracking process. We expect people with experience in the regular classroom to be beneficiaries of a promotion process internal to a single school system, whereas those engaged in professional development are more likely to use professional contacts to advance. Former teachers are likely, therefore, to be embedded in an organizational system that emphasizes the unity of regular and special educational purposes and a philosophy that places regular education problems ahead of the distinctive perspective of special education. Those spending time in professional development are likely to work in organizational situations where the distinctiveness of special education is emphasized and problems of the regular schools are downplayed, factors important to setting special education goals.

These differences in outlook are examined in Table 6, which reports on a group of attitude questions that explored what respondents to the questionnaire thought were the most important and rewarding aspects of their work. The questions differentiate between the school-oriented and profession-oriented respondents, since people from those two groups strongly endorse different statements. As I have suggested they would, those psychologists who spend time in professional development activities show a predisposition in their responses to see student problems rooted in the organizational dynamics of schools. They claim to find the possibility interesting and challenging that school staff members have partly caused student problems and, thus, such complications are a source of stimulation in their work. Although they are perhaps critical of them, these respondents also find educators' difficulties natural, interesting, and a point of entry for the psychologist who wishes to help.

Former teachers are most definite in saying that diagnosis is the main job of the school psychologist and that psychologists should work out of their own offices, rather than traveling from school to school. I take this as evidence that these respondents view testing as a discrete

TABLE 6. **Measures of Professionalism Correlated with Measures of Attitudes and Behaviors Psychologists Report with Respect to Various Aspects of Testing**

	Number of Years Teaching (Teacher)	Hours Spent in Professional Development (Inservice)
1. Student problems are made worse by teachers and principals (1 = Often)	.03 (211) p < .34	− .16 (185) p < .02
2. How do you feel when you find that student problems are exacerbated by the school? (1 = Challenged; 4 = Frustrated)	.04 (209) p < .27	− .16 (184) p < .02
3. Testing is best conducted in the psychologist's office, not in the student's school. (1 = Agree Strongly)	− .22 (218) p < .001	.09 (190) p < .12
4. Diagnosis is the most important part of a school psychologist's work. (1 = Agree Strongly)	− .18 (218) p < .006	.04 (190) p < .28
5. I become involved in organizational politics. (1 = Often)	.15 (216) p < .02	− .26 (189) p < .001

Pearson Correlation Matrix: missing values are excluded from the analysis.

measurement activity that produces objective results that stand alone. In other words, they are not disposed to supplement their psychometric data with data on the child's social life. Perhaps that is because other members of the interdisciplinary diagnostic team are responsible for collecting that data.

Notice that for the first four items in Table 6, members of the opposing segments are neutral. That is, former teachers do not deny that teachers and principals sometimes make student problems worse nor are they always frustrated when they encounter such situations. People who spend a lot of time in professional development activities are only mildly hostile to the idea of testing children in a central office, and they are neutral about the claim that diagnosis is their most important function. We see this neutrality because, with the exception of Item 3, all of these statements refer to unavoidable and broadly acknowledged features of the school psychologists' work. People in opposing segments are not denying that they confront the same reality. They only differ in how they assign value to different aspects of that reality. Former teachers would say it is a sad fact that some teachers and principals exacerbate student problems. They also would probably say it is not their job as psychologists to do anything about it. Similarly, most profession-oriented psychologists would acknowledge that diagnostic work is the activity of their job. They may not like that fact very much, but they acknowledge it.

The sharp difference between the two orientations is demonstrated in Item 5, the question about whether respondents often engage in organizational politics. This involvement is a natural extension of the criticism of educators implied in the questions about whether school organization contributes to student problems. By the same token, the questions school-oriented people agreed to suggest that the psychologist's work should be clearly defined, differentiated from the work of other educators, and somewhat insulated from any power struggles that may go on among the regular educators. They consequently suggest that psychologists should stay out of organizational politics. All of this information supports the notion that the school-oriented/profession-oriented distinction reflects less a conflict rooted in different ideologies or points of view about education than differences in the amount of engagement with other school actors between members of the two segments.

Limitations of the Segmentation Argument

The segmentation argument is appealing because it suggests that one's orientation to school psychology is the main thing responsible for what is good or bad about the occupation. If people were selected on the basis of their commitment to the profession-orientation, one might argue, then the kind of passive school psychologist I have described would be eliminated because it is school-oriented psychologists who most support routinized testing and who seem to pursue a narrow bureaucratic role. People who are school-oriented could gradually be replaced, which would eliminate this flaw of passivity.

Drawing characterological conclusions from the segmentation argument ignores the complexity of examples I have provided to this point. On one hand, school-oriented people like Donna Blackman or Maria Higgins show that psychologists interested in education can be as active, innovative, and strategically oriented as any of the profession-oriented people. On the other hand, Sam Osterweis has to be classified as profession-oriented, and he is as disengaged from the school scene and as inclined to routinized, objective testing as any of the Chicago people I met.

The passivity we have seen among people who are former teachers is not an automatic product of their way of thinking about schools. Rather, they are passive because they are alienated and frustrated by their situations at work. They wish to be cooperative, safe, and helpful but that cooperativeness opens them to exploitation.

When I say school psychologists are exploited I do not mean to depict regular educators as harsh, dishonest people. Regular educators, naturally, do not go around trying to figure out how to maximize the success of special education programs. They have their own problems, and they worry about resolving them. When school psychologists appear, seeking to be supportive and helpful, regular educators are likely to ask for assistance that will be helpful to their own programs. If school psychologists do not forcefully define a role for themselves, regular educators are likely to be somewhat confused about what school psychologists are really supposed to do and therefore are likely to act on the basis of what they imagine a school psychologist's job is. They are likely to ask them to test and to help remove difficult children from the regular program.

School psychologists who want their work defined by administrators find themselves isolated, forced into more routine work, and left uninvolved in the real and important business of schools. The school-orientation is weak to the extent that it does not inform psychologists about how to manage the politics of their role. The weakness is not in the conviction that school psychologists ought to support the educative process, the philosophical statement that most distinguishes this orientation from the profession-orientation.

Blanket acceptance of the profession-orientation also ignores conflict between the formal profession of psychology, represented most vigorously by the American Psychological Association (APA), and less highly credentialed providers of psychological services like school psychologists.[9] Masters' level school psychologists who dabble in psychotherapy or present themselves as "real" psychologists to their school-oriented colleagues would probably be attacked by representatives of the profession of psychology for false marketing and practicing without a license.

The APA has sought for some time to require licensure for those who provide psychotherapy and to limit insurance copayment to services provided either by psychiatrists or Ph.D. psychologists. Certified social workers have recently become eligible to receive insurance copayments in some areas. Most other non-Ph.D. providers, including M.A. level school psychologists, face continual attack. Indeed, one of the sponsors of this study, the School Section of the Illinois Psychological Association, was considering withdrawing from the IPA to form its own organization in response to perceived hostility from Ph.D. psychologists.

These fights are in part battles over turf and simple credential power. But they also reflect discomfort with a mushrooming industry of lay psychotherapy. Christian counselors, drug and alcohol abuse counselors, spouse and child abuse shelters, and health self-help groups are examples of a trend that has exploded since the mid-1970s when public funding for mental health services began to be curtailed. People who themselves have suffered a problem for which others require treatment have gained increasing legitimacy as therapists who can help others recover or cope with their problem. Alcoholism, disability, or religious conversion, rather than training in psychological theory and clinical internships, are the curriculum preparing self-help counselors to be therapists.[10]

There also is a psychological services "industry" that grows and adapts to changes in government and insurance reimbursement practices. Low-cost alcohol treatment, for example, becomes profitable when, as happens now in Pennsylvania, the government allows "certified" alcoholics nine months on welfare and medical assistance payments that will cover their psychotherapy.[11] Reimbursement rates for these low-income substance abusers are too low for the time of Ph.D. psychologists. Fully certified psychologists serve middle-class or wealthy people whose health insurance will pay for a higher level of care.

Meanwhile, the government has relaxed its criteria for certifying organizations providing psychotherapy since, given fiscal austerity, there are few alternative ways of managing low-income, disruptive people with substance abuse problems. In such a climate, the government has little power or inclination to regulate service providers. Some providers may give excellent service, but the industry is guided primarily by what service providers must do to make money and who is available in a given area willing to work on a fee contingency basis to provide psychological counseling. Pop psychology, the college of hard knocks, and fractured versions of major psychotherapeutic traditions may well inform treatment practices.

There are school psychologists, seeking to be therapists either in schools or in their free time, who are part of this burgeoning, informal psychotherapy industry. Their required M.A. no doubt allowed some of them to develop clinical skills, making them better equipped to tap into the formal body of psychological knowledge than other psychological service providers with little formal training. At the same time, school psychology as a field heavily emphasizes psychometrics. Many practitioners continue to hold the outmoded view that these are objective measures whose results are meaningful without regard to the context in which they are given or the social and emotional conditions that govern the life of a subject. To the extent that a positivist attitude toward diagnosis governs training in school psychology, Ph.D. psychologists in other branches of the discipline are going to be doubtful that an M.A. in school psychology prepares one for anything but pychological testing— and even their testing results are likely to be taken with a grain of salt by many Ph.D. psychologists.

I do not say these things to criticize school psychologists who have a strong profession-orientation. When the profession-orientation leads people to be more sensitive to organizational dynamics and politics and to the social psychology of school failure, the orientation strikes me as a pragmatic, useful approach. Furthermore, the career trajectory of those holding the profession-orientation often takes these practitioners into more advanced clinical training. Working as a school psychologist is probably a useful sort of internship for someone who ultimately will become a Ph.D. clinical psychologist. To the extent these people are supervised by competent clinical psychologists so that their school work truly functions as a professional internship, the shortcomings are reduced that follow from undertrained people trying to apply ideas that are borrowed from clinical psychology.

At the same time, there are aspects of psychotherapy that are probably misplaced in schools. Most school psychologists have such large case loads that they cannot give intensive attention to any single person over a long period of time. One of my school-oriented respondents argued that if school psychologists wish to "play psychotherapist," they might well cause harm by not being available to a child when a crisis occurs. Private clinicians are not always available immediately to their clients during crises either, so this criticism may not stand.[12] It does seem, however, that with a caseload of several thousand it would be difficult for school psychologists to regularly provide individual treatment without neglecting other responsibilities.

School psychologists must fit their activities into the program of their school system. It may be that no one supervises psychologists very closely and that an individual has considerable latitude to innovate and create programs that will meet school needs. But a psychologist who takes advantage of this freedom to provide intensive services to a handful of people is not doing *school* psychology. They may be helpful to those few students or teachers one serves, but if one asks in abstract terms why a school system should employ a psychologist, such a limited intervention approach hardly provides a justification. If we ask why psychologists exist in schools, it cannot be to provide psychotherapy except in schools for exceptional children like the ACORN TMR School that Arnold Cohen served.

We cannot say there is a "correct" way to practice school psychology because the needs of local school systems vary and because, for the most part, services respond to what the traffic will bear. We will see in chapter 6 that the consumers of psychological services may join with school psychologists to create social control mechanisms that limit the diversity of practice styles, that impose on school psychologists some standards of accountability in terms of the quality of their services, and that help them continue to develop necessary intervention skills. But unless there are specific organizational mechanisms that impose a tradition of commitment to learning, to professional ethics, to accountability, and to values that emphasize psychotherapeutic values of serving the individual client, the family and the organizational systems in which that client lives, there is danger that a profession-orientation will be little more than an instrument of legitimation, power, and access to opportunities for making money on extra jobs.

It is important, therefore, that we be clear when we distinguish benefits of a profession (rather than a school) orientation that might come from intellectual substance rather than from those that come from organizational process. The benefits I am talking about come from the latter and occur in two ways. First, a profession-orientation predisposes psychologists to cynicism about educators and thus encourages a strategic, covert approach to their work. The cooperative orientation pursued by school-oriented psychologists traps them into a narrow bureaucratic role because of the time demands imposed by the testing regime.

Second, a profession-orientation encourages psychologists to make their opportunities for career development dependent on relationships with professional peers. Ideas are likely to be the currency of interaction among psychologists who do not work for the same school system. So if one depends on these people to improve one's job situation, one is encouraged to take a more intellectual approach to work than if one depends on the routinized advancement patterns that evolve in a large bureaucracy. Ideas and performance are probably less important for career advancement if one is school-oriented and counting on bureaucratic advancement than if one is profession-oriented. I do not mean to say that this pressure means all profession-oriented people will be intellectual giants. At the same time, they are likely to face subtle or not so subtle pressure to carry on a dialogue in the language of professional psychology. When, as in the ACORN cooperative described in Chapter Six, that pressure is "not so subtle," it can jolt psychologists out of the rut of a narrow testing role.

Thus, a profession-orientation is not just an interest in psychotherapy and a desire to practice therapy in schools or elsewhere, although this interest may play a part. Professionalism has structural consequences. It encourages people to be organizational activists, and it changes the structure of risks and payoffs so that people do not accept rigid organizational relationships. The actual content of professional knowledge is somewhat arbitrary. What counts is that practitioners see their work as a creative intellectual activity and that they are subject to some coercion and control from their peers.

CHAPTER 6

How Organization Affects Psychologists' Work Orientation

One of the main issues this book addresses is why school psychologists working with black children so consistently conduct child studies in a manner that gravely risks serious assessment error and misclassification of those children as cognitively or emotionally handicapped. A major factor is that most of the psychologists who serve black children work in a large city school system—Chicago. Within Chicago, all children are tested rapidly. Indeed, white children receive somewhat more rapid testing than do black children, but outside Chicago the pattern is reversed. White children receive a somewhat more leisurely psychological evaluation than black, although minority students still receive much slower testing than do their Chicago peers.

It is tempting to say that the only reason testing practices affect race is that there is de facto segregation in the schools. Chicago school psychology is different from school psychology elsewhere. Although Chicago psychologists test rapidly, almost uniformly, neither my interview nor my survey data show that psychologists are under any compulsion to follow a particular testing style. That local tradition encourages rapid testing does not change the findings of psychometric research or the violence done to children. Psychologists continue the practice even though their time is not closely monitored and they are free to move from school to school, frustrating any close supervision of how they spend their time. There was no statistically significant difference in the survey responses of Chicago respondents from those working elsewhere on questions concerning the closeness of supervision or the relevance of supervision to actual job tasks. Because they have tenure in the school system, psychologists who refused to test rapidly could not, presumably, be fired.

Although there may be no formal constraints forcing psychologists to test quickly, school employees of all kinds recognize that informal pressures and punishments abound for those who lose favor with the powers that be. One may be transferred to a particularly dismal setting if one is out of favor or to an exciting, challenging setting if one has a place in the sun with administrators. Psychologists may be made to feel like outsiders in the schools they serve and deprived of opportunities to work in a collegial way with the regular school staff. Regular program supervisors can ask officials of the special education hierarchy to investigate one's competence and may even initiate an effort to have one fired. Even if such attempts fail, the harrassment is frightening and anxiety-producing. Psychologists often see themselves in a vulnerable organizational position. They tend to avoid at all costs becoming a target of attack by regular educators.

Most school psychologists work under this pressure. Adopting a school orientation is one way to set up one's work life so that one feels less threatened and more an accepted part of the school system. Psychologists who undertake the strategic activities I described in Chapter Four are taking risks, although I have suggested that those risks can have great payoffs in terms of satisfaction with one's work and in a feeling of control and power over one's job. What needs to be explained is why it is so much easier for psychologists working outside the city to accept these risks and to pursue an aggressive approach to their work. The explanation is to be found in the different organizational structures of urban and nonurban school systems.

This is partly a matter of size. Strategic action is likely to be more rewarding and effective in a small school system where the organization is more personal. A bright, energetic, charismatic person can become influential in such a system whatever formal position he or she holds. This is much more difficult in larger systems where interest group politics dominate and diminish the potential for people whose organizational positions give them no special leverage to become influential leaders in the system.[1]

Another important organizational difference has to do with the structural location of special education programs inside and outside cities. The large cachement area city school systems encompass allows the creation of comprehensive special education departments within the school system. Chicago has a special education department structurally equivalent to the primary and secondary education departments. The special education department contains separate subdivisions for school psychology, school social work, and special instruction, including several special schools.

Outside cities, the school districts are smaller and generally depend on educational service centers for some part of their special educational services. Most of the psychologists I described in earlier chapters were affiliated with ACORN—in Illinois the centers are called cooperatives. These are organizations incorporated as regional school systems and consequently are partially independent of the regular school systems they service. Although representatives of local school superintendents may sit on the board of an organization like ACORN, educational service centers (ESCs) often gain substantial autonomy.[2] This is partly because they have a legal mandate to monitor the due process provision of the Education for All Handicapped Children Act as it is implemented by local school systems.

ESCs also gain autonomy because to survive, these organizations usually generate a variety of different services. Reimbursement for services ESCs provide to local districts tends to be slow because money comes from the state and normally is provided only after a service has been given. This creates chronic cash flow problems since the ESC staff must be paid on time. Creating a variety of programs with different cash flow patterns allows an ESC to borrow from ongoing programs to pay for services where reimbursement lags. Thus, across the country one sees educational service centers providing a diverse range of educational services: one center is a local ERIC data base center; another center provides educational TV signals and video services to local school districts; a third center provides job training and counseling to unwed mothers; a fourth center has become the regional microcomputer consulting facility for local school districts.

These services are important to school psychologists because they give the ESC an organizational identity separate from the local school systems it serves. The autonomy comes partly from having its own buildings, independent legal status, and control over its own budget. More important, in the last ten years they have become centers of educational entrepreneurship. Local school systems benefit if an effective grantsperson/entrepreneur runs the ESC. However, such entrepreneurs usually demand independence from the close supervision and control of their board so they can search out and quickly develop promising opportunities.[3]

Within educational service centers, school psychologists may be central personnel. In Illinois they provide one of the most important services the centers sell—psychological assessment. Special education generally is a major interest of these organizations, and psychologists are likely to be important consultants to instructional programs. In addition, psychologists receive more sophisticated training than many other school employees. They can help the center director write grant proposals, they can design research and intervention programs, and they may take on administrative responsibility for new programs. The psychological staff provides a flexible pool of talent that can be shifted in and out of service to regular districts. Such staffing flexibility is critically important for a soft-money organization to be successful.[4]

I do not mean to suggest that all ESCs are entrepreneurial organizations or that school psychologists are always central personnel. There is great variation in the way these organizations are set up. Whatever their arrangement, they give psychologists independence from the direct control of the regular school district. Knowing people in different ESCs (and psychologists do meet people in other centers) also provides an information network on matters of professional interest. News about job openings travels through this network, allowing people to escape particularly unpleasant job assignments. Centers also become mutually reinforcing. A center that is particularly entrepreneurial or committed to the professional development of its staff is likely to encourage participation among people working in other centers.

This arrangement tends to encourage a profession-orientation among psychologists. It does so in part because there are clear payoffs for psychologists who apply their knowledge eclectically. They can become part of the entrepreneurial effort of the service center. It also encourages a profession-orientation because service centers move career rewards outside of a single organization.

This happens in two ways, First, psychologists usually have more than one organizational affiliation. They are simultaneously employees of one or more regular school districts and employees of the service center. They consequently cannot adopt a simple conception of what their organizational situation is. Such a simple perspective is, conversely, encouraged in large school systems.

Second, to change jobs psychologists usually must change organizational affiliations. If they move from one assignment to another within the domain of the service center, they are likely to leave one regular district and move to another. This makes the ESC, not the regular school district, seem like their primary job assignment. They also are likely to move from one ESC to another sometime in their careers—at least most of those I interviewed had done so. Relationships with other psychologists are likely to be critically important for finding an attractive new assignment. This is different from a large city system where movement usually occurs within the system. To transfer to a new assignment in the city, networks of regular educators are usually as important as those including other psychologists.

To make the organizational importance of service centers clearer, we shall examine the case of ACORN in more detail. ACORN is unusual in having an especially strong staff of psychologists and clear recognition that psychologists work for both the cooperative and the local districts. Another cooperative I studied, BART, did not make this simultaneous responsibility as clear and as a consequence, the psychologists tended to feel more vulnerable to control by their regular school employers.

The value in studying ACORN is that we can see, on one hand, the risks psychologists feel in opposing their regular school employers and, on the other hand, the countervailing pressure a strong professional organization can create to force psychologists to adopt a strategic rather than a bureaucratic approach to their work. By seeing this process working in exaggerated form at ACORN, we better understand the sharp differences in activism we have seen throughout the earlier chapters between psychologists who adopt the school- and professional-orientation. The informal organization of work for psychologists outside cities more nearly approximates the ideology of the profession-oriented segment. The informal organization of work in cities more closely approximates the ideology of the school-oriented segment. For psychologists to be active rather than passive, ideology and organization must converge. We see this happen in ACORN.

The ACORN Special Education Cooperative

ACORN fits the model of an entrepreneurial organization that makes its staff of psychologists central to its organizational development efforts. Located on the fringes of the Chicago Metropolitan area, the cooperative served fourteen small suburban school districts. Despite being in the suburbs, these school districts were diverse in terms of wealth, race, urbanism, and industrial concentration. Several were bedroom communities, clustered around the commuter rail line to Chicago. One was a heavy industrial community. Two were small towns that had existed prior to suburban expansion and continued to assert their small town independence.

ACORN employed fourteen psychologists to serve these districts but not on a one-to-one basis. Some staff members, like Arnold Cohen, served two districts. Others worked primarily in special education facilities operated by ACORN. Some of these people felt strong loyalties to the districts that employed them. Most of the psychologists, however, saw ACORN as their primary employer and their assignment to particular local school districts as temporary duty.

An important part of ACORN's organizational life was a requirement that all of the psychologists work one day per week in the ACORN central office on Fridays. Having one scheduled office day is standard practice for school psychologists and, working out of a central office, this tradition in many places has become an important source of collegiality.[5] In ACORN the Friday office day was partly a precaution to ensure that psychologists would be given free time by local districts to complete test scoring and other paperwork essential to a child study. The cooperative also used it as an opportunity to provide member psychologists with a regular program of in-service training. Even people like Donna Blackman, who normally did not work out of the ACORN office, were required to attend biweekly in-service training sessions.

A striking feature of ACORN was the remarkably strong rapport that existed among the psychologists. This arose partly from informal social activities the cooperative sponsored. After biweekly two-hour Friday group training sessions, the whole psychological staff typically went out for an extended lunch. Often the group traveled some distance to be outside of any member districts so that the psychologists could share a few bottles of wine, relax, and pretend they were beginning the weekend early together. At the annual state psychological association meetings, the cooperative rented the most luxurious suite it could find and all of the psychologists would camp out there together in sleeping bags. Through these events, ACORN encouraged the psychologists to believe that the staff should live well together. This was not a gray, impersonal bureaucracy.

Also, the two chief psychologists, both Ph.D.s, played the roles of mentor and sponsor for the younger psychologists. The two men had begun a private clinical practice together and they encouraged younger members of the staff to work with them at night and on weekends to gain experience. They also encouraged younger people to enter Ph.D. programs so that eventually they would be able to start their own clinical practices. For most of the staff members, therefore, working in public schools was only part of their overall job experience. ACORN felt more like a graduate program in psychology than like a dull, rule-bound organization grinding out psychological examinations.

This would be no more than an interesting vignette, except that it became apparent not everyone was an enthusiastic supporter of the regime. Donna Blackman did not like the arrangement because, school-oriented as she was, she found that the strong psychology orientation of the chief psychologists did not support or enrich her primary interest. Others were uncomfortable because they did not fit the models of professionalism and career goals that seemed to be advocated through ACORN's in-service training program.

If one did not support the ideology that was dominant in ACORN and if one had the wrong occupational career trajectory, then the in-service training program seemed to become as much an ongoing test of loyalty to the local version of the profession-orientation as a means of improving skills. Although speakers presented lectures on topics of collective interest, most of the Friday sessions focused on testing techniques. In particular, the group regularly discussed the administration and scoring of Rorschach tests. That they focused on the Rorschach emphasized the clinical orientation of the staff. A projective test, the Rorschach was used by most of the staff members to discover the sorts of relationships a child was having special difficulty managing and why a child was failing. Questions such as Was a student having trouble dealing with male or female authority figures? and Was a child retreating in the face of ambiguous situations? focus attention on the social and emotional context of a child's performance more than on the objective characteristics of cognitive performance.

Each week, one psychologist presented a case protocol gathered from his or her school work. The presenter described a child, how the case came to attention, and what results were achieved on other test batteries. Then the presenter described administration of the Rorschach in detail. The ten Rorschach inkblot pictures have been standardized since their introduction in the 1930s.[6] There is vast psychiatric experience interpreting subjects' responses to these pictures and associating them with different forms of psychopathology. In presenting a case, a psychologist described how the subject responded to each picture—how long he took to answer, how he reacted physically to the image, what he said, how the psychologist prompted him to answer more fully and precisely what the respondent saw in the picture. The psychologist then interpreted the subject's behavior and response to the group. After describing the response to each picture, the rest of the group offered further interpretations. If the chief psychologists found some flaw in the administration technique, they suggested ways the presenter could improve his or her technique.

Most of the psychologists participated in these case discussions with enthusiasm. To be sure, the presenter was receiving a test of sorts. But most of the psychologists saw these presentations as intellectual play, and competed to find subtle and insightful interpretations of responses. They questioned the presenter about the subject's background and used this new information to launch new hypotheses about why a child had started crying uncontrollably in class or had shown a history of total failure dealing with math problems. Presenters who were confident of their ability fielded these questions energetically, defended their interpretations, and tried to show they had anticipated the thoughts of other psychologists. Younger presenters who thought the Rorschach valuable might stand aside, accepting gracefully the advice of more experienced psychologists and listening appreciatively as the older ones reconstructed their case before the group.

Although these sessions were group play, the way the psychologists performed and participated also uncovered subtle conflicts over approach and status. This always happens in a group with fixed membership that works together over a long period of time, as small-group social psychologists have demonstrated.[7] The chief psychologists were the obvious social leaders in these meetings. But others, like Sam Osterweis, who usually was somewhat standoffish in the group, came to the fore as intellectual leaders of the group, vying actively for the floor. Those who normally seemed warmly accepted by the group were peculiarly quiet. As I interviewed each psychologist, it became clear that everyone watched these performances and interpreted them in terms of individuals' strengths and weaknesses as psychologists. The in-service training sessions were not just information-sharing sessions. They provided a complex theater in which people learned about each other and formed judgments about professional competence.

These judgments, in turn, became part of the lore of the organization. Everyone carried understandings about how others judged every member of the psychological staff along with their own private feelings of sympathy or disapproval. These were continually exposed to new information, revised through the in-service sessions, and reinforced as controversies arose in a staff member's relationship to their regular school assignment. In certain cases, these implicit understandings became critically important in determining an individual's fate. Consider the following two examples.

Tom Blanchard and the Addison Elementary School District

Tom Blanchard is one of the people with longest tenure as a psychologist for ACORN. He came there to work in the 1960s after finishing his master's degree at one of the prestigious universities of the midwest. He soon began his doctoral program there as well while working as a therapist in the student counseling program. He moved to

ACORN for the greater income he could earn. Now about forty, he sees himself as being at a critical point in his career. He fears it will become increasingly difficult for him to find high quality school psychology jobs in the future. In the next year or so he will have to decide where he wants to work for the remainder of his career.

Blanchard talked about these issues during my interview with him because he had recently been "fired" by his local school district and was now reassigned to the ACORN special school, a program for trainable retarded (TMR) children on the first floor of the ACORN building. This was humiliating to him as, apparently, it was intended to be by Dr. O'Rourke, the chief psychologist.

Blanchard had become involved in a disagreement with the special education director for the Addison Elementary District, Mrs. Adelle Murphy, when she insisted that he take on a heavy testing load. Opposing her demand seemed consistent with ACORN policy, but when she complained to O'Rourke, he supported Murphy rather than Blanchard and agreed that Blanchard was behaving in an unprofessional manner. O'Rourke immediately removed Blanchard from Addison, replacing him with another psychologist, and assigned Blanchard to a placement internal to ACORN, the TMR School. This way he would not further embarrass the cooperative and he could be more closely supervised. In Blanchard's view, O'Rourke had come to doubt him because he, O'Rourke, had not thought Blanchard was an enthusiastic enough participant in the in-service sessions, and presumably felt that Blanchard did not have the proper, professional attitude towards school psychology. To Blanchard, being required to submit to the paternalistic Rorschach training sessions was an affront to a person as senior as he. That discomfort, he observed ruefully after the fact, was minor compared to his present humiliation. So he was considering other job options.

Blanchard reviewed for me the incidents that led up to his predicament. Like other psychologists working for ACORN in the 1960s, he was assigned to the central psychological office when he first came to work for the organization. Psychologists were not assigned to any particular district. Rather, whoever was available would evaluate children as districts requested services. All of them wrote up their child study reports and had them typed in the central office. This meant that the psychologists could easily talk over interesting or difficult cases and, because the demand assignment system meant that each person was sent to all of the districts at one time or another, it was easy for them to make relevant suggestions about how to handle a case. Although psychologists then did little more in schools than "test and run," there was a strong atmosphere of collegiality at ACORN. They were insulated from the complex social lives of the schools they served, so the psychologists became more and more committed to preserving what they saw as the objectivity of projective and intelligence tests.

In the late 1960s, special education programs expanded both in their variety and in the number of children served. At first, psychologists continued to work entirely out of a central office. But as school officials requested their services more and more often, they began to think of psychologists less as representatives of a consulting service and more as part of their school staffs. Districts began asking that only one psychologist be assigned to them so that person could coordinate services better with other educators. Blanchard was initially assigned to the Addison High School District under the new arrangement. After a year there, he began working part time for the Addison Elementary School District with its two elementary schools and a junior high. This time-splitting arrangement continued until the ACORN psychological staff was decentralized and assigned full-time to districts. Blanchard then began working only in the Elementary District where he remained for six years until replaced during my observation period.

Addison is an area of upwardly mobile, working class, and white collar families. Parents expect the school system to provide their children with a strong academic program to compete with those of near-by communities where there are professional families. Some parents think that quality education requires the latest "experimental" programs—in the early 1970s this included such things as sex education, "Transactional Analysis for Tots," and learning disability programs. Other parents are traditionalists, however, and school officials fear innovations will be attacked as too radical.

Blanchard describes the district as one in which there is pressure to be up-to-date and to "do" things, but where too often administrators have little idea of what they want to accomplish or how to achieve their goals. When Mrs. Murphy, a new special education supervisor, was hired in Addison from outside the district two years ago, she found herself in a difficult situation. She was new to special education, having worked in regular programs previously, and she was also new to the district. Yet she was expected to be innovative and to steer clear of the political shoals in the district. As she planned her programs, she relied heavily on Blanchard's knowledge of the personalities of principals and administrators and on his familiarities with current trends in special education. They became close friends—at least so he thought.

Two things changed conditions in the district for Blanchard. First, there were a number of personnel changes in supervisory and principalship positions with the result that he no longer had a group of friends running the schools with whom he could act as intermediary for the special education supervisor. Second, Murphy apparently became uncomfortable with her dependency on him. Perhaps to show her authority, when the new personnel came in Murphy charted a course that would be independent of Blanchard's influence. She not only cut Blanchard out of program planning decisions but became personally somewhat hostile toward him.

There also was a change in state funding policies for special education that required the Addison School District to rethink its special education programs and reevaluate many of its special students. Special education programs are financed jointly by state and local school funds. In the past, children with unusual or severe handicaps could be referred by small school districts to private special schools, if they lacked appropriate programs for them, with the state paying a disproportionate share of the bill. Addison, like many other districts, had used this arrangement as a way of avoiding having to set up the variety of special programs recently required under state and federal law and demanded by some parents. Finding that this private school placement program was becoming expensive, the state decided to phase out the program, requiring instead that all children be educated in public facilities. Either districts would have to provide programs or organizations like ACORN and the larger, regional special educational organizations that serve low incidence cases would have to educate the children. Under this new pressure from the state, ACORN warned districts with insufficient programs that they would soon be responsible for children who had been neglected in local programming.

Activated by the state and by ACORN, Murphy decided that special programs should be provided more in conjunction with programs in regular classrooms. Choosing this "mainstreaming" approach, Blanchard reflected later, gave her the opportunity to claim she was following the latest special education trends without having to really expand programs. She was under pressure to contain costs and recognized that totally overhauling the district's special education program might be seen as radical change. Blanchard also suspected that Murphy had a better understanding of and more sympathy for regular, as compared with special education, program needs. Thus she opted for cosmetic rather than fundamental change.

Perhaps mainstreaming solved Murphy's problems, but it put double pressure on Blanchard. Time limitations imposed by ACORN and by the state required that those children outside districts be reevaluated within the year. In Addison, not only children with unusual problems placed in private schools would have to be reassessed. In line with both state and federal laws, all of those mildly handicapped children whose programs were to be altered would also have to be tested and considered by screening committees. In order to provide space for the more severely handicapped children now in private schools, the mildly handicapped children would be the ones most often mainstreamed. On top of this, Mrs. Murphy ordered Blanchard to get to know and to work closely with regular class teachers in arranging the reintegration of current special education students into the mainstream.

It was not just the increased work load that Blanchard found difficult to handle. The previous policy at Addison had allowed him to continue functioning as he and his colleagues had in the early days of ACORN. Placing so many children outside of the Addison schools had made his testing independent of what went on in the regular program. The new demands that he work with teachers and help them with problems arising from mainstreaming required an attentiveness to the organizational processes of schools that never before had been necessary for him. Blanchard acknowledges that he did not really know how to approach teachers and that his new responsibilities made him feel uncomfortable.

More important in his view, however, was the expectation that he would subordinate the interests of children referred to him and the integrity of special education programs to the self-interested demands of regular program officials. This interfered with his professional values. To his mind, the whole point of school psychology is for an independent and objective observer using data-gathering methods that do not rely on educators to consider teachers' placement recommendations. This is not just a matter of protecting the rights of children. He argued that learning handicaps are so colored by the school setting that one can tell if disabilities are independent of school experiences only through triangulation. Administrative considerations may be important in classifying a child, but should he incorporate those concerns when evaluating a child, Blanchard felt he would be no more neutral than the other educators. His job, he asserted, is to try to look at the child independently of the pressures and the definitions of situations that emerge from the flow of school life. If he lets himself be too strongly guided by administrative concerns, those things that allow him to make a distinctive contribution to education would be lost.

Rather than spend a lot of time working with teachers, Blanchard decided it was most important that he spend his time carefully reevaluating students. He could work with teachers after he was sure that each child had been appropriately placed. Murphy was incensed that he would not drop all of his testing and rush off to work with teachers.

Blanchard said she seemed to have no idea of the time demands she was making. She stopped communicating with him, and Blanchard found it difficult to obtain any administrative help in his work. After several months of frustration, he went to Mrs. Johnson, the ACORN director, and asked her if she could find out what was happening and help him gain more cooperation from his supervisors.

Bringing Johnson into the episode eventually led to Blanchard's replacement. When she was hired, Johnson's charge from local superintendents was to make psychologists more responsive to the districts while maintaining high professional standards. She was an aggressive, entrepreneurial leader who wanted ACORN to be independent of local district control. The expansion of special education programs had made the local districts want to increase their control over ACORN, its programs, and the resources it controlled. To block the expansion of district influence in the cooperative, Johnson had insisted that the districts have only policy-making power. ACORN would require that high professional standards be maintained but beyond that, districts could make specific demands about what they wanted from the special education staff and the programs they shared with ACORN. Once policy was formulated, ACORN was responsible for selecting, training, and supervising staff. Assignments would be negotiated with the local districts, although according to an elaborately formal arrangement for specifying the time and task responsibilities of psychologists and other staff loaned to districts.

This arrangement provides a buffer for ACORN, giving it the power to protect its staff members when local districts make inappropriate demands. At the same time, when a district complains about a staff member, the cooperative must be able to argue that this person was adhering to the professional norms of the organization. ACORN's autonomy derives from the claim that only the cooperative is competent to train and evaluate staff. If district representatives are unhappy with someone's performance, the cooperative asserts that any other staff member would have done the same thing. If, however, someone seems to be violating the professional norms of the organization, ACORN has to admit to the error. Otherwise the argument that all staff members are equivalent loses legitimacy. Put more pragmatically, although ACORN has considerable power to protect staff members against district complaints, it is useful to the organization for it to occasionally admit that one of its people made a mistake and to pull that person in for retraining.

To Johnson, district complaints about Blanchard seemed to reflect his refusal to accept the new ACORN policy of limiting the autonomy of psychologists and submitting to district requests for service. Johnson's sympathy encouraged Murphy to question whether Addison should continue to employ Blanchard. In mid-December of the year I was studying ACORN, Blanchard was fired by Addison and replaced by Tony Black, a second-year psychologist. Dr. O'Rourke suggested to Blanchard that he might be better off seeking a job outside of the cooperative. He had tenure in the organization and could not be forced to leave, but both Johnson and Dr. O'Rourke made it clear that if he did leave, they would ensure he would find a good job, "appropriate" to his skills as they had with others who had left ACORN under pressure. This might not be possible later, they suggested. In the meantime, Blanchard was to take over Tony Black's work in the TMR School. This would keep him away from regular educators, give him the experience he now lacks working with teachers and children, and keep him nearby so he could be closely supervised by O'Rourke.

When I interviewed other ACORN psychologists, particularly the younger ones, there was consensus that the firing of Blanchard was justified. They reported that for some time Dr. O'Rourke and Dr. Al Simmons, the other senior psychologist of the cooperative, had complained that Blanchard was too old-fashioned in his approach and was unwilling to develop new skills required of psychologists if they are to be effective. Reassignment to the TMR school, they felt, was good for Blanchard. Working totally inside ACORN, he would not cause so many difficulties for the cooperative in its relations with the districts. He could be closely and directly supervised by Dr. O'Rourke. There also is little need for testing in that facility, so Blanchard would be forced to learn to work with teachers and to help out with children who present classroom problems.

The younger psychologists also see a lesson in the episode about how to conduct themselves in the regular districts. All of the psychologists are encouraged by O'Rourke and Simmons to remember that theirs is an inherently political job. School psychologists provide services regular educators are not likely to fully understand or to accept. In addition, because they are somewhat outside the core school programs, they must be aggressive about advancing their programs while being aware of their vulnerability. They may be attacked at any time, just as Blanchard was. They must avoid taking rigid, ideologically inspired positions on issues. Rather, they should try to provide services that fulfill the requests of their host districts while also meeting the psychological needs of children.

I visited Tony Black in one of the Addison Elementary Schools early in the fall following Blanchard's dismissal; it appeared that the problems surrounding changed programs for the special children had been amicably resolved. Black had begun by quickly screening the children in the district special classes who were targeted for mainstreaming—pretty much in the way I described Betty Sue Wheeler doing it in Chapter Four. Children with minor problems were returned to regular classrooms without careful psychological examinations. Black reasoned that those with serious learning problems would probably be referred again anyway, and he could give them full child studies at that time. Until then, they would be left in regular classes receiving part-time special instruction. Their cases then would be reviewed at the end of the year as part of the routine district review of special education cases.

Black himself had been fired by a district after his first year on the job, and was reassigned to the TMR School at ACORN. He found the reassignment an important opportunity to work with teachers and to explore ways of providing them with support services in their classrooms. He also had learned much about managing relations with school personnel, particularly from Dr. Simmons. Simmons made it clear that it was foolish to fight openly against the wishes of regular district administrators, for they always controlled the overt power in schools. Psychologists must influence school affairs indirectly, making friends with key people and taking advantage of the fact that school people usually did not understand psychometric techniques and were a little afraid of psychologists. Reiterating what he had told me when I observed him in his school (Chapter Four), Simmons told Black that there are times when appearing authoritative in making a recommendation is more important than having carefully collected, objective data to support your report.

In contrast to Blanchard, Black's approach to working in Addison was consistent with Simmons's philosophy. He chose to concentrate on making school programs more sensitive to psychological issues and to downplay the importance of careful psychometric assessment. He also probably violated the due process provisions of the Education for All Handicapped Children Act. Black also quickly resolved any crisis of confidence in ACORN that Blanchard's recalcitrance might have caused. By acknowledging Blanchard's errors and quickly replacing him with a psychologist prepared to meet the school district's service demands, the Addison administrators continued to see ACORN as an effective vehicle for providing specified educational services and as an organization capable of policing its own staff.

Meanwhile, Blanchard did not ultimately resign from ACORN. During a follow-up interview a year later, he no longer worried about being humiliated before other psychologists. He accepted that he was more of an outsider than he was before. At the same time, he found his new work in the TMR School challenging. Working with teachers is difficult and puzzling, he reported. He was uncomfortable with the passivity of his classroom observer role and wanted to get involved with the activities he was watching. He was reluctant to do this, however, because he feared he would be too critical. He recognized that individual teachers have diverse personal styles of working. Although he might not approve of particular things they do, to interfere might be harmful because their patterns of instruction would be disrupted. He was also aware that being too critical could discourage the teachers. He spent most of his time working with students individually and trying to figure out effective ways of helping in classrooms.

It appears that Blanchard is being successfully "rehabilitated." After several years of work in the ACORN TMR School, perhaps he once again will be sent out into a regular district. This partly reflects ACORN's genuine commitment to retraining rather than punishment of staff. Perhaps more importantly, disasters like Blanchard's seem reasonably common in school psychology. Most of the psychologists who have worked in ACORN for more than four or five years have been thrown out by a client district at least once. In more than a few cases, the cost of continued district acceptance of ACORN has been that the psychologists who were victims of these conflicts were forced to take the blame for incidents which, several of the psychologists acknowledged, reflect persisting problems in certain regular school districts. Blanchard's position in the TMR School will be needed later when some other person has to be "sanitized." Having been retrained, Blanchard will be an acceptable replacement at that time.

Ann Thomas and the Greeley Elementary School District

Like Tom Blanchard, Ann Thomas, now in her mid-forties, has worked in the ACORN area since the early 1960s and has more psychological experience than most of the staff. Others identify her as a member of the clique of older, conservative psychologists who are seen as an opposition faction to the leadership of Mrs. Johnson, Dr. O'Rourke, and Dr. Simmons. The other members are Tom Blanchard and Sam Osterweis, who is an outspoken critic of the present regime. Because she has known them a long time, she often socializes with the other members of her "clique" and sympathizes with their problems. Like them, she has few career ambitions beyond working as a school psychologist and, because of this, is seen as a negative role model by younger psychologists.

Thomas speculated during our interview that her identification with the two most outspoken critics of ACORN leadership could get her in trouble. She worried that the ACORN leaders might be vindictive. In fact, she had been satisfied with ACORN and with her role in it. She valued the continuing training that membership in the cooperative provides. She was intrinsically interested in psychology and had found the in-service meetings an important source of new ideas. At the same time, ACORN was intrusive, in her view, and she disliked the attempts O'Rourke and Johnson made to control her way of working in Greeley. They did not understand the interactional and political problems one faces in a district, she thought. Thomas has found that if she is away from the schools for a week, she is already out of touch. How can people who do not spend time in the district really understand the choices she must make on a daily basis? She worried that being identified as part of an opposition clique would cause her concrete work problems to be overlooked should a crisis develop between her and her district supervisors. She did not fully trust O'Rourke and Johnson to value her methods of practice over her loyalty (or, rather, her lack of loyalty) to them.

Actually, Thomas saw her style of school psychology as quite different from the objective-testing commitment Osterweis and Blanchard revealed in their work. Like most school psychologists, she spent much of her time giving tests and participating in the referral of children to special classes. She was concerned that children be properly evaluated, and after fifteen years of testing did what the other psychologists recognized as a competent job. However, she had relatively little confidence in the objectivity of tests. They can help one to make some initial judgment but, more than most of the others I interviewed, she tried to obtain background data on children and to follow them after placement to make sure they received the services they needed.

Thomas used a lot of energy in trying to learn about the problems people—teachers as well as students—had coping in the Greeley Schools. In this, her outlook was like that of Drs. O'Rourke and Simmons. Unlike her ACORN supervisors, however, Thomas's concern with the social contexts in which psychological problems arose was not based in cynicism about the intelligence or sensitivity of teachers and school administrators. Rather, she thought it was inevitable in schools that individual needs would not always be recognized or that the organization would fail to adjust to meet the personal problems of some employees and students.

Thomas's concerns are based in her teaching experience. She worked in a classroom for two years after leaving college. She sympathized with teachers, and they often came to her seeking advice or the name of a psychotherapist with special sensitivity to the problems of people in their occupation. Like many teachers, Thomas had little confidence that administrators, using as they must the same rules to deal with everyone, could be sensitive to the problems that develop in particular school contexts. She suggested that the mix of children in a classroom and different combinations of teacher and principal personalities in school makes each setting unique. To provide effective support, one consequently must work hard to know the many settings of educational practice within a school system, and one must respect the fact that everyone is responding to a complex interactional situation. She believes that outsiders cannot get enough information to judge teachers. A support person like the school psychologist should be most concerned with discovering individual needs that are being ignored and filling them in a nonjudgmental manner.

With this approach, Thomas inevitably seemed to step on administrators' toes. She mentioned a recent conflict with a junior high school principal who resented her attempt to intervene on behalf of a child in his school. The student had neurological problems and was from a family in which several other children had been Thomas's clients. Although she had known the family for a number of years, she had not had contact with any of its members for some time. She encountered the child at the junior high when a teacher asked for help. The teacher thought the girl was seriously depressed, in addition to having apparent problems with the mechanics of her school work. When she discovered who the child was, Thomas realized that the student had been incorrectly placed in the junior high school. The student had previously been assigned to a special education class. Apparently, her parents had enrolled her in the junior high without consulting anyone. Thomas immediately began preparations to have the child moved into a special class and arranged for her to begin seeing a therapist.

The principal of the school was angry with this arrangement because he felt only he should have the authority to initiate action concerning a student. Thomas pointed out that this case involved an assignment error and that there was a serious and immediate problem. Had she not acted, she and the special education program could have been found at fault if the parents, realizing the error, had sued the school system. Thus, in addition to helping the child, she was acting within her authority as the ACORN representative. Nonetheless, the principal took the matter up with the district superintendent and tried to have her disciplined.

Just as she encountered this sort of jurisdictional problem when administrators in the regular school program try to override her authority as the ACORN representative, she found that Dr. O'Rourke sometimes tried to impose his ideas on how she should act as part of the regular school program. He seemed to expect her to be a missionary for ACORN. He did not appreciate that she would sometimes become caught in role conflicts in which she must mediate between the two organizations for which she was working. If she were to be seen as one of the critics in the school psychology group, she could also been seen as siding with the district in its disputes with ACORN. She was under pressure from both ACORN and the district. She feared that if ACORN turned on her the district would, too, and she would be disciplined, as Blanchard had been. This made her wonder whether she should accept an offer from her district to work full time there, cutting her affiliation with ACORN. At least then she would have one less interest group to worry about when deciding how to act in difficult situations.

Thomas's ambivalence about ACORN was brought to a head shortly before my interview with her, when events occurred that were similar to those that surrounded Tom Blanchard's undoing. The special education director in Greeley, Dr. Robert Neal, had been appointed three years earlier at the new superintendent's initiative. He was a psychologist, but Ann Thomas thought he was too ambitious and too impressed with himself. During his tenure there had been a number of battles with the special education staff, and the previous spring he had taken a month off because of an ulcer condition. This year the superintendent, who had been the director's patron, was replaced. Dr. Neal began avoiding contacts with special education staff members, and many of his decisions appeared peremptory and arbitrary.

Meanwhile, during the summer Thomas was notified that one of the school district counselors would be assigned to her as a psychological intern. State law requires that one year of internship must be served after receiving a master's degree in psychology and before beginning work as a school psychologist. The counselor, Eileen Gibbons, was popular in the district and had worked in it for ten years. When Thomas pointed out that psychological interns were generally trained by Dr. O'Rourke at ACORN, Dr. Neal told Thomas that ACORN tried to control district affairs too much. Greeley could train its own psychologists and did not need the cooperative's interference. Feeling she had no choice, Thomas reluctantly agreed to train Gibbons.

Shortly, however, Dr. O'Rourke learned of the internship plan and called Thomas into ACORN. He saw the internship as an effort by the regular educators to control the special education program and the way school psychology is practiced in Greeley. Gibbons is just the sort of person O'Rourke says he refuses to hire, her primary allegiance being to the school district and to the superintendent. O'Rourke accused Thomas of buckling under pressure from the regular educators to train Gibbons. He accused Thomas of being too involved in the administrative problems of her district and not sufficiently critical of its special education policies. She ought to be an advocate within the program but instead, he asserted, she was being coopted to work against her best interests as a psychologist.

As the year got under way, these cross-pressures worsened. At in-service meetings, O'Rourke often mentioned Thomas's "sellout," since Gibbons was not attending ACORN's in-service sessions and he felt it essential that inexperienced psychologists attend them. Thomas had, in fact, asked Dr. Neal whether Gibbons could also come to ACORN on Fridays. He had refused and suggested that once trained, Gibbons would be free of ACORN control, unlike Thomas.

Increasingly, Thomas felt her supposed membership in the opposition clique at ACORN was being cemented, if only because O'Rourke's hostility was making the climate of opinion among the psychologists such that Blanchard and Osterweis were her main source of sympathy and support. At the same time, she took Dr. Neal's desire to have a psychologist free of ACORN control to mean that in Gibbons she was actually training her own replacement. If it came to Greeley trying to fire her, Thomas was less and less confident that ACORN would defend her. Increasingly, she felt that her personal and professional rewards from membership in the cooperative had to be accompanied by a commitment from ACORN administrators that they would respect standards of behavior that were collectively developed by supporting psychologists in conflicts with local district officials. Without this commitment, the costs of participation in ACORN, in terms of her relationship to her regular district, were too high.

Ann Thomas finally spoke to Mrs. Johnson and explained the bind she faced. She was angry at O'Rourke's criticisms since she felt there was little choice for her but to accept her district's demand to train Gibbons. At the same time, she objected to digging her own grave by training a replacement. Though she recognized that Johnson might undercut her, she asked the ACORN director to find out what plans the district had for Gibbons.

Johnson was immediately sympathetic and supportive. A number of districts have continually sought ways to circumvent ACORN's influence over special education policy. As ACORN director, Johnson continually insists that the psychologists be concerned with serving the districts as well as being independent and competent as psychologists. She thus saw Thomas's efforts as positive and not as a challenge to the authority of O'Rourke's leadership.

When she called the superintendent, she learned that no particular plans had been made about what to do with Gibbons. She explained O'Rourke's concerns about the training conditions for the intern and asserted that any psychologist in the ACORN area, though they may work for a district, still must meet ACORN's training requirements before the cooperative would allow children to be referred by them to special education programs. As the regulatory agent for the state, the cooperative can block any regular district special education program. After hearing this, the superintendent began relating the problems he had been having with Dr. Neal since taking over Greeley. Johnson reported Thomas's complaints about Dr. Neal, and before the conversation was completed there was agreement that Dr. Neal, not Ann Thomas, was the one who needed replacing. They agreed that Gibbons would be a good special education director since she knew the district well. This also would give everyone a good excuse for not insisting that she be trained at ACORN. She would not be actually working as a school psychologist but rather would be doing administrative work. For this purpose, perhaps it was appropriate for Gibbons to be trained within her own district. It was agreed, however, that she should attend the Friday in-service meetings, which she did for the remainder of the year.

With the situation thus clarified, Thomas was more secure in ACORN. Johnson had also convinced the superintendent to extend Thomas's contract with the Greeley district another year to protect Thomas from the possibility that Dr. Neal might act vindictively. Despite this successful resolution, Thomas remained concerned about the uncertainty of support psychologists receive from the ACORN supervisors. She felt fortunate that her crisis involved the broader principle of what districts may do to make their special education programs independent of ACORN and that Johnson was obliged to defend her. She recognized that Dr. O'Rourke and other psychologists thought that her methods of practice suffered because she was committed to service in the district. She would have preferred that this issue be openly discussed in meetings and would have liked franker acceptance of the dilemmas faced by psychologists who work for two organizations. Without this discussion of constitutional issues, she feared that decisions about competence would be made on basically political grounds. If that happened, it would be in her best interests to leave the cooperative and work wholly within her district.

Professional Organization

One might be uncomfortable with a certain ruthlessness implicit in these two cases. Both Tom Blanchard and Ann Thomas seem like thoughtful, caring people caught in an uncomfortable conflict of organizations, seemingly at the mercy of their superiors' whims. Blanchard was reassigned for insisting that the law be obeyed. We might admire him for being willing to suffer the consequences that follow from resisting the temptation to sell out to political pragmatism. The harshness of these cases is important, however, because it highlights two important things about the lives of school psychologists and the nature of ACORN.

First, it is easy to see that the incidents that so threatened Blanchard and Thomas are likely to arise periodically for school psychologists. They are caught between two organizational value systems, and they lack the power to force other players to accept their judgment about how a value conflict should be resolved. Real risks follow.

Second, ACORN forces its staff members to be accountable to its organizational values. Its ability to do this is not automatic since regular school systems do not willingly give up authority over any of their programs or parts. Also, ACORN's ability to exert authority over the psychology staff rests fundamentally in consensus among those psychologists about what constitutes good practice and whose competence among their numbers is likely to be questioned. The psychologists have the option of allying themselves closely with their regular school districts and resisting close ACORN control, an option chosen by Donna Blackman and seriously considered by Ann Thomas.

These two factors make it possible for ACORN to work as a professional organization. A professional organization is one that constitutionally is more like a voluntary association than an industrial organization that buys labor through contracts and that has the understanding that superiors have the right to define subordinates' job tasks and responsibilities. ACORN does have some contractual authority but, since staff psychologists can force the organization's supervisors to negotiate with regular school system administrators what work demands they may make on psychologists, contractual power is limited. Psychologists accept the power of their ACORN supervisors because they think, on balance, they gain more from being ACORN employees than they lose subjecting themselves to the risk of a punishment like Blanchard's.

They gain two things. First, in ACORN psychologists are central rather than marginal. Marginality is both an organizational and a psychological phenomenon. Psychologists can be organizationally marginal in regular school districts and use that marginality to build influence and enhance their effectiveness if they do not feel psychologically marginal to the organization as well. If they feel that their work is peripheral, ineffective, and only a by-product of the vagaries of red tape, there seems little point in taking risks or trying to change regular school practices.

ACORN emphasizes the distinctiveness and importance of the psychology part of school psychologists' work. Not only does it provide an ideology explaining why the occupation is important and how one can magnify one's importance in schools. ACORN also emphasizes that psychologists are unified by a common interest, by a collective hobby, by sharing a sort of play that none of the members share with anyone outside the group—or rather outside the profession. Defining psychology as something people do because they enjoy it rather than because they are trying to achieve an external goal makes one's commitment to the distinctive values of the profession more robust. If goal achievement is the main reason you work hard, you might be convinced that the goals you have set for the organization are parochial or misguided. If you are doing psychology because you like it and you think that others will benefit from your efforts even if those efforts do not further the formal goals of the school system, then one is likely to press on even in the face of opposition from regular system staff.

Second, the group of psychologists controls decisions made by the leaders, however harsh the punishments may be and however idiosyncratic the values promoted by ACORN supervisors may appear. This may not be obvious since the top office holders at ACORN are leaders of the informal social life of the group as well and did not openly consult with other staff members before deciding how to treat Blanchard and Thomas. The psychologist group works closely together and self-consciously seeks to define and cultivate a characteristic set of values about practice. This happens in office conversation, during in-service training sessions, and during social hours staff members share. Drs. O'Rourke and Simmons dominate sessions where values are debated and defined, and their point of view holds sway. But it is important that their leadership is continually tested. Blanchard and Osterweis may object to the leaders' ideology about school psychology, but they have had a fair chance to bring the other psychologists around to their point of view. Failing to do so, they have been put on notice that they should either accept the dominant ideology or recognize that they are skating on thin ice. As long as they maintain the support of their regular school supervisors, as Osterweis has done, they can follow their established norms of practice. If they fall into a conflict with regular educators where those values are questioned, they cannot expect ACORN support.

By the same token, if individuals show that they accept ACORN's clinical values or if a conflict arises not bearing on those values, the cooperative has substantial power to protect those psychologists. That power is partly legal. But more importantly, the cooperative asserts to districts that in the same situation any of its members would behave the same way. Districts may try to convince Mrs. Johnson that they object to a personality, that they doubt an individual's competence. She is likely to argue in response that they are in error. They really are not objecting to *individual* behavior. Rather, they are reacting to the consequences of a group policy internalized and accepted by staff members. Psychologists do inevitably confront situations defined, as Thomas argued, idiosyncratically by the context of their practice. The key to ACORN's authority, however, is its claim that because of its screening and training programs, its supervisors are confident that all psychologists would make comparable judgments in similar situations. Districts would not gain anything by replacing one psychologist with another, Johnson tries to claim. Rather, district supervisors should perhaps look at the performance of their own staff members where the assertedly appropriate professional values of the psychologists have been challenged. This occurred in Thomas's case and ended in Dr. Neal's termination.

Forming a voluntary association focused on defining values of practice, ACORN psychologists have built a robust organization capable of defending their way of working from a critical clientele. We see here in concrete, political terms what theorists of the professions assert is the basis of power in professions. Talcott Parsons and Everett Hughes argued that the core of professional authority and power is that these occupations are moral communities focused on techniques of practice, self-regulating and self-protective.[8] Powerful criticisms have been launched at the structural functional theory of professions over the past quarter century, seriously undermining the claim that professions like medicine have a consensual moral basis or that they are self-regulating.[9] Accurate though the criticisms may be for a huge, wealthy, and powerful occupation like medicine, they tend to overlook the pragmatic political benefits of normative consensus among professionals.

Professionalism among ACORN psychologists is not a form of credential competition. The professionalism of these psychologists does not come from lofty academic training or great social and economic prestige. It represents a high stakes game about which they are ambivalent. Because their settings of practice are usually hidden from the direct observation of other experts and because their decisions are judgmental and rooted in idiosyncratic situations that others cannot fully understand, school psychologists (like other professionals) can nearly always avoid having their methods of practice closely scrutinized and harshly evaluated. Accepting close scrutiny of one's routine methods of practice by informed expert colleagues—something that occurs routinely at ACORN—can be very threatening. Not only are one's identity and prestige tied up in claims of expertise, but exposing one's practice to criticism opens the possibility that others will find mistakes or failures of competence. There are strong incentives for most professionals to avoid honest scrutiny, frank criticism, and mandated correction of flaws. ACORN shows that under certain organizational conditions, this tendency to seek privacy can be overridden by a collective desire among a group of professionals to use normative consensus as protection against a clientele that is both demanding and truly interested in receiving high-quality service.[10]

Professional versus Bureaucratic Organization

ACORN is an unusual organization—educational service centers are not usually so active professionally—and an important example because it throws the structure of professional organization in sharp relief. We are used to thinking of professionalism as a personal attribute, as a claim of status, or as a vaguely defined interest group lobbying for the social and economic power of an occupation. All of those factors are at play with school psychologists as well. But what gives the profession-orientation so much power within this occupation is the pragmatic organizational force professional affiliation has for members. In ACORN we see the full array of organizational benefits professionalism can provide.

Not only do members share a common interest and receive protection, but their work in the cooperative also ties them into regional and statewide professional associations. These associations offer psychologists opportunities for improving their professional credentials and for building networks that can help them find new jobs if they desire them. Several of the ACORN psychologists had migrated around the suburbs of Chicago from cooperative to cooperative. Some of the younger psychologists felt they had learned all they could from the in-service training sessions and thought they had sacrificed some income working in ACORN.

Other cooperatives may not have the organizational influences that make ACORN powerful, but they and their staff members do capitalize on specific elements. Members of BART, a coop adjacent to ACORN, were extremely active in the Illinois Association of School Psychologists, which allowed members to use the professional job network freely and to enjoy the intellectual stimulation of professional contacts even though their cooperative did not confront regular districts on issues of professionalism. ACORN and other cooperatives sometimes exchanged staff for reasons of personal and organizational convenience. O'Rourke and Johnson really could have placed Blanchard in another organization more supportive of his school psychology beliefs where his recent work history would not haunt him. Other young psychologists had moved on to nearby cooperatives as present staff members wished to do. They regularly returned to participate in the Friday in-service sessions and thus constituted a far-flung intellectual network of which ACORN was the hub. There were other cooperatives in other corners of the metropolitan area, organized somewhat like ACORN, that served a similar regional function as the intellectual center for school psychology. Individuals could be isolated from intellectual peers in their immediate work settings and still be nurtured by the intellectual and moral community fostered by a place like ACORN.

Not all psychologists in the suburban area made use of these opportunities for professional affiliation. Some preferred working closely with educators. Others simply were not willing to take the risks professional alliances entail and preferred being low-profile members of their school bureaucracies. At the same time, dual organizational affiliations, the need for small districts to patronize an organization that could provide specialized educational services, opportunities to jump from organization to organization among the many small suburban school districts, opportunities for personal influence in those districts, and the ideological heterodoxy that is possible where many small organizations rather than one monolithic one prevail all make the decentralized, voluntaristic qualities of professional organization attractive. School psychologists would join professional associations to gain a benefit, but a consequence is that they also would be presented with the ideology of professionalism and encouragement to see themselves more as psychologists than as educators. The organizational structure of psychology in the suburbs fed the ideology of professionalism that grew from the tendency of suburban school districts to recruit people directly from psychology graduate programs. In the suburbs, the unity of personal career patterns and organizational encouragement gave cohesion to the profession-oriented segment.

For Chicago psychologists, most of the incentives ran the other way. There was a professional association of school psychologists, the Chicago Association of School Psychologists (CASP) that, incidentally, was very helpful in this study. But this association had little capacity to protect its members or, for that matter, to seriously challenge or shape their orientation to work. This is partly because members disagreed about what constituted the best approach to school psychology. Not only did many members favor a school orientation, but it was often the case that the psychologists with Ph.D.'s were school-oriented. Since these psychologists remain in urban school psychology for a long time, they gradually built up credential seniority. Their training is not inferior to that of O'Rourke and Simmons, the way Blanchard's or Osterweis's was.

In addition, the professional association had no meaningful role in arranging or managing the job assignments of psychologists. Where ACORN both promoted professional training and negotiated with school districts on behalf of psychologists, CASP was separated from the administrative hierarchy of the Bureau of Child Study, the school psychology department of the Chicago Public Schools. Furthermore, all of the school psychologists' job assignments were controlled by the bureau. In the suburbs, psychologists often changed jobs, moving from school district to school district and cooperative to cooperative. The School Section of the Illinois Psychological Association was an important networking forum, allowing psychologists to make contacts with potential employers in the loosely structured collection of school districts that surrounded Chicago. Within the city, opportunities for new job assignments were controlled by a single administrative hierarchy so the professional association could not play the mediating role that gave it power in the suburbs.

The ineffectiveness of CASP as a professional organization was made worse by the continual crises that buffeted the Chicago schools. During this time, the school system went bankrupt and the teaching staff was integrated by the use of a lottery system that reassigned teachers to schools throughout the city. Chaos prevailed, and in that atmosphere it was hard for school psychologists to find anyone very concerned about their narrow occupational problems. Important decisions were made in negotiations between the teachers' union, the administration, the school board, outside legal authorities, and powerful citizen interest groups.[11] Changes affected a whole stratum of the administrative system.[12] Local school needs did not cause much of a ripple on this pond, and no school psychologist, however charismatic or influential, could make much of an impact on the systemic confusion that prevailed. Under these circumstances, laying low and accepting that other people were responsible for the decisions that affected your life simply reflected the brutal realities of life in that school system. The organizational conditions supported a school-oriented ideology of school psychology. Trying to impose a professional-orientation under these conditions was like spitting into the wind.

This chapter has focused in much more detail on the organizational conditions that support a profession-orientation in the suburbs as compared with the school-orientation of the city. One might question this allocation of attention since the main policy question is why urban school psychologists test children, and most problematically minority children, so rapidly. I asserted earlier that there are no direct administrative orders for rapid testing. Urban school psychologists are not any more closely supervised than are their nonurban colleagues. Given the clarity of the evidence that rapid testing distorts test scores and the enormous concern that intelligence tests are biased when used with minorities and that they foster racial overrepresentation in stigmatizing special education classes, why do urban school psychologists continue this questionable practice?

When I interviewed Chicago psychologists, their unequivocal response was that there was no issue. They acknowledged that they could interact with teachers as suburban psychologists do and that they could test in a more lengthy fashion. They do not because that is not the way things are done in the Bureau of Child Study and because the regular educators they serve do not want them done that way. School psychologists are there to support regular educators. That is the nature of their job. Tests are objective measures. That is the way they are understood. People may criticize and offer research findings to challenge the standard operating procedures of the Chicago schools, but those people have not spent time in urban schools, they do not understand the problems, and they are promoting the self-interested perspective of professional psychology. Those people outside the system are hostile to teachers and to school psychologists, so they are not really giving friendly suggestions. Although ignoring these suggestions may not be quite right, professional psychology has not offered much useful advice about how to work in urban schools or how to manage the role of the urban school pscyhologist so it is only practical to ignore its preachings.

I was so impressed with the sensible, if discouraging, pragmatism of these people that the question for me became, What would lead a school psychologist to ignore the dangers and inconveniences of conforming to regular school demands and adopt the profession-orientation? Having answered this question, we can see the limitations of the city school psychologists' role. There is some freedom and flexibility, but most work in large organizations is meaningful because it is part of a complex division of labor. One looks for the reasons that motivated the policymakers of one's organization to create one's role. If those reasons are unarticulated, one tends to supply them. Isolated in their work and coming from backgrounds as teachers, it is hard to imagine Chicago psychologists striking out on their own, inventing community psychology, and challenging the power of an overwhelming regular school hierarchy. Weak in a huge bureaucracy, it is no surprise that the psychologists have sought refuge in being bureaucrats. Unfortunately, children suffer.

CHAPTER 7

The Diffusion of Responsibility in School Psychology

In this concluding chapter, I wish to sharpen the focus on these issues by showing how the descriptive strands of the earlier chapters define moral dilemmas common to professional workers in modern organizations. Because our attention thus far has been focused on such specific questions as what is appropriate testing or how can school psychologists effectively expand their role, it is easy to see this discussion as one concerning only problems in school psychology. The discussion applies as well to air traffic controllers, operators of nuclear power plants, physicians in hospitals, and other practitioners who must interpolate between the concrete, specific rules of bureaucratic organizations and the fluid, judgmental guidelines of their technical knowledge. Bear with me, then, as I summarize material in the book.

The Bankruptcy of School Psychology

We have seen that school psychology is full of promise. We also have seen that as a systematic intervention to help children, school psychology is basically bankrupt. This is most clearly true in cities, where practitioners spend most of their time giving psychometric tests for the purpose of placing children in classes for the mentally retarded and the learning disabled. In the suburbs, there are many examples of creative, energetic practice where school psychologists seem to make an important contribution to the educational systems they work in. At the same time, the nature of their contribution is unsystematic. It depends on whether an aggressive, well-trained, creative person happens to work in a district school or whether the educational service center that serves a school district is committed to effective psychology. As one reader of this manuscript pointed out, cities have no monopoly on bureaucratic school psychology.

Many school psychologists practice testing in a manner that violates longstanding standards of competence and responsibility in professional psychology. Rather than being independent and student-centered, the child study process in cities is administrative make-work, rubber-stamping the referrals made by regular educators and cloaking them in objective, scientific legitimacy. The legal reforms mandated by the Education for All Handicapped Children Act in 1975 have become a maze of red tape that at best is a waste of time. At worst, the red tape further entrenches practices that are harmful for children of low-income and minority families whether they live in the city or in the countryside.

We know that intelligence tests systematically yield low scores for these children and that there is reason to think the instruments are culturally biased.[1] Perhaps, as I suggested in Chapter Two, a sensitive examiner can see beyond these biases and use tests in a constructive way that helps even those students whose psychological skills do not equip them to shine when tested. Hurried testing, especially in cities where low-income and minority children are most likely to be considered for special class placement, seems to ensure that these children will receive anything but careful testing. Instead, the limitations of blacks, Hispanics, and the poor are magnified. Because special education classes can stigmatize, and generally offer a curriculum that is paced more slowly than the regular curriculum, labeling is dangerous to children. Carefully designed programs coupled with a system of evaluation and placement that is sensitive to individual needs can help some children. Programs hurt that are casually designed and administered. When the children hurt are primarily poor and from minority groups, as they are in cities, the practice is institutional racism.

What I have said about special education is not new. My discussion represents an established position in social science mirrored in the legal decisions and congressional testimony that led to the enactment of PL 94-142.[2] The data presented in this book contain two new findings. The first is conclusive evidence that intelligence testing in Chicago is routinely conducted in a hurried and presumably irresponsible manner. We do not have comparable data on other cities, but there has been suggestive research on large cities in California and Pennsylvania that indicate my findings could be replicated elsewhere.[3]

The second finding is that outside of cities (although more in the suburbs than in rural areas), school psychology can be child-centered, careful, and helpful. This enlightened school psychology occurs in an unsystematic, ad hoc fashion, and it is hard to argue that school psychology is essential to education in nonurban areas. Despite such a qualification, the positive contributions of school psychology are likely to be surprising to veteran observers of this occupation. Psychologists in universities and private clinical practice who hold doctoral degrees have almost universal disdain for school psychologists, and they voice little confidence that any good comes from their work.

Although the empirical findings of this study deserve attention from special education policymakers and from those who train school psychologists, I think the most important questions raised here are, Why do urban school psychologists persist in destructive practices? and Why do we find such sharp differences in the practice of school psychology froom place to place?

Confronting the Risks of Rapid Testing

It is hard to imagine that school psychologists are unaware of the risks inherent in their work. Academic criticism suggesting that intelligence tests are culturally biased and legal attacks on testing practices in special education have been so widespread and well publicized that those administering tests in schools must know about these complaints. Indeed, during the course of this research a suit was directed at the Chicago Public Schools that called attention to the possible damage caused by testing practices with Hispanic students. Some of the psychologists I interviewed reported receiving explicit instructions from their supervisor not to answer my questions, information that suggests most people knew that hard questions were being asked about their work from many quarters.[4] With this level of awareness, I find it especially puzzling that misuse is so widespread. This is not a question of the occasional school psychologist being ill-informed or ill-prepared for his or her work. We are witnessing a systematic, institutionalized phenomenon.

One of the striking findings is the conviction with which urban school psychologists assert that their testing practices are necessary and legitimate. To summarize earlier chapters, I argue that their conviction comes from three sources.

First, the Chicago psychologists I interviewed work in a school psychology department with a history of doing research on objective psychometric measures. This tradition discourages skepticism about the accuracy of tests.

Second, urban school psychologists in general are more inclined than their nonurban counterparts to see themselves as educators, to view possibilities for career advancement within their present school system, and to believe that their primary job is to support and cooperate with the regular school program.

Third, urban school psychologists see themselves as noninfluential functionaries in a sprawling bureaucracy. People other than themselves make the policy decisions that define and shape school psychologists' work. Consequently, those people are morally and legally responsible for whatever consequences flow from the services school psychologists provide. In short, however powerful the criticism of their testing practices may be, Chicago school psychologists accept the world view and the authority of the school system they work in.

As I talked with Chicago psychologists, I was impressed with their seriousness and conviction. Many of my respondents were bright and articulate. They were impressed with the enormous problems that confronted the Chicago schools and urban education generally. The situation was so desperate that many felt obligated to do whatever they could to help regular educators. The atmosphere of crisis that pervaded the schools also seemed to make everyone feel vulnerable to the same problems. School psychologists did not see themselves as separate from teachers and principals. All are buffeted by the waves of crisis generated by bankruptcy or systemwide desegregation.

To place themselves outside the education process or to see themselves as better than educators, a stance seemingly cultivated by their profession-oriented colleagues, seemed wrong to many of those I interviewed. They were committed to the school system and wanted to see it get better. That was why they were willing to participate in this study even though the ongoing lawsuit meant that being frank with me clearly threatened their position in the Chicago schools.[5]

It was this conviction about the propriety of their work coupled with information that challenges the propriety of their work that led me to think of Everett Hughes's article, "Good People and Dirty Work."[6] Hughes explored the reasons that "good" Germans willingly allowed Hitler's solution to the Jewish question to proceed without rebelling. He argues that by allowing the establishment of a class of caretakers and by segregating them and their work with the Jews from public scrutiny, good Germans were both sponsoring the atrocities that occurred and creating a situation in which they were likely to happen. A similar situation might occur in any society, said Hughes. The notion that "good" people can do terrible things without feeling responsible for the consequences of their actions gained broader meaning in the days of Watergate and the Contra investigations.

The Variability of Practice in School Psychology

It is, of course, an enormous distortion to compare school psychologists with Nazis. That is not my intention. However, misclassification of children destined for special class placement cannot be taken lightly, and psychologists too often do abandon their responsibilities. Their situation is made morally ambiguous by the fact that such displacement of responsibility is common in modern society. The contemporary dilemma faced by good people who work in bureaucratic settings is that they do not know what they can do to stop practices they find abhorrent or unethical. The conditions of their work allow them to diffuse their sense of responsibility. School psychologists either choose not to see that there is a problem or they pass the blame on to regular educators.

One reason this happens is that in practice the "moral way" often is not clear. I tried to show in the case examples that "good" school psychology often demands breaking the rules. In Chapter Four I suggested that intentional misadministration of tests or distortion of results in reporting the conclusions of a child study sometimes represents good practice. In Chapter Six I related how Tom Blanchard was fired for insisting on being careful as he tested children destined for reassignment to a new special education class. I suggested that ACORN epitomizes responsible school psychology even though it punished Blanchard for his "responsible" stand.

As I explained in Chapter Three, Merton argues that this value ambiguity is common in professional and social service work.[7] Indeed, the need to make definite decisions in the face of contradictory demands is, in his perspective, a major source of creativity and structural definition in occupations. He talks about certain "coordinate norms" characterizing different occupations. These are values that seem necessary but that end up contradicting each other in many concrete situations. Merton talks about the physician's need to be at once scientifically objective about patients' illnesses while being emotionally available and sympathetic to them. Caring about a patient demands being upset about the tragedy of their illness, but effective therapy requires distancing oneself and treating patients as "physical objects" rather than "selves." This theme is repeated in the symbolic interactionist and structural functional occupational studies I discussed earlier whose theme is that occupational identity comes, first, from common sharing of certain characteristic work dilemmas and, second, from the evolution of a work culture that provides individuals with support and protection as they try to resolve those work dilemmas.

In these studies, moral ambiguity is both ever-present and the basis of a robust informal organization of work. Police or teachers or budgetary officers or doctors band together to talk about their work dilemmas, to find support for their troublesome decisions, and to organize protection in case outsiders question the legitimacy of their actions. Challenges happen because those actions insiders would usually agree are necessary violate legal rules, formal instructions, or commonly recognized (outside of the occupation, that is) rules of the game. Work culture validates one's feeling that a particular situation posed a real dilemma and necessitated breaking the rules. Work groups are moral communities to the extent that their cohesiveness grows out of shared ambiguity at work.

The main thrust of this book is to argue that this sort of moral community, this banding together to address moral ambiguities at work, is a variable. The problem with school psychology is that the occupation does not foster creation of a moral community. Each practitioner is isolated and left to confront the value conflicts of his or her work alone. Given the marginality of their position, it becomes enormously hard for school psychologists to recognize the value conflicts inherent in their work or the moral complexity of decisions they must make. When the core organizational system is overwhelmingly powerful, as it is in cities, self-protectiveness makes it seem foolish to challenge the system. Following a course of action consistent with the parochial value system of one's occupation seems self-destructive if 1) it threatens one's job security and if 2) there is little chance that one's action will build into a program or systematic course of action. It would be like preaching prohibition at a vintner's convention.

School psychology has better chances of success outside of cities because organizational conditions allow an occupational culture to form. That is the point of the ACORN example. ACORN has no monopoly on ideological correctness where school psychology is concerned. I have no idea whether Mrs. Johnson and Dr. O'Rourke were right or wrong when they punished Tom Blanchard. What makes ACORN powerful and valuable is that it fosters an occupational culture among its school psychologists precisely by emphasizing the idea that value conflicts define the job.

Dr. O'Rourke brings a definite set of values to his work and may well make unfair judgments on occasion. But his leadership was not based on demands that his staff members follow an orthodoxy he defines. What he was most concerned about and what generated respect among his staff members is that his people recognize the moral ambiguity of their work and struggle to find the correct value stance when confronted with a difficult situation.

More than asking whether people were following the correct rules, O'Rourke worried about whether people were thinking in a flexible way about the principles that govern their work. When people treat rules as rigid guidelines, he asserted, it is only a matter of time before a school psychologist is dominated by the regular school system. Effective school psychology has to be dynamic and creative. Blanchard failed in the eyes of his superiors because he seemed to be rigid in the application of values rather than flexible, creative, and sensitive to the moral ambiguities of the situation.

The data in this study, both quantitative and qualitative, support O'Rourke's theory. If we accept that the rate of testing is a valid measure of the quality of child studies, then psychologists who assume a passive stance are significantly more likely to test rapidly than those who assume an active stance. Passivity is expressed operationally as a reluctance to become engaged in organizational politics, a desire to work in an insulated setting (one's office rather than the schools one services), reluctance to accept that student learning problems may be caused by failures of teaching or school organization, and little constructive interaction with those regular and special program staff who oversee one's work.

Activeness is expressed in the reverse of these things and in a desire to provide diverse psychological services, escaping a narrow testing role, a desire to become involved in the interactional dynamics of schools and to relate one's diagnostic work to those dynamics, and an effort to maximize one's organizational position—weak though it usually is—to work as an advocate for children and other school actors. People who are passive accept that their role is given, usually seeing it defined in terms of regular program needs. Active people believe that they must create a role for themselves, trying to shape it so they can do work consistent with the values and skills they have been taught as psychologists.

I showed in Chapter Five that whether people take an active or a passive role in their work, it is most affected by three things: 1) their personal professional training and socialization, 2) the structure of career advancement opportunities they confront, and 3) specific incentives and constraints work organizations present that define personal risks and benefits that flow from activism or passivity.

Often trained first as teachers, Chicago school psychologists tend to have stronger allegiances with educators than with psychologists. Working in a large organization where most advancement opportunities will be internal to that organization, Chicago psychologists have little choice but to follow the traditional advancement patterns of their school system and curry favor with its powerful members, people who usually are most concerned with regular education. Those people who work in smaller districts can afford to take the local power structure less seriously because their natural career advancement opportunities will require that they change districts. Finally, large cities offer few rewards to those who launch innovative programs and services. The system is rigid and slow to change, so the rewards for creativity are small. At the same time, seeming to be an empire builder or a power seeker is dangerous to psychologists. Cooperativeness and conformity are safer and more appreciated by those one works with. This may also be true in small nonurban districts. However, there are opportunities for psychologists to build personal influence within their school systems, there are particular districts that seek and even demand unconventional psychology, and the dual allegiance psychologists face because they are affiliated with educational service centers can make passivity more risky than activism.

The administrative conditions outside of cities make organizational activism possible, or maybe they even encourage it. However, this approach to work cannot be mandated on a large scale through legislation like PL 94-142. Activism depends on individuals wanting to work creatively, wanting to shape and challenge (however covertly) the dominant practices of the school districts that employ them, and viewing moral dilemmas as central challenges in their work. We can encourage activism in training programs and through staff selection and promotion policies. We can also encourage it with organizational arrangements that produce equally powerful joint affiliation for workers. This would legitimate value dilemmas and protect people as they make serious efforts to resolve them. There is no professional system, however, that guarantees universal competence. Even in the strongest settings of medical practice, all that usually happens to those judged less competent is that they are pushed into less desirable settings of practice. As long as there is school psychology there will be people who wish to do little more than test children and be left alone.

Although no one can ever mandate activism, systems like those in Chicago and most other large cities almost guarantee passivity. One might try to mimic the conditions that prevail outside of cities and thereby try to reform urban school psychology. I do not think this would work. It would be hard to overcome a century of tradition in Chicago—traditions deeply embedded in the *whole* school system about what testing means, how it should be done, and who should be recruited to administer the tests. It also would be hard to make school psychology values seem as important as the urgent problems that face the regular school program.

Were I the philosopher king, I would abandon school psychology and probably special education as it exists in cities. I would consider creating freestanding, independent organizations to offer special educational services. However, the monopoly on education enjoyed by a large urban school system is so powerful that it is hard to imagine even legally independent special education organizations maintaining autonomy. They would become captives as beltway-bandit consulting firms are captives of federal government bureaucracies. For *special* education—and other peripheral school programs—to work, I suspect we would need revolutionary change in the structure of urban *regular* schools.

School Psychology in Sociohistorical Context

This talk of reform assumes, of course, that the point of special education and school psychology is actually to help children, either those with organically based handicaps or those who are entangled in destructive school conflicts. As Carrier suggests, it might make more sense to view the rationale for special education in political and historical terms.[8]

Most sociological observers have treated special education as a variety of social control in schools.[9] That is, schools as organizations have an ongoing need to generate cohesion and commitment among students. Special education fosters cohesion by removing or controlling students perceived to interfere with maintaining order whether they do this by being discipline problems or by frustrating teachers as they fail to learn. The control perspective suggests that although special education may not be there to do what it says it is doing, at least it is serving a necessary function for schools. Another interpretation is that intelligence testing and labeling are important mainly for culturally symbolic reasons. In this perspective, the manifest substantive activity in schools does not matter very much. What counts is how people outside of schools think about the process of education and how their ideas about education work to legitimate the structure of inequality in society.

Social Control

The need for social control emerges in somewhat different ways at the various organizational levels of schools. Numerous classroom observers have seen conflict as a central theme in student-teacher relationships.[10] Similarly, teacher-principal, teacher-parent, and principal-central office relations all have important elements of conflict. Schools thrive when there is consensus and acceptance of the authority of the staff. When that authority breaks down, schools become uncomfortable and sometimes dangerous places.[11] Disruption is dangerous, and consequently schools need mechanisms for challenging and controlling it. Special education is one of those mechanisms of control.[12]

In this perspective, children are referred to special education not because they suffer some clearly defined handicap but because they have come to be seen as a "problem" by school officials. They may be problems because they fail to learn in the way teachers expect—perhaps because they suffer neurological lesions that interfere with their capacity to process information as learning disability theorists propose. Children may be problems because they are disruptive and because they pose discipline problems. They also may be problems for reasons that have little to do with their own behavior. Students may be goaded into hostile or self-protective action. Or they may just be labeled by a teacher or principal with his or her own reasons for wanting to identify some problem children.[13]

If we see special education as social control, the classification apparatus, within which school psychologists work, exists primarily to legitimate and sanitize an activity that the schools cannot publicly admit they are carrying out. To keep things under control, schools may need time-out rooms, safety-valve arrangements, and entertainments that will appeal to children who are otherwise uninterested in school. But when schools seek budgetary approval or when they explain their punitive actions, the simple need for social control is not publicly acceptable. Schools need labels to sell these programs and to convince people, in- and outside of schools, that if children are being stigmatized or given slower-paced instruction, that is happening for good reasons.

Legitimation for Inequality

The social control perspective suggests that special education exists to meet certain illegitimate but necessary organizational needs. An alternative view, inspired by Marxist reinterpretations of the role of schooling in capitalist society, asserts that the major function of education is to reproduce the class structure from generation to generation, ensuring that the children of the elite will also be elites.[14] This happens in two ways.

First, the process of education discourages poor children from learning while it rewards the cultural style of the middle class. Poor children are convinced that they have few chances for upward social and economic mobility because they are stupid and our society is a meritocracy.[15] Meanwhile, middle-class and wealthy children are taught the social skills they will need to survive at the middle and higher levels of complex organizations and in professional work. Schools pass on to these children the "cultural capital" of the elite.

Second, schools certify achievement and allocate credentials that foster career advancement. When they do this, they reward appropriate behavior or attitude as much as they do cognitive achievement.[16] As people progress through the educational system, the mere fact that they attend a prestigious school is enough to confer on them the status they need to advance in their educational or professional career. Possessing a desirable credential has a greater effect on career advancement than does objective performance. Although the educational system is somewhat open to advancement by talented lower-class people, the strong social component in credential allocation ensures that children from less favored backgrounds will be blocked out of the opportunity to advance into many high-prestige jobs.

This system works to the extent that people believe the myth of meritocracy. If people see schools as open institutions committed to equal opportunity and if they believe that the rewards schools have to hand out are given on the basis of objective intellectual competition, then the inequality in skills and credentials that results from education is understandable and acceptable. In this critical perspective, schools must create a variety of programs and symbols to foster the myth of meritocracy.

One of the most important myths of the open competition model of schooling is that there is a set of objectively indentifiable traits we can call intelligence. These traits can be measured objectively using IQ tests. Further, the myth says, intelligence is something that is part of one's personal heritage. It is partly inherited and partly fostered by the social and cultural climate one lives in as a small child. We believe that some people have a lot of intelligence, that others have less of it, and that it is normally distributed in society. A key part of this belief is that poor people on average have less intelligence than rich people, which is a reflection on their impoverished cultural heritage and their lower genetic potential. Schools are important as a vehicle for those few smart lower-class children to escape their background and as a source of positive socialization that may combat the destructive influences of lower-class culture.

Special education, intelligence testing, and school psychology make an important symbolic contribution to the meritocratic ideology. Learning disability theory is useful for explaining why middle-class children might fail despite their positive genetic and social endowments. A specific flaw in their ability to process information blocks them from succeeding in school. With proper instruction, they still have the capacity to achieve—look at the late Governor Rockefeller and other high-achieving persons with learning disabilities. The presence of special education shows that schools are committed to giving everyone equal opportunity and an education appropriate to their needs and abilities. Its presence also emphasizes the continuing validity of using IQ measures to assert the existence of class differences in intelligence.

In the critical perspective, it really does not matter what the reality of special education is. There is no way for the outcomes of actual programs to be publicly known, fed into the policymaking process, and somehow made accountable for their activities. What special educators actually do is not relevant for their legitimizing function to be performed, and so no machinery to guarantee accountability need exist. Because their most important function is symbolic, all that is important is that the programs exist, that money be spent, and that children be processed so that schools can demonstrate their continued commitment to this expression of equal educational opportunity and meritocratic advancement. There is no fixed relationship between the size of programs and their ability to validate symbols. When there is widespread public interest in and political support for programs, budgetary expansion is likely. When interest wanes, budgetary decline is likely although it will be limited by statutory restrictions and ongoing public support for programs.

At any rate, in the critical perspective there is no relationship between program size or program structure and actual need (if there is any need at all).[17] What programs actually look like and do is determined by the internal organizational pressures of schools, by the academic traditions and intellectual fads that hold sway among policymakers, and by pressures for organizational isomorphism.[18] The rationales that govern program design are not likely to make sense when held up to serious scrutiny. They are useful mainly because they legitimate programs politically, and they serve to generate commitment among practitioners.

An Assessment of Latent Function Explanations

In a classic essay, Robert K. Merton once distinguished between the manifest and latent functions performed in social systems.[19] Manifest functions are those justifications that are publicly stated and that supposedly represent a rational definition of how tasks link together and collectively produce definite, necessary social products. Merton suggested that manifest functions are usually a pale description of what actually goes on in social systems. The job of the social scientist, he sugggested, is to look for latent functions. These are activities carried out in a social system but not publicly acknowledged. Often they are not even recognized by participants. Astute observers, however, perceive these latent functions and draw upon the facts of organizational life to show how they operate and produce their less visible, perhaps illegitimate products.

Thus far I have given an assessment of the effectiveness of school psychology in terms of its manifest functions and have identified two latent function theories of why school psychology, intelligence testing, and special education exist in schools. The latent function theories are attractive because what school psychologists do—especially in a city like Chicago—is far from what enlightened theory suggests they might or should do.

Most sociological field studies of special education have been rooted in the social control theory. Tomlinson's work and my earlier study of special classes show its usefulness for making sense of the details of everyday life in schools.[20] Carrier and Berk, Bridges and Shih, however, argue that the social control theory is inadequate to explain why special education exists and how overall student referral patterns have evolved.[21] In their analysis of Chicago records, Berk, Bridges, and Shih could not find support for a claim that children are placed in special classes for disciplinary reasons. IQ scores were the best predictor of placement.[22] Coupled with my findings, their results suggest that although testing is rapid, unreliable, and disconnected from ongoing student programs, intelligence testing has substantial authority in the public schools and that it confers power on school psychologists. The symbols are powerful even though the substance is empty.

This seems to mean that we ought to understand the history and changes in special education in terms of the symbolic needs of schools. Special education has grown primarily when there have been waves of immigration of culturally nonmodal rural people into urban areas. The first period of growth was 1890 to 1920; the second followed the black urban migration of the 1940s and 1950s. Special education has expanded in response to assertive political demands for more equal opportunity in schools. It is sold as an effort to fine-tune education for those poorly equipped to succeed in mainstream education. In its enactment, special education demonstrates the inferiority of new migrants compared to native urbanites, and it helps regular educators manage their social control problems. After the migration slows and the public outcry dies down, special education programs gradually diminish, achieving a stable, maintenance level of program size.

The trouble with this explanation is that it does not explain the vitality of school psychology outside of cities. In a place like ACORN, school psychology and special education actually seem to be doing what they are supposed to be doing. Outside cities we need an evolutionary theory of organizational development like Lindblom's notion of disjointed incrementalism.[23] Policies are put in place in response to publicly perceived social problems. Then as political fads change and practitioners struggle to implement the policy, there is a gradual evolution of practice. Over time, policy adapts in response to ongoing public demand, the operating difficulties of program administration, and the availability of resources. There usually are successive revisions of formal policy to reflect political and practical reality. Then eventually programs are institutionalized, gaining a certain permanence.

The trouble with an incrementalist explanation is that it works best in social services where small, fragmented organizations predominate. In an organizational monolith like the Chicago public schools, new policies are just demolished unless they have powerful support and speak to the core concerns of the organizational system. There has been some cosmetic change in school psychology in the face of PL 94-142 reforms, but the real practices of special educators have been impervious to federal change efforts. No doubt special education and school psychology are maintained in Chicago in part because they are legally mandated. They are also maintained, I am sure, because special education has genuine symbolic value in all school systems. The main value of these programs *is* symbolic, however. There is nothing to force accountability on the Chicago schools, and so special education is mostly form with little value.

The Omnipotent Planner

The major selling point of this book is that it purports to show how the actual practice of testing and student evaluation in schools departs from "correct" practice. Two sources of authority define what ought to be good practice in school psychology. One is legal, embodied in legislation, litigation, and administrative regulations—The Education for All Handicapped Children Act of 1975. The other is scientific, based in research and methodological propositions that guide the use and interpretation of psychometric tests. Showing how practice departs from correctness allows us to see how racial minorities come to receive inferior treatment in the public schools and, despite reform, continue to be exposed to the risks of stigmatization and misclassification in special education classes.

At the same time that I have been excoriating urban school psychologists for what amounts to malpractice, I have argued that no school psychologist in his or her right mind really wants to follow the dictates of "correct" practice. We do not want psychologists to take the guidelines that govern test administration too seriously because it is dangerous to act as though the instruments are objective measures. We are not quite sure what they measure or what errors they contain, so one should interpret all test results with caution. Probably tests are most useful if we use them as instruments of discovery. They help us understand why a child fails by providing a standardized environment for observation and a set of tools with which we may test hypotheses about the causes of failure. Tests also need to be supplemented by information about a child's real life. One needs to know something about a child's family situation, his or her classroom relationships, history in school, and so on. Tests should be used artfully rather than according to some lockstep set of rules.

This suggested use fits with what psychologists have learned about tests and testing over the last nine decades. It also makes sense because psychologists are participants in a complex organizational system who, over time, develop commitments, relationships, and priorities of their own. The role of the psychologist is very limited in certain respects because it is marginal and not centrally involved in the main business of educating children. At the same time, that very marginality frees psychologists of constraints that hamper more "important" educators. No one quite knows who the psychologist is responsible to, what he or she is supposed to do, or even where he or she is supposed to be on a given day since they usually float from setting to setting. This freedom coupled with training to be observers of troubled social settings equips psychologists to see disruption and conflict that others may be blinded to. It also is likely to liberate them from the competition and alliances that prevent members of the school core from doing anything when they find themselves caught in debilitating conflicts. At the same time that they have little formal power, their freedom provides opportunities for intervention not available to many other actors around schools.

Those opportunities are necessarily somewhat ad hoc. Admittedly, as I have shown in this book, individual psychologists tend to favor certain sorts of involvement in schools. Some like helping teachers with curricular development; others like hobnobbing with superintendents; and others like to listen to people talk about their emotional problems, helping out when they can. But whatever mode of intervention they prefer, most activist psychologists jump into the fray when the situation demands their involvement or presents them with a problem. Most psychologists I met were at some time in their careers confronted with the full range of situations I have described in this book.

This argument follows Lipsky and Weatherley's suggestion that school psychologists are street level bureaucrats. Their activities are defined by the idiosyncracies of the situations they encounter and by a combination of common sense and technical skill they bring to bear on problems. The term "street-level bureaucrat" refers to the whole range of occupations whose members provide social services directly to clients. The nature of their work requires that they use personal discretion and judgment in deciding when and how to intervene. This being the case, however, it is nearly impossible to articulate a policy to govern their practice. If practitioners are continually "ad hocing it," to use the ethnomethodological term, how can anyone, and especially people outside of the occupation, set goals, press for high quality practice, or criticize performance?[24] This problem is exacerbated because, adapting to the conditions of work that prevail in them, school systems have developed "loosely coupled" authority systems at the same time that they have rigid, tradition-bound formal structures. People jealously guard turf and standard operating procedures while fiercely resisting direction from administrative superiors.

The analytical struggle of this book has been to find ways of understanding school psychology that make the occupation seem less anarchic. In general, it is true that school psychologists, like others who work in education, are free of supervision and direction. They have latitude to freelance, and in some circumstances face serious punishment if they take the safe route and avoid being innovative, political, and energetic in their work.

At the same time there is structure to the occupation. It may be true that policymakers and administrative superiors do not usually have the power (or the inclination) to define the psychologist's role or to mandate that specific tasks will be carried out at work using specific methods. But the technology of their work imposes limits on what school psychologists can do and the fabric of interdependence that ties psychologists to regular school staff members creates informal obligations. Between the two, psychologists can find their time at work severely restricted and directed even though they are subject to no specific human authority. Constraint "falls out" of the system.

One lesson, then, is that if we wish to understand what directs the course of work in loosely structured occupations that encourage workers to use discretion, we should give careful attention to the technical structure of work. With school psychologists, as in Stinchcombe's earlier study of steel plant engineers, time budgets are mostly powerful when they tie up time. If workers are locked into a tight set of obligations, we know exactly what they will be doing. But if their work by its nature requires creativity, judgment, and ingenuity, then that close control is likely to translate into rigidity and worker passivity. Rather than anticipating and attacking problems, workers tend to believe tasks are allocated to them by some distant authority that has real responsibility for his or her work. Denying responsibility and treating one's work as passive and bureaucratic is the way that "good people" end up accepting "dirty work."

A second lesson of this study is that social control, rooted in moral communities, occurs within worker communities. The values that such communities articulate and accept guide workers as they make their judgmental decisions about practice. This is an old truism of organizational analysis dating back at least to the Hawthorne studies.[25] Moral communities are self-protective for workers. They tell people how to behave and define "signature dilemmas" so that workers understand the kinds of problems they share with their peers. Understanding that certain problems are common allows discussion of how to attack them and what constitutes a "good" intervention, and it allows the community to protect individuals who are attacked by outsiders for behavior that peers judge appropriate.

Informal worker communities arise spontaneously, and they are usually self-governed and self-controlling. I have argued that this same organizational mechanism lies at the heart of professional organization. I have presented professionalism not as credentialism or a body of intellectual knowledge. Rather, it is a style of voluntary organization among workers in which the informal structure of work groups becomes a formal organization that is the agent of the workers. Particularly when the workers share a body of academic knowledge, folding formal and informal work organizations in on each other tends to focus attention on the relationship between abstract technical knowledge and practice. This does not guarantee that practitioners will be sophisticated or even competent in their use of these abstract ideas. It does, however, push workers into developing self-consciousness about the values that govern their work and into believing that values play an important role in governing their work. They are not just ad hocing it. They are trying to apply a definite code of knowledge and behavior to work problems— they are trying to *be* psychologists or doctors or whatever.

Given the fluidity of street level bureaucratic work, encouraging people to articulate values for their work—whatever those values might be—and encouraging them to abide by those precepts seems to me important. It is important not because people ought to be moral. Rather, people need to be encouraged to pull back from the short view and think about what they are really doing in their work. If people just ad hoc it, they tend to have no systematic understanding of what they are doing, how they do it, or what constitutes good work. Thus the opposite of following strong values at work is not immorality or even incompetence. It is anomie—thoughtless management of details without a sense of their meaning, consequences, or importance.

The challenge in school psychology lies in encouraging practitioners to be responsible. Responsibility requires psychologists to have an idealized sense of purpose in their work, the dangers it poses and a commitment to maintaining the integrity of their role in the face of role conflicts. These are all abstract concepts, free of predetermined substance. They refer not to any set of moral universals but rather to a way of working that is active rather than passive.

To some extent we can influence the activeness of workers and maybe even influence their work values in some cases. One way to intervene is to remove barriers, like those in Chicago, that prevent people from assuming responsibility. Another way is to establish organizations like ACORN that provide incentives for workers to form professional associations that exercise firm control over methods of practice.

Realistically, however, most practice will be outside both of these kinds of determinative settings. We know this from our studies of medicine in which the majority of practitioners work autonomously with little peer review or control. Tight monitoring of practice occurs in some settings but, according to the research, only when students are being trained or where an organization seeks to maintain high status in the medical community. In most situations, street level bureaucrats or professionals are left to work in a way they think is best. For these people, we have to rely on training and early professional socialization to inculcate a desire to maintain high standards and to upgrade knowledge and skill. Some people do it, some do not.

Organizations like ACORN are professional socialization settings for school psychology. One of their functions is to intensively train young psychologists who, seeking more independence, responsibility, and pay, move on to less controlled practice settings. Policymakers might work to establish centers of professionalism within regions, hoping that gradually there will be a continual diffusion of professional values into less closely monitored school settings.

These centers are not really a solution to the deeper problem of policymaking. We academics and people in government seek generalizations that elucidate, explain, and suggest interventions for social problems. This encourages us to lay down proper procedures or rational interventions. Usually these interventions tend to be overly rigid and ill-suited to the realistic problems of practice that workers confront. So we try again, either becoming increasingly frustrated or gradually losing interest in the issue that once seemed like such a pressing problem.[26] Policymaking—whether it involves creating norms for intelligence tests, trying to find a humane way of helping children who fail in school, or formulating regulations to govern how children will be placed in those classes—seems doomed to produce outcomes that are different from those which were intended. Like it or not, school systems will mostly run out of control. That is to say, the people who work in them and receive services in them will work out together what they will do. Technological fixes will not work very well.

Is this a problem? It is if your job is to find out *the* truth or to solve the problems of society. This study of school psychology suggests that reality is too complex and multidimensional for either of these approaches to be realistic. We have seen that there are some troublesome practices in school psychology that ought to be stopped. We have seen that there is some strong professional control operating in school psychology, but that seems to be an infrequent occurrence. We have learned that schools have a need for social control and that special education sometimes serves that need. Testing and school psychology legitimate that use.

This suggests that school psychology exists primarily for symbolic purposes. If that is the case, does it make sense to talk about "high-quality" school psychology? Perhaps that value forms over essential content. Indeed, all of the talk I have provided about how school psychologists could be social psychologists for the schools might be misplaced if the main function of the occupation is to legitimate an activity schools cannot admit in a forthright way that they are doing even though it is organizationally necessary. In the end, school psychologists have to be committed to the overall success of schooling and education rather than being narrowly committed to some professional ideal of their work.

The truth is that all of these things are true, and they all matter. Contradictions abound, as they must. We need policymakers because local systems have to be held accountable and because we need to bring a broader view to bear on narrow technical activities. But policymaking will be distorted and incomplete because broad, general analyses will not capture the essential contextual details that make street level bureaucracy creative, judgmental work. We have to realize that educational policy will always be customized to fit the political realities, professional preferences, and student needs of different localities.[27] We should not be upset about this because the point of policymaking is not to "fix" things. Rather, social science and policy analysis are ways of generating a dialogue between the general and the specific—between the nation and the locality, between the profession and the practitioner, between the pressures of today and the long-term consequences of one's actions.

Mail Questionnaire for the Illinois School Psychology Project

SURVEY OF ILLINOIS SCHOOL PSYCHOLOGISTS

Sponsored by:

Alcohol, Drug Abuse and Mental Health Administration
National Institutes of Heath

and

The School Section, Illinois Psychological Association

Principal Investigator:

Carl Milofsky, Ph.D.
Department of Education
University of Chicago
Member, Illinois Psychological Assn.

INSTRUCTIONS

Please follow the procedures and instructions outlined below in answering this questionnaire. This will insure that your answers can be aggregated with those of your colleagues and then compared.

1) In completing this questionnaire, you will find two types of questions:

  a) Questions with numbers (codes) following the answer categories. These questions should be answered by circling the appropriate code.

                FOR EXAMPLE: YES . . . . . ①
                                NO 2

  b) Questions that require you to supply a number or a name. In such instances, write the answer in the space provided.

                FOR EXAMPLE: ENTER # MONTHS: __9__

2) Please answer <u>all</u> questions <u>unless</u> otherwise instructed. At many points in the questionnaire, your answer to a question will determine whether you are to proceed to the next question or skip it. These instructions are:

  a) located in parentheses between the answer category and the code,

    FOR EXAMPLE:

    2. Prior to becoming a psychologist, did you have any experience as a public school teacher or in another public school position?

                        YES . . (ANSWER A & B) 1   15/
                        NO . . . (GO TO Q. 3) 2

        IF YES:
        A. For each of the following positions, please indicate whether you held

    3. Did you every have a full-time job or seriously consider a career in a field other than psychology or education? IF YES: Please indicate in which field. CIRCLE ALL THAT APPLY.

  or b) in boxes before or after questions,

    FOR EXAMPLE:

        IF YOU NOW PLAN TO DEVOTE MOST OF YOUR CAREER TO SCHOOL PSYCHOLOGY
        BUT DIDN'T WHEN YOU BEGAN YOUR M.A. PROGRAM, ANSWER Q. 10.
        OTHERWISE, GO TO Q. 11.

    10. Some psychologists change their career goals after they have begun graduate work. Sometimes family demands interfered with their career goals, sometimes role

If there is no instruction, always proceed with the next question.

<u>INTRODUCTION</u>

A. Which of the following describes the kind of work you did in psychology during the 1976-77 and/or 1977-78 school years? CIRCLE ALL THAT APPLY.

SCHOOL PSYCHOLOGY IN A PUBLIC SCHOOL:
FULL TIME OR PART TIME 1   6/

SCHOOL PSYCHOLOGY IN A NON-PUBLIC SCHOOL:
FULL TIME OR PART TIME 2   7/

ACADEMIC TEACHING OF PSYCHOLOGY 3   8/

PRIVATE CLINICAL PRACTICE   4   9/

OTHER: PLEASE SPECIFY _____ 5   10/

IF YOU WERE <u>NOT</u> WORKING IN SCHOOL PSYCHOLOGY,
EITHER FULL TIME OR PART TIME DURING 1976-77
<u>OR</u> 1977-78, PLEASE RETURN THIS QUESTIONNAIRE
IN THE PREPAID ENVELOPE PROVIDED. THANK YOU.

B. Were you working in school psychology, either full time or part time, during the 1977-78 school year?

YES 1   11/

NO . (READ THE INSTRUCTION BELOW) . . 2

<u>IF NO</u>:

WHENEVER QUESTIONS ASK FOR YOUR CURRENT STATUS OR ACTIVITIES
AS A SCHOOL PSYCHOLOGIST, PLEASE ANSWER FOR THE 1976-77 SCHOOL
SCHOOL YEAR.

CAREER CHOICE

1. In making a career choice, many things often act together in influencing a
    decision. In thinking about the factors that led you to choose psychology as
    a career, which one of the following was the most important, which one the
    second most important, and which one the third most important?

CIRCLE ONE CODE ONLY IN EACH COLUMN

	MOST IMPORTANT 12/	2ND MOST IMPORTANT 13/	3RD MOST IMPORTANT 14/
THE AVAILABILITY OF JOBS IN PSYCHOLOGY AND RELATED FIELDS	1	1	1
THE SUBSTANTIVE CONTENT OF THE FIELD . .	2	2	2
THE STATUS AND FINANCIAL OPPORTUNITIES WHICH COME WITH BEING A PSYCHOLOGIST . .	3	3	3
ENCOURAGEMENT FROM PEOPLE WHO FELT I WOULD BE GOOD AT PSYCHOLOGY OR THE EXAMPLE OF IMPORTANT PEOPLE IN MY LIFE . .	4	4	4
A SERIES OF MORE OR LESS UNPLANNED CHOICE DURING COLLEGE	5	5	5
A DESIRE TO WORK WITH PEOPLE	6	6	6

2. Prior to becoming a psychologist, did you have any experience as a public school teacher or in another public school position?

YES . . (ANSWER A & B) 1   15/

NO . . . (GO TO Q. 3) 2

IF YES:

A. For each of the following positions, please indicate whether you held such a position prior to becoming a psychologist. IF YES: Please indicate the number of years you held the position.

	YES: ENTER # YEARS	NO	
REGULAR CLASS TEACHER	_____	0	16-17/
SPECIAL EDUCATION TEACHER . . .	_____	0	18-19/
SCHOOL PRINCIPAL	_____	0	20-21/
SCHOOL COUNSELOR	_____	0	22-23/
SCHOOL ASSISTANT PRINCIPAL . .	_____	0	24-25/
OTHER ADMINISTRATIVE POSITION .	_____	0	26-27/

B. Were each of the positions you have indicated above in the same county in which you are presently working?

YES 1   28/

NO 2

---

3. Did you every have a full-time job or seriously consider a career in a field other than psychology or education? IF YES: Please indicate in which field. CIRCLE ALL THAT APPLY.

YES: MEDICINE 1   29/

RESEARCH IN PHYSICAL OR BIOLOGICAL SCIENCIES 2   30/

CLERGY OR RABBINATE 3   31/

BUSINESS - SALES OR MANAGEMENT 4   32/

ENGINEERING 5   33/

OTHER: PLEASE SPECIFY _____ 6   34/

NO: DID NOT HAVE OR CONSIDER OTHER CAREER 7   35/

4. How old were you when you began your graduate training in psychology?

ENTER AGE: _____   36-37/

---

5. When you <u>began</u> your graduate program in psychology, what degrees did you expect to receive after you had completed all of your graduate work? CIRCLE ALL THAT APPLY.

    M.A. OR M.S. IN
    PSYCHOLOGY OR
    SCHOOL PSYCHOLOGY 1   38/

    PH.D. IN PSYCHOLOGY 2   39/

    J.D./LL.B. 3   40/

    M.B.A. 4   41/

    M.D. 5   42/

    OTHER: PLEASE SPECIFY:

    _____ . . 6   43/

6. When you <u>began</u> your graduate program in psychology, to which <u>one</u> of the following applications of psychology did you plan to devote most of your career? CIRCLE ONE CODE ONLY.

    SCHOOL PSYCHOLOGY 1   44/

    PRIVATE CLINICAL OR
    CONSULTING PRACTICE . . . 2

    ACADEMIC TEACHING OR
    RESEARCH 3

    EDUCATIONAL
    ADMINISTRATION 4

    OTHER: PLEASE SPECIFY:

    _____ 5

---

7. <u>At this time</u>, do you plan to go on to obtain a Ph.D. in psychology or some other graduate degree, or do you already have a Ph.D. in psychology? CIRCLE ALL THAT APPLY.

    PLAN TO GET PH.D. IN
    PSYCHOLOGY 1   45/

    PLAN TO GET OTHER
    DEGREE (PLEASE SPECIFY)

    _____ 2   46/

    ALREADY HAVE PH.D. IN
    PSYCHOLOGY 3   47/

    DO NOT PLAN TO GET
    ANOTHER GRADUATE
    DEGREE 4   48/

8. <u>At this time</u>, to which <u>one</u> of the following applications of psychology do you plan to devote most of your career? CIRCLE ONE CODE ONLY.

    SCHOOL PSYCHOLOGY
    (GO TO Q. 10) 1   49/

    PRIVATE CLINICAL OR
    CONSULTING PRACTICE . . . 2

    ACADEMIC TEACHING OR
    RESEARCH 3

    EDUCATIONAL ADMINIS-
    TRATION 4

    OTHER: PLEASE SPECIFY:

    _____ 5

IF YOU DO NOT PLAN TO DEVOTE MOST OF YOUR CAREER TO BEING A SCHOOL PSYCHOLOGIST:

9. Which one of the following phrases best describes the way you view your
   present occupation as school psychologist in terms of your long-range career
   plans? CIRCLE ONE CODE ONLY.

> IT PROVIDES ME WITH FINANCIAL SECURITY WHILE
> I BUILD MY PRIVATE PRACTICE OR FINISH
> WORK ON MY PH.D. 1   50/
>
> FAMILY DEMANDS PREVENT ME FROM CONTINUING ON
> TO THE NEXT STAGE OF MY CAREER AT THIS TIME 2
>
> MY WORK AS SCHOOL PSYCHOLOGIST WILL PROVIDE ME
> WITH IMPORTANT EXPERIENCE IN MY LATER CAREER 3
>
> IT IS JUST A TEMPORARY JOB FROM WHICH I WILL MOVE
> ON AS SOON AS I FIND THE KIND OF JOB I AM
> LOOKING FOR 4

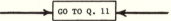

GO TO Q. 11

> IF YOU NOW PLAN TO DEVOTE MOST OF YOUR CAREER TO SCHOOL PSYCHOLOGY
> BUT DIDN'T WHEN YOU BEGAN YOUR M.A. PROGRAM, ANSWER Q. 10.
> OTHERWISE, GO TO Q. 11.

10. Some psychologists change their career goals after they have begun graduate work.
    Sometimes family demands interfered with their career goals, sometimes role
    role models worked the change, sometimes the individual enjoyed a certain kind
    of work s/he had not been exposed to before, and so on. In thinking about the
    factors that led you to change your career plans, which one of the following
    was the most important? CIRCLE ONE CODE ONLY.

> FAMILY RESPONSIBILITIES 01   51-52/
>
> THE AVAILABILITY OF JOBS 02
>
> THE SUBSTANTIVE CONTENT OF THE FIELD 03
>
> THE WORK ENVIRONMENT 04
>
> OTHER: PLEASE SPECIFY: _____
>
> _____ 05

WORK ACTIVITIES AND RELATIONSHIP WITH OTHER STAFF

11. The following phrases describe activities or situations which psychologists might encounter in their work. For each, please indicate the frequency with which the activity occurs in your work: does it occur often, sometimes, rarely, or never?

	OFTEN	SOME-TIMES	RARELY	NEVER	
(1) I HAVE OPPORTUNITIES TO CONDUCT PSYCHOTHERAPEUTIC WORK WITH CHILDREN AND PARENTS.	1	2	3	4	53/
(2) I DISCUSS EVALUATION METHODS (TESTS, ETC.) AND THE RESULTS OF CHILD STUDIES FOR SPECIAL EDUCATIONAL REFERRALS WITH OTHER PSYCHOLOGISTS.	1	2	3	4	54/
(3) I SERVE AS A RESOURCE PERSON FOR PARENTS AND SCHOOL OFFICIALS REGARDING SOCIAL OR PSYCHO-LOGICAL SERVICES AVAILABLE FROM AGENCIES OTHER THAN THE PUBLIC SCHOOLS.	1	2	3	4	55/
(4) I BECOME INVOLVED IN THE ORGANIZATIONAL POLITICS OF SCHOOLS.	1	2	3	4	56/
(5) QUESTIONS THAT TEACHERS AND PRINCIPALS ASK ME SHOW THAT THEY HAVE A GOOD UNDERSTANDING OF MY PROFESSIONAL SKILLS AND OF THE RANGE OF SERVICES I MIGHT PROVIDE.	1	2	3	4	57/
(6) TEACHERS AND PRINCIPALS ASK ME FOR ADVICE ON ISSUES INVOLVING MY GENERAL JUDGMENT MORE THAN MY PROFESSIONAL ONE.	1	2	3	4	58/
(7) I MAKE SUGGESTIONS OR TALK TO PEOPLE TO TRY TO RESOLVE OR REDUCE THE EFFECTS OF DISAGREEMENTS AMONG SCHOOL STAFF MEMBERS.	1	2	3	4	59/
(8) I BECOME INVOLVED IN SO MANY DIFFERENT KINDS OF ACTIVITIES AND RELATIONSHIPS THAT I DON'T HAVE SUFFICIENT TIME TO DEAL WITH EACH ONE.	1	2	3	4	60/
(9) I HAVE EXPERIENCES WHICH GIVE ME OPPORTUNITIES TO IMPROVE MY PROFESSIONAL SKILLS.	1	2	3	4	61/

A. Thinking about each of these activities, which one activity or situation do you find the most rewarding when you experience it? It may be something you experience infrequently. PLEASE CIRCLE ITS DESCRIPTION.   62-63/

B. Which activity or situation do you find the most frustrating when you experience it? PLEASE CROSS OUT ITS DESCRIPTION. DO NOT CROSS OUT AN ACTIVITY YOU ENJOY BUT DO NOT HAVE ENOUGH CHANCE TO DO.   64-65/

12. How frequently does your job give you the chance to do the things you do best?

OFTEN 1   66/

SOMETIMES 2

INFREQUENTLY 3

NEVER 4

13. For each of the following statements regarding the role of psychotherapy in the schools, please indicate whether you agree with it strongly, agree somewhat, disagree somewhat, or disagree strongly.

	STRONGLY AGREE	SOMEWHAT AGREE	SOMEWHAT DISAGREE	STRONGLY DISAGREE	
SCHOOL PSYCHOLOGISTS SHOULD NOT ENTER INDIVIDUAL OR GROUP THERAPY RELATIONSHIPS WITH SCHOOL CHILDREN IF TIME LIMITATIONS WOULD MAKE IT DIFFICULT TO BE AVAILABLE WERE A CRISIS TO OCCUR	1	2	3	4	67/
PSYCHOLOGISTS MUST BE PREPARED TO USE PSYCHOTHERAPEUTIC SKILLS TO INTERPRET THE EMOTIONAL PROBLEMS OF CHILDREN WITH LEARNING PROBLEMS.	1	2	3	4	68/
PSYCHOLOGISTS MUST USE THERAPEUTIC SKILLS TO INTERVENE IN SITUATIONS WHERE PARENTS OR CHILDREN ARE ACTING IRRATIONALLY AND REGULAR SCHOOL STAFF CANNOT HANDLE THE SITUATION.	1	2	3	4	69/
PSYCHOLOGISTS MUST BE ABLE TO HELP RESOLVE THE EMOTIONAL PROBLEMS OF TEACHERS OR PRINCIPALS WHICH CONTRIBUTE TO THE INCIDENCE OF STUDENT LEARNING PROBLEMS.	1	2	3	4	70/
SINCE SCHOOLS DO NOT HAVE THE RESOURCES TO PROPERLY ADDRESS AND RESOLVE EMOTIONAL PROBLEMS, IT IS BEST FOR PSYCHOLOGISTS TO SIMPLY ASSIST THOSE NEEDING HELP BY MAKING REFERRALS.	1	2	3	4	71/
PSYCHOLOGISTS OFTEN LACK THE NECESSARY SKILLS TO PRACTICE THERAPY IN SCHOOLS AND SHOULD STICK TO DIAGNOSIS.	1	2	3	4	72/

"PRIMARY SERVICE ASSIGNMENT" IN THE FOLLOWING QUESTIONS REFERS TO THE SCHOOL DISTRICT, SPECIAL PROGRAM, OR ADMINISTRATIVE ASSIGNMENT IN WHICH YOU SPEND MOST OF YOUR TIME WORKING DURING ANY GIVEN MONTH.

14. Are you a regular member of one or more staffing teams--teams that discuss the nature of student problems and make pupil program decisions--in your primary service assignment?

                                    YES   1   73/

                                    NO . . (GO TO Q. 20) .   2

15. Which of the following statements best reflects your experiences with staffings? CIRCLE ONE CODE ONLY.

     SINCE MOST DECISIONS ARE MADE BEFORE THE MEETING
     HAPPENS, THEIR MAIN FUNCTION IS TO INSURE THAT
     MANDATED ADMINISTRATIVE PROCEDURES HAVE BEEN
     PROPERLY FOLLOWED 1   74/

     STAFFING ARE OFTEN DIFFICULT AND CHALLENGING FOR
     PSYCHOLOGISTS BECAUSE SCHOOL OFFICIALS MAY DISAGREE
     WITH THE PSYCHOLOGIST'S RECOMMENDATIONS 2

     STAFFINGS ARE GENERALLY PRODUCTIVE OPPORTUNITIES
     FOR SCHOOL PERSONNEL WITH DIFFERENT SPECIALTIES TO
     COME TOGETHER, SHARE KNOWLEDGE ABOUT PARTICULAR
     CHILDREN AND COLLECTIVELY DECIDE WHAT PROGRAM WOULD
     BE BEST FOR THEM 3

     THE PSYCHOLOGISTS' PRESENCE AT STAFFINGS IS
     IMPORTANT PRIMARILY BECAUSE THEY, AS THE STUDENTS'
     ADVOCATES, INSURE THAT THE BEST INTERESTS OF THE
     STUDENTS ARE SERVED, WHICH MIGHT NOT BE THE CASE IF
     ONLY EDUCATIONAL PERSONNEL ATTENDED 4

     STAFFINGS ARE A WASTE OF TIME SINCE THE SKILLS OF
     PSYCHOLOGISTS ARE NOT REQUIRED TO DEAL WITH THE
     MAJORITY OF CASES; THE FEW PROBLEM CASES COULD BE
     HANDLED IN OTHER WAYS 5

16. In your experience, how important are staffings in providing a forum in which parents are involved in planning the education their children receive and may challenge school decisions?

                         VERY IMPORTANT 1   75/

                         SOMEWHAT IMPORTANT 2

                         NOT VERY IMPORTANT   3

                         NOT AT ALL IMPORTANT 4

17. Who is most responsible for the management of staffing meetings held in your
    <u>primary service assignment</u>?

    THE SCHOOL PSYCHOLOGIST   1   6/

    THE SCHOOL SOCIAL WORKER   2

    THE PUPIL PERSONNEL DIRECTOR OR
    DISTRICT REPRESENTATIVE   3

    THE SCHOOL NURSE   4

    A SPEECH OR LD TEACHER   5

    IT VARIES FROM SCHOOL TO SCHOOL   6

    THE STAFFING TEAM SHARES RESPONSIBILITY . .   7

    OTHER: PLEASE SPECIFY _____

    _____   8

18. How often do you follow the progress of children in special programs after
    they are placed through staffing meetings you attend in your primary service
    assignment outside of mandated yearly re-evaluations?

    MORE THAN 75% OF THE TIME   1   7/

    50-74% OF THE TIME   2

    25-49% OF THE TIME   3

    LESS THAN 25% OF THE TIME   4

19. How satisfied are you that program decisions made by the staffing team in
    your primary service assignment are carried out in later special or regular
    educational programs to which the students are assigned?

    VERY SATISFIED   1   8/

    SOMEWHAT SATISFIED   2

    SOMEWHAT DISSATISFIED   3

    DISSATISFIED   4

20. Do you feel that, as members of the staffing team, psychologists have a respon-
    sibility to make sure that children placed in special programs actually receive
    the programs prescribed for them?

    YES   1   9/

    NO   2

21. What proportion of your time are you free to allocate as you wish?

    75% OR MORE   1   10/

    50-74%   2

    25-49%   3

    24% OR LESS   4

22. <u>Of this discretionary time</u>, how much of it do you spend developing and implementing programs you have helped design which are not a part of the classification process?

ALMOST ALL--OVER 90% . . . . . . (ANSWER A) . . 1   11/

MOST OF IT--60-89% . . . . (ANSWER A) . . 2

ABOUT HALF--40-59% . . . . (ANSWER A) . . 3

SOME OF IT--10-39% . . . . (ANSWER B) . . 4

ALMOST NONE OF IT--UNDER 10% . . (ANSWER B) . . 5

IF ABOUT HALF OR MORE OF THE TIME:

A. Which of the following statements best describes the reception your efforts to create new programs generally receive from regular school staff members? CIRCLE ONE CODE ONLY.

THEY USUALLY SUPPORT MY EFFORTS 1   12/

THEY ARE USUALLY MOST SUPPORTIVE IF THEY CAN
SEE IMMEDIATE PAYOFFS IN MY SOLUTIONS 2

MANY ARE SKEPTICAL OF MY EFFORTS BUT THEY
DO NOT OFTEN INTERFERE 3

OFTEN THERE IS ACTIVE RESISTANCE TO MY EFFORTS . 4

IF SOME OR ALMOST NONE OF THE TIME:

B. Which of the following statements best describes the reason why you infrequently or never attempt to create new programs? CIRCLE ONE CODE ONLY.

I FEEL THIS ACTIVITY SHOULD NOT BE A MAJOR
PART OF THE PSYCHOLOGIST'S ROLE 1   13/

THE NEED TO FIND IMMEDIATE PAYOFFS WHICH WOULD
MAKE SUGGESTIONS ATTRACTIVE TO SCHOOL STAFF
MEMBERS MAKES ME FEEL I WASTE A LOT OF
TIME WHEN I TRY PROGRAM CREATION 2

MY PROGRAM CREATION EFFORTS IN THE PAST HAVE
USUALLY BEEN BLOCKED OR SIDE-TRACKED DUE TO
SCHOOL POLITICS AND/OR A LACK OF INTEREST
AMONG SCHOOL PERSONNEL 3

MY CASELOAD AND OTHER DEMANDS ON MY TIME
LEAVE LITTLE TIME OVER FOR PROGRAM CREATION . . 4

23. In general, when you do undertake this kind of activity, do you find it rewarding, do you feel neutral about it, or do you find it frustrating?

REWARDING 1   14/

NEUTRAL 2

FRUSTRATING 3

24. Do regular school officials in the district(s) or the supervisors of the special program in which you work generally <u>expect</u> you to use your psychological skills to help deal with school problems in this way?

YES	1	15/
NO	2	

25. Some psychologists report that the problems students exhibit are often stimulated or exacerbated by the ways in which teachers or principals have dealt with the children. In the district(s) where you presently work, how frequently is this the case with children referred to you?

OFTEN . . . . . . (ANSWER A & B) .	1	16/
SOMETIMES . . . . . (ANSWER A & B) .	2	
INFREQUENTLY . . . (ANSWER A & B) .	3	
NEVER . . . . . (GO TO Q. 26) . . .	4	

IF SUCH PROBLEMS OCCUR:

A. Which of the following statements comes closest to your evaluation of why such problems occur? CIRCLE ONE CODE ONLY.

THE WORKING CONDITIONS IN SCHOOLS ARE OFTEN DIFFICULT AND THE RELATIONSHIPS AMONG STAFF MEMBERS ARE COMPLEX SO THAT SUCH PROBLEMS ARE SOMETIMES UNAVOIDABLE	1	17/
TEACHERS TEND TO BE ISOLATED BY THE NATURE OF THEIR CLASSROOM RESPONSIBILITIES; WITHOUT SUPPORTIVE PEOPLE TO TALK TO AS A SOURCE OF SUGGESTIONS ABOUT PROBLEMS THEY ENCOUNTER, SUCH PROBLEMS WILL OCCUR	2	
THE PROBLEM STEMS LARGELY FROM THE INCOMPETENCE OF STAFF MEMBERS	3	
IT'S NOT A QUESTION OF ORGANIZATIONAL PROBLEMS OR INCOMPETENCE: SOMETIMES PEOPLE JUST DON'T GET ALONG OR HAVE PERSONAL PROBLEMS WHICH AFFECT THEIR WORK	4	

B. When such problems occur, do you find them very challenging, somewhat challenging, somewhat frustrating, or very frustrating?

VERY CHALLENGING	1	18/
SOMEWHAT CHALLENGING	2	
SOMEWHAT FRUSTRATING	3	
VERY FRUSTRATING	4	

ORGANIZATIONAL WORK HISTORY

26. Which of the following types of organizations best describes the one in which you have your present primary service assignment? CIRCLE ONE CODE ONLY.

                AN ELEMENTARY AND/OR JUNIOR HIGH SCHOOL DISTRICT 1   19/
                AN INDEPENDENT HIGH SCHOOL DISTRICT 2
                A UNIFIED SCHOOL DISTRICT (BOTH 1 AND 2) 3
                A SPECIAL EDUCATIONAL COOPERATIVE OR BUREAU OF CHILD
                  STUDY ADMINISTRATIVE OFFICE 4
                A SPECIAL EDUCATIONAL SCHOOL OR PROGRAM 5
                A DIAGNOSTIC CENTER 6
                A NON-PUBLIC ELEMENTARY OR SECONDARY SCHOOL 7
                OTHER: PLEASE SPECIFY _____ 8

    A. In which school district do you have your present primary service assignment? IF YOUR ASSIGNMENT COVERS MORE THAN ONE DISTRICT, ANSWER FOR THE DISTRICT WHERE YOUR OFFICE IS LOCATED.

                                ENTER # OF DISTRICT:_____   20-23/

27. What is the name of the special education unit which supervises your work? "Special education unit" in this and the following questions refers to the administrative unit which was primarily responsible for hiring you and placing you in your program or district assignment. It need not be the organization which provides you with job benefits and gives you your paycheck.

                ENTER NAME: _____   24-26/

28. In what year were you first employed by this special education unit?

                                ENTER YEAR: 1 9_____   27-28/

        ┌───┐
    ───→│ IF YOU WERE FIRST EMPLOYED DURING THE   │←───
        │ CURRENT SCHOOL YEAR, 1977-78, GO TO Q. 32   │
        └───┘

29. What is the length of your current job tenure? That is, as of last June, how many consecutive years had you worked in a position which has been supervised by this special education unit, regardless of any changes in the schools or districts in which you have worked?

                                1-3 YEARS 1   29/
                                4-6 YEARS 2
                                7-10 YEARS 3
                                11-20 YEARS 4
                                20 YEARS OR OVER . . . 5

30. Through the period of your tenure, have you had a <u>primary service assignment</u> other than that to which you are now assigned?

YES . (ANSWER A THROUGH D) . . 1   30/

NO . . . . (GO TO Q. 31) . . . 2

IF YES:

A. How many changes in your primary service assignment have you had during the period of your job tenure? THE SAME ASSIGNMENT AT DIFFERENT POINTS IN TIME SHOULD BE COUNTED SEPARATELY.

ENTER # OF CHANGES: _____   31-32/

33/R

B. What is the length of your job tenure in your present primary service assignment? That is, how many consecutive years had you held the assignment as of the end of last year?

1-3 years . . (ANSWER C & D) . 1   34/

4-6 years . . (ANSWER C & D) . 2

7-10 years . .(GO TO Q. 31) . . 3

11-20 years . (GO TO Q. 31) . . 4

21 or over . (GO TO Q. 31) . . 5

C. Which of the following statements best describes the reason you left your last primary service assignment and took your present one? CIRCLE ONE CODE ONLY.

    MY PRESENT PRIMARY SERVICE ASSIGNMENT OFFERED AN
       OPPORTUNITY TO WORK IN A DIFFERENT KIND OF SPECIAL
       EDUCATIONAL PROGRAM WHICH I THOUGHT I WOULD ENJOY
       MORE THAN MY LAST ONE. 1   35/

    THERE WAS A DISPUTE WITH MY SUPERVISORS OR COLLEAGUES
       IN MY LAST ASSIGNMENT (E.G., I DID NOT LIKE THEIR
       METHODS, ETC.) WHICH LED TO MY NEW ASSIGNMENT . . . 2

    MY PRESENT PRIMARY SERVICE ASSIGNMENT OFFERED AN
       OPPORTUNITY FOR ME TO WORK WITH STUDENTS OF
       A HIGHER CALIBER 3

    MY PRESENT PRIMARY SERVICE ASSIGNMENT WAS MADE AS
       THE RESULT OF AN ADMINISTRATIVE TRANSFER (E.G.,
       PART OF A STAFF RACIAL INTEGRATION PROGRAM, OR AS
       THE RESULT OF AN ADMINISTRATIVE DECISION UPON
       WHICH I COULD HAVE HAD NO INFLUENCE) 4

    I THOUGHT MY PRESENT PRIMARY SERVICE ASSIGNMENT
       WOULD PROVIDE ME WITH MORE JOB SECURITY OR IT
       WAS A HIGHER ADMINISTRATIVE OFFICE 5

D. How satisfied are you with your <u>present</u> primary service assignment as compared to your <u>last</u> assignment? Are you more satisfied with your present assignment than your last, about as satisfied or less satisfied than with your last assignment?

MORE SATISFIED 1   36/

ABOUT EQUALLY SATISFIED . . . 2

LESS SATISFIED 3

31. During the period of tenure in your present primary service assignment, has your degree of autonomy changed, and if so, in what direction?

    YES, I NOW HAVE MORE AUTONOMY 1   37/

    YES, I NOW HAVE LESS 2

    YES, BUT IT TENDS TO FLUCTUATE FROM YEAR TO YEAR . 3

    NO 4

32. Please estimate the percentage of students you serve in your primary program assignment that belong to each of the racial/ethnic groups listed below. IF NONE IN A GROUP, ENTER A "0."

    BLACK . . . . _____ %   38-40/

    HISPANIC (I.E., MEXICAN, CUBAN, PUERTO RICAN). _____ %   41-43/

    WHITE . . . . _____ %   44-46/

33. Is there a wide variation from the racial/ethnic composition you have indicated above among the various schools or settings in your primary service assignment?

    YES 1   47/

    NO 2

34. Please estimate how many parents of the students you serve in your primary service assignment fall into each of the following employment categories.

	ALL OR MOST	MANY	SOME	ALMOST NONE OR NONE	
PROFESSIONAL (e.g., jobs requiring post-graduate work)	1	2	3	4	48/
WHITE COLLAR (e.g., office or management work)	1	2	3	4	49/
FACTORY OR OTHER BLUE COLLAR: PERMANENTLY EMPLOYED	1	2	3	4	50/
FACTORY OR OTHER BLUE COLLAR: INTERMITTENTLY EMPLOYED	1	2	3	4	51/
UNEMPLOYED	1	2	3	4	52/
DON'T KNOW THEIR EMPLOYMENT STATUS	1	2	3	4	53/

IF YOU ARE A SUPERVISING PSYCHOLOGIST, GO TO Q. 48.

WORK SUPERVISION

The following questions explore how school psychologists are supervised in their work.

35. How well does your supervising psychologist from your present <u>special education unit</u> know the job of psychologists?

VERY WELL 1   54/

FAIRLY WELL 2

NOT SO WELL 3

NOT AT ALL WELL 4

36. To what extent does your supervising psychologist in the <u>special education unit</u> have the freedom of action necessary to do his/her job well?

S/HE HAS ALL THE FREEDOM NECESSARY . 1   55/

S/HE HAS SOME FREEDOM 2

S/HE HAS LITTLE FREEDOM 3

S/HE HARDLY HAS ANY FREEDOM 4

37. Taking into account any limits on his/her actions, how well does your supervising psychologist in the <u>special education unit</u> do his/her job?

VERY WELL 1   56/

FAIRLY WELL 2

NOT SO WELL 3

NOT AT ALL WELL 4

38. How responsible is your supervising psychologist in the <u>special education unit</u> for defining your primary service responsibilities? Is s/he primarily responsible, somewhat responsible, hardly responsible, or not responsible at all?

PRIMARILY RESPONSIBLE . . 1   57/

SOMEWHAT RESPONSIBLE . . 2

HARDLY RESPONSIBLE · · · 3

NOT RESPONSIBLE AT ALL . 4

39. What organizational position is held by the person (or persons) who is (are) <u>primarily</u> responsible for supervising you in your primary service assignment? IF NO ONE PERSON OR TYPE OF PERSON IS PRIMARILY RESPONSIBLE, CIRCLE "6." CIRCLE ONE CODE ONLY.

> THE SUPERINTENDENT OR EXECUTIVE DIRECTOR
> OF YOUR DISTRICT OR COOPERATIVE   1   58/
>
> YOUR DISTRICT REPRESENTATIVE, PUPIL PERSONNEL
> OFFICER, OR OTHER DISTRICT SPECIAL EDUCATION
> OFFICER   2
>
> THE DIRECTOR OF A SPECIAL PROGRAM IN WHICH
> YOU WORK   3
>
> YOUR SUPERVISING PSYCHOLOGIST IN THE SPECIAL
> EDUCATION UNIT (E.G., YOUR COOPERATIVE,
> BUREAU OF CHILD STUDY, ETC.) . (GO TO Q. 43) . .   4
>
> A SUPERVISING PSYCHOLOGIST WORKING IN THE
> PRIMARY SERVICE ASSIGNMENT   5
>
> NO ONE TYPE OF PERSON IS PRIMARILY
> RESPONSIBLE . . . . . (GO TO Q. 47)   6

40. How well does the person(s) supervising your primary service assignment know the job of the school psychologist?

> VERY WELL   1   59/
>
> FAIRLY WELL   2
>
> NOT SO WELL   3
>
> NOT AT ALL WELL   4

41. To what extent does the person(s) supervising your primary service assignment have the freedom of action necessary to do his/her job well?

> S/HE HAS ALL THE FREEDOM NECESSARY . .   1   60/
>
> S/HE HAS SOME FREEDOM   2
>
> S/HE HAS LITTLE FREEDOM   3
>
> S/HE HARDLY HAS ANY FREEDOM   4

42. Taking into account any limits on his/her action, how well does the person(s) supervising your primary service assignment do his/her job?

> VERY WELL   1   61/
>
> FAIRLY WELL   2
>
> NOT SO WELL   3
>
> NOT AT ALL WELL   4

43. How good is the person(s) who supervises your primary service assignment at dealing with people s/he supervises?

VERY GOOD	1	62/
FAIRLY GOOD	2	
NOT SO GOOD	3	
BAD	4	

44. Think about the amount of supervision you receive from your primary service supervisor: do you get a lot of supervision, pretty much, not much, or hardly any supervision at all?

A LOT OF SUPERVISION . .	1	63/
PRETTY MUCH	2	
NOT MUCH	3	
HARDLY ANY AT ALL . . .	4	

45. Thinking about the supervision you <u>do</u> receive from your primary service supervisor, to what extent does it focus on things which concern your supervisor in his or her own job (like getting along with school principals) as opposed to things which concern you and the problems you encounter in your work?

MOSTLY MY SUPERVISOR'S PROBLEMS, RARELY MINE	1	64/
OFTEN MY SUPERVISOR'S PROBLEMS, BUT SOMETIMES MINE	2	
ABOUT HALF MY SUPERVISOR'S PROBLEMS, HALF MINE	3	
OFTEN MY PROBLEMS, ONLY SOMETIMES MY SUPERVISOR'S	4	
MOSTLY MY PROBLEMS, RARELY MY SUPERVISOR'S	5	

46. How supportive is your primary service supervisor(s) of special education
     in general: does s/he support it actively, accept it, tolerate it, or is
     s/he unsupportive?

                              SUPPORT IT ACTIVELY 1   65/

                              ACCEPT IT 2

                              TOLERATE IT 3

                              ARE UNSUPPORTIVE 4

---

47. Which one of the following staff groups is <u>most</u> supportive and which one <u>least</u>
     supportive of your work as school psychologist?

                                        CIRCLE ONE CODE ONLY IN EACH COLUMN

	MOST SUPPORTIVE	LEAST SUPPORTIVE
YOUR PRIMARY SERVICE SUPERVISOR	01 66/	01 67/
YOUR SCHOOL PRINCIPALS	02	02
REGULAR PROGRAM TEACHERS	03	03
SPECIAL PROGRAM TEACHERS	04	04
SCHOOL SOCIAL WORKER	05	05
PUPIL PERSONNEL TEAM MEMBERS (EXCLUDING SOCIAL WORKER)	06	06
OTHER PSYCHOLOGISTS	07	07
YOUR SPECIAL EDUCATION UNIT SUPERVISOR	08	08
YOUR DISTRICT SUPERINTENDENT	09	09
OTHER: PLEASE SPECIFY _____		
_____	10	10

> IF YOU WERE FIRST EMPLOYED AS A SCHOOL PSYCHOLOGIST
> DURING THE CURRENT SCHOOL YEAR, 1977-78, GO TO Q. 42

TIME ALLOCATION

For Q's. 48-52, you may find it helpful to refer to your "School Psychologist's Annual Report, 1976-77."

48. <u>During an average month in 1976-77</u>, how many hours did you work?

ENTER # HOURS: _____   68-70/
BEGIN DECK 3

    A. Of these hours, how many <u>hours per month</u> were you involved in each of the activities listed below? THE TOTAL NUMBER OF HOURS SPENT IN THESE ACTIVITIES SHOULD EQUAL THE NUMBER INDICATED ABOVE.

HOURS PER MONTH		HOURS PER MONTH	
PRESCHOOL SCREENINGS . . _____	6-8/	INDIVIDUAL COUNSELING . _____	30-32/
INDIVIDUAL PSYCHOLOGICAL EVALUATIONS . . . . . _____	9-11/	GROUP COUNSELING . . . _____	33-35/
GENERAL EDUCATIONAL OR PSYCHOLOGICAL SCREENINGS . . . . _____	12-14/	IN-SERVICE TRAINING PARTICIPANT . . . . . _____	36-38/
BEHAVIORAL ANALYSIS . . _____	15-17/	IN-SERVICE TRAINING LEADER . . . . . . _____	39-41/
OBSERVATIONS IN CLASS-ROOMS . . . . _____	18-20/	RESEARCH . . . . _____	42-44/
TEACHER CONSULTATION . . _____	21-23/	INVOLVEMENT WITH COMMUNITY AGENCIES . _____	45-47/
PARENT CONSULTATION . . _____	24-26/	PROFESSIONAL DEVELOP-MENT (CONVENTIONS, PROFESSIONAL	
GENERAL ADMINISTRATIVE CLERICAL DUTIES . . . _____	27-29/	ORGANIZATIONS) . . . _____	48-50/

49. For how many children did you provide <u>individual child study</u> in 1976-77? INCLUDE <u>ONLY</u> THOSE CASES IN WHICH YOU DID ALL <u>THREE</u> OF THE FOLLOWING TASKS:

        (a) used individual psychological evaluation techniques;
        (b) discussed findings in staffings and case conferences; and
        (c) wrote a report showing findings and recommendations.

CHILDREN PROVIDED INDIVIDUAL
CHILD STUDY IN 1976-77 . . . . . _____   51-53/

    A. Of all children for whom you provided individual child studies during 1976-77, what percentage were found eligible for special education programs? programs?

ENTER % FOUND ELIGIBLE: _____% 54-56/

    B. How many hours does an average individual child study take?

ENTER # HOURS: _____ 57-58/

50. What was the total number of children you saw, for any reason, in 1976-77?
     INCLUDE INDIVIDUAL CHILD STUDY CASES.

                                 TOTAL # CASES SEEN: _____   59-61/

     A. Of all the children you saw, please estimate the percentage that were
         or had previously been found eligible for special education programs.

                                 ENTER % FOUND ELIGIBLE: _____%   62-64/

51. At the end of the 1976-77 school year, what was the number of referrals which
     had to be carried over because you were unable to attend to them?
                                 ENTER # CASES: _____   65-66/

52. At the end of the 1976-77 school year, what was the number of referrals for
     which you had completed evaluations but which had to be carried over because
     administrative procedures (typing, staffings, etc.) had not been completed?

                                 ENTER # CASES: _____   67-68/

53. To how many programs or positions are you assigned? INCLUDE YOUR PRIMARY SERVICE
     ASSIGNMENT.

                                 ONE 1   69/
                                 TWO 2
                                 THREE 3
                                 FOUR OR MORE 4

54. What is the total number of individual schools you serve?
                                 ONE 1   70/
                                 TWO 2
                                 THREE 3
                                 FOUR 4
                                 FIVE 5
                                 SIX   6
                                 SEVEN OR MORE 7
                                 NONE 8

55. Please estimate the total number of students in all the schools you serve.
                                 LESS THAN 200 1   71/
                                 200-500 2
                                 501-1,000 3
                                 1,001-2,000 4
                                 2,001-4,000 5
                                 4,001-6,000 6
                                 MORE THAN 6,000 7

COLLEGIAL RELATIONS

The following questions refer to opportunities you have to meet and talk with
other psychologists.

56. How many psychologists (including yourself) are employed in
your present primary service assignment?

OF SCHOOL PSYCHOLOGISTS . . . . _____   6-8/

OF PSYCHOLOGISTS WORKING IN
ADMINISTRATIVE OR OTHER EDUCATIONAL
CAPACITIES . . . . _____   9-10/

57. The following is a list of settings in which school psychologists sometimes
have contact with one another. During an average month, how many times
do you see other school psychologists in each setting?

	# TIMES PER MONTH				
	ONE OR LESS	TWO	THREE	FOUR OR MORE	
SHARED OFFICE SPACE	1	2	3	4	11/
STAFF MEETINGS IN THE SPECIAL EDUCATION UNIT FOR ADMINISTRATIVE OR IN-SERVICE TRAINING PURPOSES	1	2	3	4	12/
MEETINGS BETWEEN DISTRICT AND SPECIAL PROGRAM PSYCHOLOGISTS CONCERNING SHARED JURISDICTION OVER CERTAIN CHILDREN	1	2	3	4	13/
MEETINGS CALLED BY PRIMARY SERVICE SUPER-VISORS FOR ADMINISTRATIVE OR IN-SERVICE TRAINING PURPOSES	1	2	3	4	14/
MEETINGS CALLED BY CITY OR REGIONAL DISTRICT	1	2	3	4	15/
MEETINGS SCHEDULED BY SCHOOL PSYCHOLO-GISTS ON THEIR OWN	1	2	3	4	16/
AS FRIENDS OUTSIDE OF WORK	1	2	3	4	17/
TELEPHONE CONVERSATIONS TO DISCUSS PROBLEMS ENCOUNTERED IN WORK	1	2	3	4	18/

A. CIRCLE THE DESCRIPTION OF THE SETTING IN WHICH YOU HAVE THE MOST
PRODUCTIVE CONTACTS WITH OTHER PSYCHOLOGISTS.   19/

B. CROSS OUT THE DESCRIPTION OF THE SETTING IN WHICH YOU HAVE THE LEAST
PRODUCTIVE CONTACTS WITH OTHER PSYCHOLOGISTS.   20/

58. Below are listed several topics concerning which psychologists might talk to each other. Of these topics, which one do you most frequently discuss with other psychologists, which one the second most frequently, and which one the third most frequently?

CIRCLE ONE CODE ONLY IN EACH COLUMN

	MOST FREQUENT	2ND MOST FREQUENT	3RD MOST FREQUENT
	21/	22/	23/
CLARIFICATION OF PROPER ADMINISTRATIVE PROCEDURES OR INTERPRETATIONS OF STATE OR FEDERAL REGULATIONS	1	1	1
ISSUES HAVING TO DO WITH OTHER MATTERS OF ADMINISTRATIVE ROUTINE	2	2	2
PROBLEMS I ENCOUNTER REGARDING THE POLITICS OF MY DISTRICT OR SPECIAL PROGRAM OR THE SUPERVISING SPECIAL EDUCATIONAL ORGANIZATION, COOPERATIVE, OR BUREAU OF CHILD STUDY	3	3	3
INTERESTING CASES WHICH PROVIDE ME WITH INTELLECTUAL STIMULATION	4	4	4
ISSUES HAVE TO DO WITH THE ORGANIZATION OF PROFESSIONAL ASSOCIATIONS	5	5	5
ISSUES PERTAINING TO A CHILD STUDY OR A STUDENT PROGRAM	6	6	6

59. The following is a list of functions which professional associations might serve for psychologists. For each function, please indicate whether for you that function is very important, somewhat important, not very important, or not at all importnat.

	VERY IMPORTANT	SOMEWHAT IMPORTANT	NOT VERY IMPORTANT	NOT AT ALL IMPORTANT	
THEY PROVIDE A FORUM IN WHICH TO DISCUSS INTERESTING NEW TECHNICAL MATERIALS SO THAT I STAY FRESH AND INFORMED.	1	2	3	4	24/
THEY PROVIDE A SETTING IN WHICH PSYCHOLOGISTS CAN DEVELOP A BROADER RANGE OF SKILLS.	1	2	3	4	25/
THEY PROVIDE A FORUM FOR LEARNING HOW THE WORK OF OTHERS IS GOING AND SUPPORTING THEM WHEN THEY HAVE PROBLEMS.	1	2	3	4	26/
THEY ALLOW FOR EVALUATION OF THE WORK PERFORMANCE OF MEMBERS AND ALLOW PSYCHOLOGISTS TO TRY TO INFLUENCE AND IMPROVE THE WORK OF THOSE WHOSE WORK IS SUBSTANDARD.	1	2	3	4	27/
PARTICIPATION IN THEM ALLOWS ME AN OPPORTUNITY TO TRAIN NEW PSYCHOLOGISTS.	1	2	3	4	28/
THEY ARE LOBBYING GROUPS, ADVANCING THE INTERESTS OF THE PROFESSION WITH OUTSIDE EDUCATIONAL OR GOVERNMENTAL ORGANIZATIONS.	1	2	3	4	29/
THEY GIVE ME A CHANCE TO SEE PROFESSIONAL FRIENDS.	1	2	3	4	30/

60. A. Ot which psychological professional associations are you a member?
         CIRCLE ALL THAT APPLY. IF NONE, CIRCLE "7."

                  NATIONAL ASSOCIATION OF SCHOOL PSYCHOLOGISTS . . 1   31/

                  AMERICAN PSYCHOLOGICAL ASSOCIATION 2   32/

                  ILLINOIS PSYCHOLOGICAL ASSOCIATION 3   33/

                  COUNCIL FOR EXCEPTIONAL CHILDREN 4   34/

                  A LOCAL PSYCHOLOGICAL ASSOCIATION 5   35/

                  OTHER: PLEASE SPECIFY _____ 6   36/

                  NONE . . . . . . (GO TO Q. 61). 7   37/

     B. How frequently do you attend a professional association meeting of
         one kind or another? CIRCLE THE LOWEST CODE NUMBER THAT APPLIES.

                         ONCE A WEEK 1   38/

                         AT LEAST ONCE A MONTH 2

                         MORE THAN TWICE A YEAR 3

                         AT LEAST ONCE A YEAR 4

                         LESS THAN ONCE A YEAR 5

---

61. To what extent is your salary an accurate reflection of your professional
     skills relative to other school personnel: very accurate, somewhat accurate,
     not very accurate, or not at all accurate?

                         VERY ACCURATE 1   39/

                         SOMEWHAT ACCURATE 2

                         NOT VERY ACCURATE 3

                         NOT AT ALL ACCURATE 4

---

62. What is the annual salary you receive in your employment as a school
     psychologist?

                         BELOW $13,000 1   40/

                         $13,000 - 15,999 2

                         $16,000 - 18,999 3

                         $19,000 - 21,999 4

                         $22,000 - 24,999 5

                         $25,000 OR MORE 6

63. Should the School Section of the IPA form an organization separate from the IPA?

                                 YES . . (ANSWER A) 1   41/

                                 NO 2

A.   IF YES: Should this new organization affiliate with the National
               Association of School Psychologists?

                                 YES 1   42/

                                 NO 2

64. To what extent are you concerned that Illinois school psychologists who

          (1) do not hold a Ph.D., or
          (2) are not certified for clinical practice under the
              grandfather clause of Illinois law

     cannot provide psychological services outside of school work?

                                 VERY CONCERNED . . (ANSWER A) . . 1   43/

                                 SOMEWHAT CONCERNED (ANSWER A) . . 2

                                 NOT VERY CONCERNED 3

                                 NOT AT ALL CONCERNED 4

A.   IF VERY OR SOMEWHAT CONCERNED: Would you be willing to contribute
     time and/or money to help repeal this law?

                                 TIME 1   44/

                                 MONEY 2

                                 BOTH 3

                                 NEITHER 4

65. Among your five closest friends, how many are school psychologists?

                                 ENTER #: . . . . _____   45/

66. In your experience as a school psychologist, how important have frequent
     and regularized contacts with other school psychologists been to doing
     the job well: has it been very important, somewhat important, not very
     important, or not at all important?

                                 VERY IMPORTANT 1   46/

                                 SOMEWHAT IMPORTANT 2

                                 NOT VERY IMPORTANT 3

                                 NOT AT ALL IMPORTANT 4

Qs. 67 and 68 further explore professional and social relationships among school psychologists. We will use the answers to these questions to learn whether there is any relationship between attitudes expressed on issues raised in this questionnaire and the kinds of people one seeks out for help on professional matters or for socializing.

67. Below is a list of situations and problems with respect to which you might seek interaction with others. For each one, please indicate:

   (a) the names of the people you would be most likely to consult on the matter, and
   (b) their job positions (e.g., Bureau of Child Study Psychologist, or Professor, Illinois State University) or relationship to you if not a psychologist.

   They need not be members of your special education or primary service units nor even psychologists. YOU MAY LIST THE SAME PERSON FOR MORE THAN ONE QUESTION. (PLEASE PRINT.)

	NAME	JOB POSITION	
TECHNICAL PROBLEMS, SUCH AS DECIDING WHAT IS THE BEST WAY OF EVALUATING A CHILD WITH UNUSUAL PROBLEMS OR SETTING UP A THERAPEUTIC PROGRAM TO RESOLVE SOME PARTICULAR PROBLEM.	_____ ...	_____	47/
	_____ ...	_____	48/
	_____ ...	_____	49/
PROBLEMS WHICH ARISE ABOUT THE WORKING CONDITIONS EXISTING IN YOUR PRIMARY PROGRAM ASSIGN-MENT?	_____ ...	_____	50/
	_____ ...	_____	51/
	_____ ...	_____	52/
HELP AND SUGGESTIONS IF YOU OR A FRIEND WERE SEEKING A NEW JOB IN SCHOOL PSYCHOLOGY?	_____ ...	_____	53/
	_____ ...	_____	54/
	_____ ...	_____	55/

68. If you and all other members of your special education unit were at a convention of the Illinois Psychological Association in Moline, who would be the three psychologists with whom you would most likely go out at night? PLEASE INDICATE NAME AND JOB POSITION.

_____ ...	_____	56/
_____ ...	_____	57/
_____ ...	_____	58/

THE PROCESS OF TESTING

During our interviews, psychologists have often spoken of the importance of intelligence and projective tests in the evaluation of children referred to special programs. In the process of our interviewing, however, we have seen and heard of a variety of approaches to the activity of testing. Psychologists differ on how objective test results are, on how to choose test instruments for use with given children, on what one should be doing while testing, and on how the test results should be communicated to regular school officials or used to improve programming for children.

69. What follows is a list of statements about various aspects of the process of testing children. Please indicate whether you strongly agree with each statement, somewhat agree, somewhat disagree, or strongly disagree.

STATEMENTS ABOUT TESTING	STRONGLY AGREE	SOMEWHAT AGREE	SOMEWHAT DISAGREE	STRONGLY DISAGREE	
GENERALLY, TESTING IS A CREATIVE PROCESS OF DEVELOPING HYPOTHESES ABOUT THE STRUCTURE OF CHILDREN'S BEHAVIOR AND OF GATHERING DATA WHICH WILL TEST THESE PROPOSITIONS.	1	2	3	4	59/
INTELLIGENCE TESTS RESULTS ARE USUALLY USED WISELY BY TEACHERS AND PRINCIPALS.	1	2	3	4	60/
TOO MANY SCHOOL PERSONNEL WHO ARE NOT PSYCHOLOGISTS ARE NOW GIVING CHILDREN PSYCHOMETRIC TESTS WHICH ONLY PSYCHOLOGISTS ARE QUALIFIED TO GIVE.	1	2	3	4	61/
PSYCHOLOGISTS SHOULD HAVE A THOROUGH KNOWLEDGE OF A WIDE RANGE OF PROJECTIVE TESTING TECHNIQUES.	1	2	3	4	62/
DIAGNOSIS IS THE MOST IMPORTANT THING PSYCHOLOGISTS DO FOR SCHOOLS.	1	2	3	4	63/
GIVEN THE ORGANIZATIONAL COMPLEXITIES OF SCHOOLS, IT WOULD NOT BE POSSIBLE TO MAKE AN OBJECTIVE DECISION ABOUT THE BEST SPECIAL EDUCATION PROGRAM FOR A CHILD WITHOUT TESTS.	1	2	3	4	64/
WHEN PSYCHOLOGISTS ARE REQUIRED TO GIVE TOO MANY TESTS, THE PROCESS TENDS TO BECOME AUTOMATIC AND MECHANICAL.	1	2	3	4	65/
PROJECTIVE TESTS ALLOW ONE TO PREDICT THE NATURE OF EMOTIONAL PROBLEMS WITH ACCURACY WHEN DOING A CHILD STUDY.	1	2	3	4	66/
INTELLIGENCE TEST RESULTS ARE AN ACCURATE WAY OF EVALUATING THE ABILITIES OF CHILDREN FOR SPECIAL EDUCATION CLASSIFICATION PURPOSES WITHOUT OTHER INFORMATION GATHERED IN CONVERSATIONS WITH PARENTS AND SCHOOL OFFICIALS.	1	2	3	4	67/

69. Continued

	STRONGLY AGREE	SOMEWHAT AGREE	SOMEWHAT DISAGREE	STRONGLY DISAGREE	
MOST PSYCHOLOGISTS IN YOUR SPECIAL EDUCATION UNIT ARE FULLY CAPABLE OF PROPERLY ADMINISTERING AND INTERPRETING NECESSARY PROJECTIVE TESTS.	1	2	3	4	68/
MOST PSYCHOLOGISTS IN YOUR SPECIAL EDUCATION UNIT ARE FULLY CAPABLE OF PROPERLY ADMINISTERING AND INTERPRETING INTELLIGENCE TESTS.	1	2	3	4	69/
MOST PSYCHOLOGISTS SHOULD PARTICIPATE MORE OFTEN IN REGULAR IN-SERVICE PROGRAMS OFFERED TO IMPROVE PSYCHOLOGICAL SKILLS.	1	2	3	4	70/
WHEN STUDENTS ARE ANXIOUS ABOUT BEING TESTED, THE RESULTS OF INTELLIGENCE TESTS MAY NOT BE VERY ACCURATE.	1	2	3	4	71/
STUDENT EVALUATIONS WOULD BE MORE EFFECTIVE IF CONDUCTED IN PSYCHOLOGISTS' HOME BASE OFFICES RATHER THAN IN SCHOOL.	1	2	3	4	72/
TESTING IS THE MOST SATISFYING ASPECT OF BEING A SCHOOL PSYCHOLOGIST.	1	2	3	4	73/
INTELLIGENCE TESTS ARE ONLY USEFUL AS STRUCTURED WAYS OF OBSERVING STUDENT PERFORMANCE ON THE KINDS OF TASKS EXPECTED OF THEM IN CLASSES.	1	2	3	4	74/
LARGE TESTING BACKLOGS CAUSE ROLE CONFLICTS FOR PSYCHOLOGISTS BECAUSE IT PUTS THEM UNDER PRESSURE TO TEST QUICKLY, BUT THEY FEEL IT IS IMPORTANT TO GIVE EACH CHILD THE TIME HE NEEDS.	1	2	3	4	75/

BEGIN DECK 5

70. What follows are some more statements about testing. For each, please indicate how frequently these situations occur.

	OFTEN	SOME-TIMES	RARELY	NEVER	
THE RESULTS OF INTELLIGENCE TESTS I GIVE ARE MISUSED IN CLASSIFICATION PROCEEDINGS.	1	2	3	4	6/
I HAVE A LARGE TESTING BACKLOG.	1	2	3	4	7/
I ENJOY TESTING CHILDREN.	1	2	3	4	8/
STUDENTS ARE MISCLASSIFIED AS SUFFERING HANDICAPS: EITHER THEY HAVE NONE OR ONES DIFFERENT FROM THOSE WITH WHICH THEY HAVE BEEN LABELED.	1	2	3	4	9/
CLASSIFICATION PROCEEDINGS INVOLVE PROCEDURES OR ACTIONS WHICH I FIND QUESTIONABLE IN TERMS OF MY PROFESSIONAL ETHICS.	1	2	3	4	10/

71. From which college and in what year did you receive your undergraduate degree?

    ENTER NAME OF COLLEGE: _____   11/

        STATE IN WHICH LOCATED: _____   12-13/

    ENTER YEAR: . . . . 1 9 ___ ___   14-15/

A. In which field did you major?

    ENTER NAME OF FIELD: _____   16-17/

B. Were you elected to Phi Beta Kappa or any other <u>national</u> academic honorary society? CIRCLE ALL THAT APPLY.

              PHI BETA KAPPA 1   18/
              OTHER: PLEASE SPECIFY

              _____ 2   19/

              NOT ELECTED TO A SOCIETY 3   20/

C. Did you graduate with honors (e.g., honors in psychology or cum laude)? IF YES: Which one?

              YES: ENTER HONOR: _____ 1   21/
              NO 2

D. During college, did you have any experience in <u>original</u> research <u>which lasted at least several months</u>? By "original research" we mean collecting and analyzing raw data or conducting an experiment, <u>not</u> writing papers based on published sources or doing experiments from a laboratory manual.

              YES 1   22/
              NO 2

72. From which college and in what year did you receive your Master's degree and/or Ph.D. in psychology?

    <u>MASTER' DEGREE</u>:

        ENTER NAME OF COLLEGE: _____   23/

            STATE IN WHICH LOCATED: _____   24-25/

        ENTER YEAR: . . . . . . 1 9 ___ ___   26-27/

    <u>PH.D.</u>:

        ENTER NAME OF COLLEGE: _____   28/

        STATE IN WHICH LOCATED: _____   29-30/

        ENTER YEAR: . . . . . . 1 9 ___ ___   31-32/

72. Continued

   A. In what area of psychology did you do your Master's degree work?

     ENTER NAME: _____   33-34/

   B. During your Master's program, did you do any <u>original</u> research <u>which lasted at least several months</u>?

                 YES 1   35/

                 NO 2

   C. How many graduate programs in psychology did you attend before receiving your Master's?

             ENTER NUMBER: _____   36/

> IF YOU HAVE YOUR PH.D. IN PSYCHOLOGY, GO TO Q. 74.
> IF NOT, ANSWER Q. 73.

73. Have you completed more than 30 units past your Master's in psychology?

                 YES 1   37/

                 NO 2

---

74. In what year were you born?

             ENTER YEAR: 1 9 ___ ___   38-39/

---

75. What is your sex?

                 MALE 1   40/

                 FEMALE 2

---

76. When you <u>graduated high school</u>, in which of the following areas did you live? CIRCLE THE LOWEST CODE NUMBER THAT APPLIES.

       CITY OF CHICAGO . . . (GO TO Q. 78) 1   41/

       CHICAGO METROPOLITAN AREA . (GO TO Q. 78) . 2

       ILLINOIS 3

       OTHER U.S. STATE: SPECIFY: _____ 4

       OUTSIDE THE U.S. 5

77. Which of the following categories comes closest to describing the type
    of place you lived in <u>when you graduated from high school</u>?

                    IN A RURAL AREA 1   42/
                    IN A SMALL CITY OR TOWN UNDER 50,000 2
                    IN A MEDIUM-SIZED CITY BETWEEN 50,000 AND 250,000. 3
                    IN A SUBURB NEAR A LARGE CITY 4
                    IN A LARGE CITY OVER 250,000 5

78. At the time you graduated from high school, were you living with your mother
    and father, or some other male or female relative? CIRCLE ONE CODE ONLY.

                    BOTH MOTHER (STEPMOTHER) AND FATHER (STEPFATHER) . 1   43/
                    MOTHER (STEPMOTHER) ONLY . . (GO TO Q. 80) . . . 2
                    FATHER (STEPFATHER) ONLY 3
                    OTHER MALE <u>AND</u> FEMALE RELATIVE 4
                    OTHER MALE RELATIVE ONLY 5
                    OTHER FEMALE RELATIVE ONLY . . (GO TO Q. 80) . . . 6

79. What was the highest grade your father (the male head of household) <u>completed</u>
    in school? EXCLUDE BUSINESS OR TECHNICAL SCHOOL.

                    EIGHTH GRADE OR LESS 1   44/

                    SOME HIGH SCHOOL 2

                    HIGH SCHOOL GRADUATE (12th Grade) . 3

                    SOME COLLEGE 4

                    COLLEGE GRADUATE 5

                    SOME POST-GRADUATE WORK 6

                    POST-GRADUATE DEGREE 7

```
IF YOU WERE NOT LIVING WITH YOUR MOTHER OR SOME OTHER FEMALE
HEAD OF HOUSEHOLD, GO TO Q. 82.  IF YOU WERE, ANSWER Q. 80.
```

80. What was the highest grade your mother (the female head of the household)
    <u>completed</u> in school? EXCLUDE BUSINESS OR TECHNICAL SCHOOL.

                    EIGHTH GRADE OR LESS 1   45/
                    SOME HIGH SCHOOL 2
                    HIGH SCHOOL GRADUATE (12TH GRADE) . 3
                    SOME COLLEGE 4
                    COLLEGE GRADUATE 5
                    SOME POST-GRADUATE WORK 6
                    POST-GRADUATE DEGREE 7

81. Did your mother (the female head of the household) work full time or part time during most of your childhood, or didn't she work during most of your childhood?

FULL TIME 1   46/

PART TIME 2

DIDN'T WORK 3

82. The U.S. Census divides jobs into the ten groups listed below. In which group would you put the job your parent (household head) had who was the <u>principal</u> wage earner of the family <u>at the time you graduated from high school</u>? IF BOTH PARENTS (HEAD OF HOUSEHOLD) EARNED AN EQUAL AMOUNT, ANSWER FOR YOUR FATHER (MALE HEAD OF HOUSEHOLD).

WHITE COLLAR {	PROFESSIONAL AND TECHNICAL	01 47-48/
	MANAGERS AND ADMINISTRATORS . . .	02
	SALES WORKERS	03
	CLERICAL WORKERS	04
BLUE COLLAR AND FARM {	CRAFTSMEN	05
	OPERATIVES	06
	LABORERS	07
	FARMERS AND FARM MANAGERS	08
	FARM LABORERS	09
	SERVICE WORKERS	10

83. Are you currently married, widowed, divorced, separated, or have you never been married?

MARRIED 1   49/

WIDOWED 2

DIVORCED 3

SEPARATED 4

NEVER MARRIED . (GO TO Q. 85) . . . 5

84. How many children do you have?

ONE 1   50/

TWO 2

THREE 3

FOUR 4

FIVE OR MORE 5

NONE 6

85. In what religion were you raised?

PROTESTANT 1   51/
CATHOLIC 2
JEWISH 3
NONE 4
OTHER (SPECIFY RELIGION AND/OR
    CHURCH AND DENOMINATION)

_____ 5

86. How often do you attend religious services?

NEVER 0   52/
LESS THAN ONCE A YEAR 1
ABOUT ONCE OR TWICE A YEAR 2
SEVERAL TIMES A YEAR 3
ABOUT ONCE A MONTH 4
2-3 TIMES A MONTH 5
NEARLY EVERY WEEK 6
EVERY WEEK 7
SEVERAL TIMES A WEEK 8

87. In politics, would you say that you are a radical, a liberal, middle-of-the-road, a conservative, or a strong conservative?

RADICAL 1   53/
LIBERAL 2
MIDDLE-OF-THE-ROAD 3
CONSERVATIVE 4
STRONG CONSERVATIVE 5

88. How would you describe yourself?

WHITE 1   54/
BLACK 2
HISPANIC (i.e., Mexican,
    Cuban, Puerto Rican) 3
OTHER 4

THANK YOU FOR COMPLETING THIS QUESTIONNAIRE

Notes

Introduction

1. Two discussions of the meritocracy are Gary Becker, *Human Capital: A Theoretical and Empirical Analysis, with Special Reference to Education* (New York: National Bureau of Economic Research, 1975); and Michael Young, *The Rise of the Meritocracy* (Baltimore: Penguin Books, 1971).

2. Some important critics of the meritocracy perspective are Christopher Jencks et al., *Inequality: A Reassessment of the Effect of Family and Schooling in America* (New York: Basic Books, 1972); James Rosenbaum, *Making Inequality* (New York: Wiley, 1976); Samuel Bowles and Herbert Gintis, *Schooling in Capitalist America* (New York: Basic Books, 1976); and Barbara L. Heyns, *Summer Learning and the Effects of Schooling* (New York: Academic Press, 1978).

3. The best-known recent example of this position in genetic psychology is in Arthur Jensen's work. See "How Much Can We Boost IQ and Scholastic Achievement?" *Harvard Educational Review* 38 (1969):1–123; and "A Theory of Primary and Secondary Familial Mental Retardation," in *Genetics and Education* (New York: Harper and Row, 1972), 204–293.

4. Jencks, *Inequality,* Appendix A, contains a statistical critique of Jensen's genetic psychology. Leon Kamin, *The Science and Politics of IQ* (Potomac, MD: Lawrence Erlbaum, 1974); and Jerry Hirsch, "To 'Unfrock the Charlatans,'" *Sage Race Relations Abstract* 6 (May 1981):1–67, provide critiques of genetic psychology by prominent psychologists.

5. Richard A. Berk, William P. Bridges, and Anthony Shih, "Does IQ Really Matter? A Study of the Use of IQ Scores for the Tracking of the Mentally Retarded," *American Sociological Review* 46 (1981):58–71.

6. See, for example, Jerome M. Sattler and Fred Theye, "Procedural, Situational and Interpersonal Variables in Individual Intelligence Testing," *Psychological Bulletin* 68 (1967):347–360; William Labov, "The Logic of Nonstandard English," in *Language in the Inner City* (Philadelphia: University of

Pennsylvania Press, 1972), 201–240; and Michael Cole and Jerome Bruner in "Cultural Differences and Inferences about Psychological Processes," *American Psychologist* 26 (1971):867–875.

7. See Reuven Feuerstein, "A Dynamic Approach to the Causation, Prevention and Alleviation of Retarded Performance," in *Social-Cultural Aspects of Mental Retardation,* ed. H. C. Haywood (New York: Appleton-Century-Crofts, 1970), for a discussion of the rationale behind a discovery approach to testing.

8. Gail Saliterman, "The Politics of Decision-making in an Incompletely Bureaucratized Organization: A Study of Textbook Selection in Public School Systems," Ph.D. diss., American University, 1971; *Dissertation Abstracts Index,* 33/02-A: 803, makes the argument about the nonbureaucratic nature of schools. On loose-coupling in school organizations, see Karl Weick, "Educational Organizations as Loosely Coupled Systems," *Administrative Science Quarterly* 21 (1976):1–19.

9. Alfred Binet and Th. Simon, *Mentally Defective Children,* trans. W. B. Drummond (New York: Congmans, Green, 1914), is the earliest description of Binet's test in English that I could find. A good biography of Binet, including a history of the development of his intelligence scale, is provided by Theta H. Wolff, *Alfred Binet* (Chicago: University of Chicago Press, 1973). Also see Seymour Sarason, "The Unfortunate Fate of Alfred Binet and School Psychology," *Teachers' College Record* 77 (1976):579–592. For a history of special education in Chicago, see Robert Slater, "The Organizational Origins of Public School Psychology," *Educational Studies* 1 (1980):1–11.

10. See Roger Hurley, *Poverty and Mental Retardation: A Causal Relationship* (New York: Vintage Books, 1969), as well as Jane Mercer, *Labeling the Mentally Retarded* (Berkeley and Los Angeles: University of California Press, 1973).

11. *Larry P. v. Riles.* See *Science,* "California Court is Forum for Latest Round in IQ Debate," v. 201 (1978):1106–1108. Mercer, *Labeling the Mentally Retarded.*

12. Peter Schrag and Diane Divoky, *The Myth of the Hyperactive Child and Other Means of Child Control* (New York: Pantheon, 1975), provides a history of parental lobbying for more effective learning disability programs. S. A. Kirk and W. D. Kirk, *Psycholinguistic Learning Disabilities: Diagnosis and Remediation* (Urbana: University of Illinois Press, 1971), provides an early discussion of learning disabilities that emphasizes this conflict between a child's characteristics and school structure. Recognition that the institution is partly responsible for student failure is also central to Arthur Jensen's discussions about the relationships between race, IQ, and heritability. See Jensen, "How Much Can We Boost IQ and Scholastic Achievement?" and "A Theory of Primary and Secondary Familial Mental Retardation."

13. A recent review of literature on dyslexia, a form of learning disabilities, is Frank R. Vellutino, "Dyslexia," *Scientific American* 256, 3 (1987):34–41. One sees from this review that our understanding of some forms of learning disability have become detailed and sophisticated. At the same time, this article

reviews a number of learning disability theories that have been discredited by psychological researchers but that one still encounters in schools—the notion that mixed dominance causes learning disabilities for example. James Carrier, *Learning Disability: Social Class and the Construction of Inequality in American Education* (New York: Greenwood Press, 1986), provides a careful review of learning disability theory from a critical sociological perspective; he also reviews some of the myths surrounding these educational problems.

14. David Kirp, William Buss, and Peter Kuriloff, "Legal Reform of Special Education: Empirical Studies and Procedural Proposals," *California Law Review* 62 (1974):40–155, provides a good history of state reforms prior to PL 94-142. Richard A. Weatherley, *Reforming Special Education: Policy Implementation from State Level to Street Level* (Cambridge, MA: MIT Press, 1979), describes implementation of the Massachusetts law, Chapter 766. Senate Report 94-168, "Education for All Handicapped Children Act," 2 June 1975, testifies to the importance of the Pennsylvania experience. For recent histories of the legislative history and implementation of PL 94-142, see Carrier, *Learning Disability,* 89–122; John C. Pittenger and Peter Kuriloff, "Educating the Handicapped: Reforming a Radical Law," *Public Interest* 66 (Winter 1982):72–96; Peter Kuriloff, "Is Justice Served by Due Process? Affecting the Outcome of Special Education Hearings in Pennsylvania," *Law and Contemporary Problems* 48 (Winter 1985):89–118; David L. Kirp and Donald N. Jensen, "What Does Due Process Do?" *Public Interest* 73 (Fall 1983):75–90; and David Neal and David L. Kirp, "The Allure of Legalization Reconsidered: The Case of Special Education," *Law and Contemporary Problems* 48 (Winter 1985):63–87. A guide to special education and its legal aspects aimed at parents is Kenneth Shore, *The Special Education Handbook: A Comprehensive Guide for Parents and Educators* (New York: Teachers College Press, 1986).

15. One of the most important points in Mercer, *Labeling the Mentally Retarded,* is this one, that most of the people placed in special education classes are not identified as handicapped anywhere but in school. She shows that there are people who are spontaneously identified as handicapped by people in the community, as does Robert B. Edgerton, "Mental Retardation in Non-western Societies: Toward a Cross-Cultural Perspective on Incompetence," in Haywood, *Social-Cultural Aspects of Mental Retardation,* 523–559. The vast majority of educational handicaps have been inventions associated with the educational system. Being school related does not mean these inventions are invalid, because schools have intellectual demands many in the population will never encounter elsewhere. It does mean, however, that the social biases built into schools will be expressed in these handicaps.

16. For a review of these difficulties see Carrier, *Learning Disability,* and James Carrier, "Masking the Social in Educational Knowledge: The Case of Learning Disability Theory," *American Journal of Sociology* 88 (1983):948–974.

17. Carl Milofsky, *Special Education: A Sociological Study of California Programs* (New York: Praeger, 1976), 52–61. Christine M. Hassell, "A Study of the Consequences of Excessive Legal Intervention in the Local Implementation

of PL 42-142," Ph.D. diss., University of California with California State University, 1981; *Dissertation Abstracts Index,* 42/07-A: 3105, makes the same observation I reported in my book.

18. Berk, Bridges, and Shih, "Does IQ Really Matter?"

19. Discussions of the sort of detailed, transactional analyses school psychologists might provide are contained in Reuven Feuerstein, "A Dynamic Approach to the Causation, Prevention and Alleviation of Retarded Performance," and Donald McIntyre, "Two Schools and One Psychologist," in *The Psycho-Educational Clinic,* Frances Kaplan and Seymour Sarason, eds., *Community Mental Health Monograph Series* 4 (Boston: Massachusetts Department of Mental Health, 1969). The term "transactional school psychology" is one I take from Seymour Sarason and John Doris, *Educational Handicap, Public Policy, and Social History: A Broadened Perspective on Mental Retardation* (New York: Free Press, 1979), chaps. 2, 3; pp. 11–39, and from John Spiegel, *Transactions: The Interplay between Individual, Family and Society* (New York: Science House, 1971). Quoting from a paper by A. J. Sameroff ["Concepts of Humanity in Primary Prevention." Paper prepared for the Vermont Conference on the Primary Prevention of Psychopathology. Burlington, VT, June 1975], Sarason and Doris define a transactional approach as follows: "Sameroff then proposes a transactional model in which a key feature is not only the effects of caretakers on a child but the effects of the child on the caretakers. We have long been aware that characteristics of children affect parents. This is a two way street called transaction" (pp. 21–22). Extending the concept of transaction to schools, Sarason and his colleagues have emphasized that the difficulties teachers and principals identify as problems in their students often are best understood as transactional in the sense that the same child in a different setting, interacting with different professionals and different peers, would not be a problem. Because special education legislation treats learning disabilities as attributes of children, a transactional perspective can be difficult to develop and to advance. It conflicts with the legal, legitimate definition of the situation if we say that the school creates the problem as much as or more than the child does.

An illustration of teachers' tendencies to downplay the importance of test results is David A. Goslin, *Teachers and Testing* (New York: Russell Sage, 1967), which reports that a sample of teachers did not closely read or use the results from tests given to their students. Whether or not teachers pay attention to test scores, the psychologists I interviewed agreed with the perception, reported by McIntyre in "Two Schools, One Psychologist," that relatively few teachers take psychologists seriously or are sufficiently interested in the results of psychological examinations to hear the subtleties in a case presentation.

20. It is common for children being tested to be anxious about the reasons for testing, uncomfortable with the test examiner, or upset for other reasons not related to the test situation. Any of these factors can lower test scores. Fair and accurate testing requires that psychologists seek ways to minimize stress and to ensure that they have adequate rapport with their subjects. This has often been demonstrated in psychometric research as Jerome M. Sattler and Fred Theye,

"Procedural, Situational and Interpersonal Variables in Individual Intelligence Testing," report in their literature review. See also, J. E. Exner, Jr., "Variations in WISC Performances as Influenced by Differences in Pre-test Rapport," *Journal of Genetic Psychology* 74 (1966):299–306; Janet Masling, "The Effects of Warm and Cold Interaction on the Administration and Scoring of an Intelligence Test," *Journal of Consulting Psychology* 23 (1959):336–341; and "The Influence of Situational and Interpersonal Variables in Projective Testing," *Psychological Bulletin* 57 (1960):65–86. A recent text with a good review of these issues is Ronald L. Taylor, *Assessment of Exceptional Students: Educational and Psychological Procedures* (Englewood Cliffs, NJ: Prentice Hall, 1984), 59–87.

Labov, "The Logic of Nonstandard English," 201–240, and Cole and Bruner, "Cultural Differences and Inferences about Psychological Processes," 867–875, argue that it is nearly impossible to establish this rapport with minority children. Whether or not they are correct about this impossibility, it seems vital that psychologists give themselves ample time for building rapport with minority subjects.

21. In Chapter Two I discuss the testing process in detail. The psychologist I observed reported it takes him three hours to complete just the test batteries he administers during a child study. It takes at least that much time in addition to score the tests and meet with all of the other people who participate in decision making. Psychologists who test black children in Illinois, however, report spending fewer than three hours on the entire process. One can check the time required for testing by looking at one of the standard test batteries like David Wechsler, *Manual for the Wechsler Intelligence Scale for Children,* rev. (New York: Psychological Corporation, 1974).

22. Cole and Bruner, "Cultural Differences and Inferences about Psychological Processes"; Labov, "The Logic of Nonstandard English"; Mercer, *Labeling the Mentally Retarded;* and Robert L. Williams, "Danger: Testing and Dehumanizing Black Children," *School Psychologist* 25 (1971):11–13.

23. Milofsky, *Special Education,* 68–93.

24. I encountered a similar style while doing my study, *Special Education,* in California. Close reading of Peter Kuriloff, David Kirp, and William Buss, *When Handicapped Children Go to Court: Assessing the Impact of the Legal Reform of Special Education in Pennsylvania* (Washington, DC: National Institute of Education, 1979). ERIC Document ED196256, shows a similar style is administered in Pennsylvania cities.

25. Berk, Bridges, and Shih, "Does IQ Really Matter?"

26. Milofsky, *Special Education.* I also have examined this issue in "Why Special Education Isn't Special," *Harvard Educational Review* 44 (1974):437–458; and in "Special Education and Social Control," in John G. Richardson, ed., *Handbook of Theory and Research for the Sociology of Education* (New York: Greenwood Press, 1986), 173–202. The point is also made in McIntyre, "Two Schools and One Psychologist."

27. In addition to Seymour Sarason's work summarized in n. 20, see Fred. F. Lighthall, "A Social Psychologist for School Systems," *Psychology in the*

Schools 6 (1969):3–12; and Fred Lighthall and J. W. Braun, *The Twenty-Second Case,* Final Report, NIMH Project 5-T21-MH-11217 (Chicago: University of Chicago, Department of Education, 1975).

28. Robert K. Merton, with Elinor Barber, "Sociological Ambivalence," in Robert K. Merton, *Sociological Ambivalence* (New York: Free Press, 1976), 3–31.

29. Arthur L. Stinchcombe, *Creating Efficient Industrial Administrations* (New York: Academic Press, 1974), 3–93.

30. My postdoctoral fellowship was funded by a grant from the U.S. Government, Alcohol, Drug Abuse, and Mental Health Administration. My sponsor was Dan Lortie. I also worked closely with Fred Strodtbeck of the Department of Sociology and Social Psychology Laboratory of the University of Chicago.

31. See William E. Henry, John H. Sims, and Lee S. Spray, *The Fifth Profession* (San Francisco: Jossey-Bass, 1971); and Peter Kuriloff, David Kirp, and William Buss, *When Handicapped Children Go to Court.* For data on overall response rates to mailed questionnaires, see Thomas A. Heberlein and Robert Baumgartner, "Factors Affecting Response Rates to Mailed Questionnaires: A Quantitative Analysis of the Published Literature," *American Sociological Review* 43 (1978):447–462.

32. Milofsky, *Special Education.*

33. Kirp, Buss, and Kuriloff, "Legal Reform of Special Education."

34. For example, a *New York Times* editorial from 17 December 1983 stated:

> Shortfalls in education budgets are not unusual. Chancellor Frank Macchiarola, considered a good manager, needed $92 million extra in 1979. Then as now, much of the added money was for "special" teaching of handicapped children, still the fastest growing budget item.
>
> Those programs serve children with physical, psychological and emotional handicaps. They provide specially trained teachers for classes limited to 12 students. The program's aims are laudable, but its increasing cost is alarming. More than 100,000 New York children now have special status. The total is growing by 10,000 a year, which explains about $50 million of Mr. Alvarado's shortfall.
>
> Children must be evaluated and placed in appropriate programs within 60 days after any teacher senses a need for help. About 2,000 more than were expected were evaluated last summer. The cost attributable to these burdensome state regulations are beyond Mr. Alvarado's reach. But he can be blamed for such costs as the premature hiring of some special education teachers. (P. 22)

Because of the provisions of PL 94-142, special education costs have been relatively immune to budget cuts under the Reagan administration's federal cutbacks in spending. The expansion reported in this editorial do not seem, however, to be continuing on a national scale.

35. I have discussed the flattening of special education growth in "Is the Growth of Special Education Evolutionary or Cyclic? A Response to Carrier," *American Journal of Education* 94, *3* (1986):313–321.

Chapter One

1. I am borrowing the imagery of Edward Shils, *Center and Periphery Essays in Macrosociology* (Chicago: University of Chicago Press, 1975).

2. I have discussed this problem in special education elsewhere. See Milofsky, "Why Special Education Isn't Special," 437–458; and Milofsky, *Special Education*. Burton Clark, *Adult Education in Transition: A Study of Institutional Insecurity* (Berkeley and Los Angeles: University of California Press, 1956), made similar observations about adult education.

3. For a discussion of the irrelevance of special education in the eyes of social scientists, see James G. Carrier, "Sociology and Special Education: Differentiation and Allocation in Mass Education," *American Journal of Education* 94, *3* (May 1986):281–312; and our exchange in the same journal, Carl Milofsky, "Is the Growth of Special Education Evolutionary or Cyclic? A Response to Carrier," *American Journal of Education* 94, *3* (May 1986):313–321; and Carrier, "Reply to Milofsky's Comments on 'Sociology and Special Education,'" *American Journal of Education* 94, *3* (May 1986):322–327. Also see Carrier, *Learning Disability*.

4. It is important to distinguish marginal roles from ones that are simply peripheral. In many organizations, peripheral roles exist that successfully maintain their autonomy and perform essential functions even though they are distinct from the central mission of the firm. Clark in *Adult Education in Transition* emphasized that marginality refers only to those situations in which actors continually revise their role definitions in hopes of making them more acceptable to members of the core and hence more secure.

5. See Janet A. Weiss, Frederick Norling, and John R. Kimberly, "The Development and Effectiveness of Educational Service Centers: A Study of JACS," unpublished paper, School of Organization and Management, Yale University (New Haven: Yale University, 1981), for a discussion of Connecticut educational service centers. The final report of this project is Janet Weiss et al., *Managing Cooperation and Complexity in Education: The Case of Educational Service Agencies. Final Report* (Ann Arbor, MI: Institute for Social Research, 1984), ERIC Document # ED242098. For a discussion of intermediate districts in Pennsylvania, see Bruce Dworkin, "Reference Group Orientation and Role Definition of School Psychologists in Educational Bureaucracies." Ph.D. diss., University of Pennsylvania, 1976, *Dissertation Abstracts Index,* 37/07A: 4644.

6. A long-standing tradition in school psychology is for people to spend four days working in schools and a fifth day in a central administrative center writing reports on the psychological examinations they had earlier carried out. In many locations, psychologists share offices or office suites, and their days in

the central office become an important time for collegial interaction. I found this pattern in my earlier study of a California school district and in the Chicago suburbs. It was a pattern that also prevailed in Chicago's Bureau of Child Study until the Chicago Public Schools were organized into a collection of neighborhood school districts and school psychology was also decentralized.

   7. In Mercer, *Labeling the Mentally Retarded,* 105, 73 percent of students in special education classes had been referred prior to the fifth grade. Since Mercer's study predated most of the special education reforms leading up to PL 94-142, her data may not still be accurate. However, because the new law mandates screening of children early in their school years and even at the preschool stage, it is likely that the pattern has not changed. Programs are designed with the expectation that most children with dramatic learning problems will be identified early.

   8. Mercer, *Labeling the Mentally Retarded,* 96–123.

   9. See Berk, Bridges, and Shih, "Does IQ Really Matter?" 46:58–71.

   10. Mercer, *Labeling the Mentally Retarded,* 96–123.

   11. Berk, Bridges, and Shih, "Does IQ Really Matter?"

   12. There is a long history of concern that IQ tests have been used as devices to oppress unpopular minorities in American society. See Leon Kamin, *The Science and Politics of IQ* (Potomac, MD: Lawrence Erlbaum, 1974). Jane Mercer (see *Labeling the Mentally Retarded*) is among the most persistent social scientists in recent efforts to demonstrate the cultural biases of IQ tests. For data on the gap between the test performances of blacks and whites, see Audrey M. Shuey, *The Testing of Negro Intelligence,* 2d ed. (New York: Social Science Press, 1966).

   13. See David L. Kirp, William Buss, and Peter Kuriloff, "Legal Reform of Special Education," 40–155, for a review of this history. Also see Senate Report 94-168, 2 June 1975, "Education for All Handicapped Children Act," *Larry P. v. Riles,* Opinion Filed 16 October 1979, United States District Court for the Northern District of California, No. C-71-2270. RFP. and *P.A.S.E. et al. v. Hannon et al.,* 1980, United States District Court, Northern District of Illinois, Eastern Division, No. 74 C 3586.

   14. See John C. Pittenger and Peter Kuriloff, "Educating the Handicapped: Reforming a Radical Law," *Public Interest* 66 (Winter 1982):72–96; and Kuriloff, "Is Justice Served by Due Process?" 89–118. Also see Fred F. Lighthall, "School Psychology: An Alien Guild," *Elementary School Journal* 63 (1963):361–374; Lighthall, "A Social Psychologist for School Systems," 3–12; and Fred Lighthall and J. W. Braun, *The Twenty-Second Case,* Final Report, NIMH Project 5-T21-MH-11217 (Chicago: Department of Education, University of Chicago, 1975). See also McIntyre, "Two Schools, One Psychologist," 21–89.

   15. See Seymour Sarason and John Doris, "Definition, Diagnosis and Action in Light of a Transactional Approach," *Educational Handicap, Public Policy and Social History: A Broadened Perspective on Mental Retardation* (New York: Free Press, 1979), chap. 3.

   16. Milofsky, *Special Education.*

Chapter Two

1. See, for example, Lewis Anthony Dexter, *The Tyranny of Schooling: An Inquiry into the Problem of "Stupidity"* (NY: Basic Books, 1964); and Robert B. Edgerton, *The Cloak of Competence: Stigma in the Lives of the Mentally Retarded* (Berkeley and Los Angeles: University of California Press, 1967).

2. One of the main themes of Mercer's *Labeling the Mentally Retarded* is that most mental retardation is associated with a particular institutional setting. The majority of those who fail in school and perform poorly on IQ tests are socially normal. That is, they are capable of functioning in their communities without being spontaneously identified by neighbors, friends, or employers as retarded. The fraction that *is* spontaneously retarded has a difficult time coping with the stigma of retardation as Edgerton, *Cloak of Competence,* shows. Most people who could be clinically defined as retarded can hide their problem, especially if they are from an ethnic minority or lower-class background. This is widely recognized in the epidemiological literature on mental retardation in the concept of "cultural-familial mental retardation." See Rick Heber, "A Manual on Terminology and Classification in Mental Retardation," *American Journal of Mental Deficiency* 64, 2 (1959), Monograph Supplement.

3. This is self-evident since IQ tests are used as one of the primary means of identifying the retarded. Before there were tests, people did not recognize the fine gradations that the tests made it possible for us to recognize. For discussion of the "discovery" of a distribution of intelligence, however, see Leo Kanner, *A History of the Care and Study of the Mentally Retarded* (Springfield, IL: Charles C. Thomas, 1964).

4. See Charles E. Lindblom and David Cohen, *Usable Knowledge: Social Science and Social Problem Solving* (New Haven: Yale University Press, 1979); and Charles E. Lindblom, "Analysis in Policy Making" and "Limits on Analysis as an Alternative to Politics," in *The Policy Making Process,* 2d ed. (Englewood Cliffs, NJ: Prentice-Hall, 1980), 11–25.

5. Stinchcombe, *Creating Efficient Industrial Administrations,* 67–69.

6. Max L. Hutt, *The Hutt Adaptation of the Bender-Gestalt Test,* 3d ed. (New York: Grune & Stratton, 1977), 6.

7. Willard Waller, *The Sociology of Teaching* (New York: Wiley, 1932), pt. 4, for example, describes this sort of manipulation as one of the effective forms of control available to a teacher.

8. David Wechsler, *Manual for the Wechsler Intelligence Scale for Children,* rev. (New York: Psychological Corporation, 1974).

9. J. F. Jastak, S. R. Jastak, and S. W. Bijou, *Wide Range Achievement Test,* rev. ed. (Austin, TX: Guidance Testing Associates, 1965).

10. Samuel J. Beck, *Introduction to the Rorschach Method: A Manual of Personality Study* (New York: American Orthopsychiatric Association, 1937).

11. Sigmund Freud, "The Psychopathology of Everyday Life," in A. A. Brill, ed., *The Basic Writings of Sigmund Freud* (New York: Modern Library, 1938), 35–178.

12. Robert Freed Bales, *Personality and Interpersonal Behavior* (New York: Holt, Rinehart & Winston, 1970).

13. Erving Goffman, *The Presentation of Self in Everyday Life* (Garden City, NY: Anchor Books, 1959).

14. See Read D. Tuddenham, "The Nature and Measurement of Intelligence," in Leo D. Postman, ed., *Psychology in the Making* (New York: Knopf, 1962), 469–525; and Read D. Tuddenham, "Intelligence," in Robert L. Ebel, ed., *Encyclopedia of Educational Research*, 4th ed. (London: Collier-Macmillan, 1969), 654–667; and see Anne Anastasi, *Psychological Testing*, 4th ed. (New York: Macmillan, 1976).

15. See Robert K. Merton, "The Ambivalence of Physicians," in *Sociological Ambivalence* (New York: Free Press, 1976), 65–73.

Chapter Three

1. Feuerstein, "A Dynamic Approach to the Causation, Prevention and Alleviation of Retarded Performance," 341–377, suggests that if one is interested in improving performance among those who fail intellectually, it is more important to understand how they make their mistakes than it is to know how many questions they get right—the basis of objective test scores. Feuerstein's discussion is the best one I have found that explains how intelligence tests might be used as projective instruments that demand an interpretive approach from the psychologist rather than an objective, impersonal approach.

2. See Robert M. Kaplan and Dennis P. Saccuzzo, *Psychological Testing: Principals, Applications, and Issues* (Monterey, CA: Brooks/Cole Publishing, 1982), 172–185, for a general discussion of the importance of rapport in testing. Sarason and Doris, *Educational Handicap,,* 11–58, provide a detailed discussion of the importance of an interactional approach if psychological diagnosis is to capture the subtleties of a child's difficulties. In an earlier work, Sarason showed that test anxiety is common and can substantially lower test scores. See Kennedy T. Hill and Seymour B. Sarason, "The Relationship between Test Anxiety and Defensiveness to Test and School Performance over the Elementary Years: A Further Longitudinal Study," *Monographs of the Society for Research in Child Development,* Serial #104, v. 31, *2* (1966). M. Deutsch, J. A. Fishman, L. Kogan, R. North, and M. Whiteman, "Guidelines for Testing Minority Group Children," *Journal of Social Issues* 20, *2* (1964):127–145, report that minority children, uncomfortable in the test setting, are prone to giving random answers and thus artificially lower their test scores.

3. Max Weber, *Economy and Society,* ed. Guenther Roth and Claus Wittich (Berkeley and Los Angeles: University of California Press, 1978), 956–983. Edgar Huse and James L. Bowditch, *Behavior in Organizations: A Systems Approach to Managing* (Reading, MA: Addison-Wesley, 1973), 9–13, refer to the Weberian tradition as "the structuralist school." Amitai Etzioni, *Modern Organizations* (Englewood Cliffs, NJ: Prentice Hall, 1964), discusses organiza-

tional theory derived from the sociological tradition. W. Richard Scott, *Organizations: Rational, Natural, and Open Systems* (Englewood Cliffs, NJ: Prentice Hall, 1981), discusses various organizational typologies and refers to those in the Weberian tradition as goal-directed rational models. Charles Perrow, *Complex Organizations: A Critical Essay* (Glenview, IL: Scott, Foresman, 1972), 1–60, discusses the development of organizational theory as rooted in the Weberian theory of bureaucracy.

5. Saliterman, "The Politics of Decision-making in an Incompletely Bureaucratized Organization," makes this argument about the nonbureaucratic nature of schools. On loose-coupling in school organizations, see Weick, "Educational Organizations as Loosely Coupled Systems," 1–19. James G. March and Johan P. Olson, *Ambiguity and Choice in Organizations* (Bergen-Oslo-Troms: Universitetsforlaget, 1976) argues that loose-coupling is inevitable in schools because uncertainty about the outcomes of alternative decisions is so high. Rather than make decisions on the basis of a clear-cut and effective technical rationality, administrators make ad hoc decisions that are not always effective and that are hard to justify to subordinates. This method makes schools quietly anarchic organizational systems.

6. Richard Weatherley and Michael Lipsky, "Street-level Bureaucrats and Institutional Innovation: Implementing Special-Education Reform," *Harvard Educational Review* 47, 2 (1977):171–197. See Michael Lipsky, *Street-level Bureaucracy: Dilemmas of the Individual in Public Services* (New York: Russell Sage, 1980).

7. The difficulty of distinguishing good from bad techniques in medical diagnosis is discussed is Arthur S. Elstein, Lee S. Shulman, and Sarah A. Sprafka, *Medical Problem Solving: An Analysis of Clinical Reasoning* (Cambridge: Harvard University Press, 1978).

8. Charles Bosk, *Forgive and Remember: Managing Medical Failure* (Chicago: University of Chicago Press, 1979), explains why there is agreement about what constitutes failure. A good discussion of the diversity of views about *good* practice is Rue Bucher and Anselm Strauss, "Professions in Process," *American Journal of Sociology* 66 (1961):325–334.

9. This conviction is sharply different from that expressed by psychologists working in suburban special education cooperatives and by the literature on due process in special education referrals. Placements in special education must be approved by the special education director, and school psychologists are agents of that director in the suburbs. The purpose of the interdisciplinary team is to ensure that students receive an educationally appropriate and least restrictive placement. This administrative machinery was explicitly created to address the problem of handicapped children who were being excluded from school while other children, who appear upon reexamination to be nonhandicapped, were placed in special classes. See U.S. Senate Report 94-168, 2 June 1975, "Education for All Handicapped Children Act"; and Kirp, Buss, and Kuriloff, "Legal Reform of Special Education," 40–155.

10. Richard DeCharms, *Personal Causation: The Internal Affective Deter-*

minants of Behavior (New York: Academic Press, 1968), provides a thorough discussion of the conceptual underpinnings of the concept locus of control or, in his terms, locus of causation. He distinguishes between people seeing the source of control over their behavior within themselves or outside of themselves, and he characterizes these two poles of control as people who, on one hand, see themselves as "origins" and, on the other, as "pawns." He explains as follows:

> The most basic postulate that we wish to present is that a man is the origin of his behavior. He is a unique locus of causality. Heider . . . has developed the proposition that man is perceived as a locus of causality under certain conditions and it is a commonplace that we *feel* that their behavior is caused ultimately by time. Our postulate states more, i.e., that man *is* the locus of causality for his behavior. Without such a postulate, behavior might be explained by external forces, but the psychological aspects of the term "motive" becomes superfluous. . . .
>
> We shall use the terms "Origin" and "Pawn" as shorthand terms to connote the distinction between forced and free. An Origin is a person who perceives his behavior as determined by his own choosing; a Pawn is a person who perceives his behavior as determined by external forces beyond his control. We hypothesize, and will try to present relevant data in later chapters, that feeling like an Origin has strong effects on behavior as compared to feeling like a Pawn. . . . (Pp. 272–274)

When I distinguish between psychologists who are professionally oriented and those who are bureaucratically or educationally oriented, I shall assert that a by-product of these orientations in the context of school work is that professionally oriented psychologists feel like Origins and are more aggressive in their work than are educationally oriented psychologists, who feel more like Pawns.

11. Fred Goldner, "Role Emergence and the Ethics of Ambiguity," in Gideon Sjoberg, *Ethics, Politics, and Social Research* (Cambridge, MA: Schenkman, 1967), chap. 11; and Rue Bucher and Joan Stelling, "Characteristics of Professional Organizations," *Journal of Health and Social Behavior* 10 (1969):3–11; and Rue Bucher and Joan Stelling, *Becoming Professional* (Beverly Hills, CA: Sage, 1977), argue that what distinguishes *professional* in organizations from other workers is their responsibility to construct roles for themselves. In what they call "professional organizations," there are institutionalized opportunities for new people to define for themselves what their work shall consist of. This is in contrast to a Weberian bureaucracy where roles are defined by their relationship to other ones in a tightly linked division of labor. In such bureaucratic organizations, roles are defined by requirements for expertise and are defined independently of the people who fill them. School psychologists with high test volumes are bureaucrats in this sense, whereas those with low test volumes operate in a setting more typical of professional organizations.

12. R. Linton, *The Study of Man* (New York: Appleton-Century-Crofts, 1936).

13. That one role may be associated with several different statuses is a point made by Henry, Sims, and Spray, *Fifth Profession,* in their study of psychotherapeutic professions—psychoanalysis, psychiatry, clinical psychiatry, and psychiatric social work. They argue that the substance of work is mostly the same in these four professions, though their institutional locations and the prestige of practitioners in each varies considerably across them.

14. Merton's notion of "sociological ambivalence," discussed in *Sociological Ambivalence,* is particularly germane here. Where Philip Selznick is concerned, not only am I referring to writings of his like *Leadership in Administration* (New York: Harper & Row, 1957), or *TVA and the Grassroots* (New York: Harper & Row, 1966). Selznick also is at the center of a case study tradition in organizational theory that Charles Perrow, *Complex Organizations: A Critical Essay* (Glenview, IL: Scott, Foresman, 1972), 177–204, calls The Institutional School. This approach to organizational research is methodologically rooted in the structural functionalism of Merton, but in many ways is parallel to the case study tradition of Chicago sociologists who had Everett Hughes as their teacher.

Being from the University of Chicago and a contemporary of leading students of George Herbert Mead like Herbert Blumer, Everett Hughes can make a strong claim to being a symbolic interactionist, although he was not at the forefront of those articulating that theoretical perspective. I am inclined to place his style of analysis more in the organizational case-study tradition of Selznick's group. At the same time, *Boys in White,* by Howard S. Becker, Blanche Geer, Everett Hughes, and Anselm Strauss (Chicago: University of Chicago Press, 1961), claims explicitly to be symbolic interactionist. Who is to argue?

15. D. Katz and R. Kahn, *Social Psychology of Organizations* (New York: John Wiley & Sons, 1966); and R. Kahn, D. M. Wolfe, R. P. Quinn, J. D. Snoek, and R. A. Rosenthal, *Organizational Stress* (New York: Wiley, 1964), are two important social psychology texts that emphasize the debilitating effects of role conflicts in organizations.

16. Jerome Skolnick, *Justice Without Trial* (New York: Wiley, 1967).

17. Merton, "The Ambivalence of Physicians," 65–72.

18. Milofsky, *Special Education,* 84–86.

Chapter Four

1. Mercer, *Labeling the Mentally Retarded,* 96–123, "The labeling process in the public schools."

2. A regular class teacher I observed and described at some length in my earlier book showed this reluctance (Milofsky, *Special Education,* 70–77).

3. Berk, Bridges, and Shih, "Does IQ Really Matter?"

4. In this section, I will try to show that although the psychologists I

observed were sometimes deceptive in their relations with regular educators, this is a perfectly legitimate and common mode of action in organizations. Some observers of professionals in organizations have made this point emphatically by talking about the fact that roles rarely are sharply defined and waiting for new occupants of professional positions. Rather, an intrinsic part of professional work in organizations is for the individual to invent or create a role and sell it to those who occupy adjacent roles and whose cooperation must be gained. See Goldner, "Role Emergence and the Ethics of Ambiguity," chap. 11; and Bucher and Stelling, "Characteristics of Professional Organizations," 3–11. A perspective that, like mine, emphasizes the difficulty of balancing ethical demands from several constituencies with differing amounts of power is Ernest Q. Campbell and Thomas F. Pettigrew, "Racial and Moral Crisis: The Role of Little Rock Ministers," *American Journal of Sociology* 64 (1959):509–516.

5. See Goffman, "Performances," 17–76.

6. George Herbert Mead, *Mind, Self, and Society,* ed. Charles W. Morris (Chicago: University of Chicago Press, 1962).

7. Erving Goffman, "The Moral Career of the Mental Patient," in *Asylums, Essays on the Social Situation of Mental Patients and Other Inmates* (Garden City, NY: Doubleday, Anchor, 1961), 125–170, describes the process by which institutions dismantle the self-image possessed by entering mental patients, forcing inmates to reconstruct their sense of self in a way that acknowledges their new status, that of someone who is mentally ill. I do not mean to suggest that school psychologists are mentally ill. Comparing people living on locked mental hospital wards with professionals in the schools may be so unlikely that all similarity is lost. I do not think so. Goffman chooses an extreme example so that it will be clear to all that one's self is a social construction, open to attack, degradation, and restructuring when the appropriate sort of social pressure is applied. What he observes in an extreme situation happens in less extreme ways in everyday life, as Goffman shows in his other books that demonstrate the theatrical, covert dimensions of routine social interaction.

8. Weatherley and Lipsky, "Street-level Bureaucrats and Institutional Innovation," 171–197; and Lipsky, *Street-level Bureaucracy.*

9. See Talcott Parsons, "Social Structure and Dynamic Process: The Case of Modern Medical Practice," in *The Social System* (New York: Free Press, 1951), 428–479; and Everett C. Hughes, "Professions," in *The Sociological Eye: Selected Papers on Work, Self, and the Study of Society* (Chicago: Aldine, 1971), 374–386.

Chapter Five

1. Senate Report 94-168, 2 June 1975, "Education for All Handicapped Children Act," reports the senate hearings on that law and provides one indication of the strong desires of the authors to minimize racial overrepresentation in special education classes. See also Kirp, Buss, and Kuriloff, "Legal Reform of

Special Education, 40–155; Weatherley, *Reforming Special Education;* and Shore, *Special Education Handbook.*

2. I use the term *segmentation* following Bucher and Strauss, "Professions in Process," 325–334. They argue that medicine and all professions are internally divided into competing, practice-oriented ideological groups or segments. They offered this argument to counter the idea that professions are morally or intellectually unified and orderly. Although technical terms can get in the way, I use this one because it emphasizes that people occupying the same status are likely to bring sharply different perspectives to their work.

3. Psychologists employed by the Chicago Board of Education who responded to my questionnaire were significantly better paid than psychologists who worked elsewhere. This is partly because those people tend to be older than the rest of the psychologists and are more likely to have accumulated credits and degrees beyond the M.A. It also happened because Chicago psychologists are likely to have longer continuous service with their school district, and they do not lose benefits as others may when they shift from one organization to another. Even with these factors set aside, many nonurban districts pay much less than do large urban districts. The cost of living may be lower, and urban districts often provide what amounts to "combat pay" since their working conditions are more difficult.

4. See Chicago Board of Education, *The Bureau of Child Study* (Chicago: Board of Education, Bureau of Child Study, 1960); Frances A. Mullen, "Fifty Years of Service to the Mentally Handicapped Children of the Chicago Schools," in *Chicago Principal's Club Reporter* 39 (1949):11–17; and Slater, "The Organizational Origins of Public School Psychology," 1–11.

5. See Mercer, *Labeling the Mentally Retarded;* and Hurley, *Poverty and Mental Retardation.*

6. See Schrag and Divoky, *The Myth of the Hyperactive Child.*

7. Weiss, Norling, and Kimberly, "The Development and Effectiveness of Educational Service Centers," provides an analysis of the structure of educational service centers. The final report of their project is Janet Weiss et al., *Managing Cooperation and Complexity in Education.* The cash flow problems of educational service centers are similar to those of other small nonprofit social service organizations I discuss in "Neighborhood-based Organizations: A Market Analolgy," in Walter W. Powell, ed., *The Nonprofit Sector: A Research Handbook* (New Haven: Yale University Press, 1987), 277–295.

8. James S. Coleman, Ernest Q. Campbell, Carol J. Hobson, James McPartland, Alexander M. Mood, Frederic Weinfeld, and Robert L. York, *Equality of Educational Opportunity* (Washington, DC: Office of Education, National Center for Educational Statistics, U.S. Government Printing Office, 1966). Good reviews of research on the problems of studying the effects of schooling are Heyns, *Summer Learning;* and Richard Murnane, *The Impact of School Resources on the Learning of Inner City Children* (Cambridge, MA: Ballinger, 1975). In both of these studies, the central issue is what to make of the tiny correlations we find between school programming and student achievement patterns.

9. Although the APA is particularly energetic in combating illegitimate providers of psychotherapy, the National Association of Social Workers also provides a vigorous program of certification and in-service training. Henry, Sims, and Spray, *Fifth Profession,* describe the four psychotherapy professions: psychoanalysis, psychiatry, clinical psychology, and psychiatric social work. I would suggest that their work is limited to those branches of the industry that are academically legitimate. There now exist a variety of therapeutic traditions that are not so graced.

10. From the original days of the psychotherapeutic professions there has been conflict between experience-based treatment and therapy rooted in academic training. Thus, early settlement house pioneers like Jane Addams, *Twenty Years at Hull House* (New York: Macmillan, 1910), and other middle-class reformers who saw helping as an expression of altruism rather than of professional work were uncomfortable with the emergence of professional social work. See Roy Lubov, *The Professional Altruist: The Emergence of Social Work as a Career, 1880–1930* (New York: Atheneum, 1969). Recently, emergence of the "self-help revolution" has led to a resurgence of experience-based treatments that emphasize the capacity of indigenous social networks to help people recover from addictions and disabilities or to cope with disease. For general discussions of the phenomenon, see Lowell S. Levin and Ellen L. Idler, *The Hidden Health Care System: Mediation Structures and Medicine* (Cambridge, MA: Ballinger, 1981); Gerald Caplan and Marie Killilea, eds., *Support Systems and Mutual Help: Multidisciplinary Explorations* (New York: Grune and Stratton, 1976); Diane L. Pancoast, Paul Parker, and Charles Froland, eds., *Rediscovering Self-Help: Its Role in Social Care* (Beverly Hills, CA: Sage, 1983); and Hope Hughes Pressman, *A New Resource for Social Reform: The Poor Themselves* (Berkeley: Institute of Governmental Studies, University of California, 1975). There are a number of focused case studies that talk about the positive and negative aspects of these treatments as they have been used with different psychological problems. Joan Hatch Shapiro, *Communities of the Alone* (New York: Association Press, 1971); and Lewis Yablonsky, *Synanon: The Tunnel Back* (Baltimore: Penguin Books, 1967), are early statements describing the benefits of this sort of therapy. Dave Mitchell, Cathy Mitchell, and Richard Ofshe, *The Light on Synanon* (New York: Seaview Books, 1980), is a later study critical of Synanon and of the tendency in a total community like this one for members to be exploited. David Rudy, *Becoming Alcoholic: Alcoholics Anonymous and the Reality of Alcoholism* (Carbondale and Edwardsville: Southern Illinois University Press, 1986); and David N. Nurco, Norma Wegner, Philip Stephenson, Abraham Makofsky, and John W. Shaffer, *Ex-Addicts' Self-Help Groups: Potentials and Pitfalls* (New York: Praeger, 1983), are recent books that recognize both opportunity and difficulty in this treatment model.

11. This example is drawn from a research project I and some colleagues have recently undertaken, examining the migration of urban substance abusers to a small rural community for purposes of recovery. One reason this mode of treatment has developed is that local self-help groups, coupled with recent

changes in welfare law, allow people to maintain themselves in an unfamiliar community, having their essential needs publicly paid for, while they receive a combination of self-help treatment through organizations like Alcoholics Anonymous and from various profit-making professional and semiprofessional psychological services. Our initial investigations have made it clear the extent to which psychology is a business working hand-in-glove with public social services and social control agencies. Although the profession-oriented psychologists I met in the present study were not benefiting from the same public funding arrangement, I am astonished by the similarity between the more entrepreneurial people I interviewed in my school psychology study and the psychological entrepreneurs we are meeting today. To say that people are business-oriented and entrepreneurial is not in any way to say that they provide poor services or that they are not psychologically sophisticated. At the same time, the business ethic under which these people work is fundamentally self-protective and self-promoting. It is different from a professional ethic—when one truly exists— which requires that people value the ideas and knowledge that informs their discipline, quality service, the well being of clients, and the protection of the professional community above their personal advancement. I want to emphasize that the professional ethic is not one that so-called professionals automatically subscribe to. I shall argue in the next chapter that most sensible professionals avoid close scrutiny and accountability if they can help it. A professional community happens when people are forced to accept the ethic for purposes of group survival. Thus, I do not mean to hold up professionalism as some altruistic ideal. At the same time, I think that services provided under a professional model are sharply different from ones that are offered under a straightforward business model.

12. This observation was made by Jaqueline Sallade through personal communication. She is a Ph.D. psychologist in private practice who also does part-time work as a school psychologist.

Chapter Six

1. I have in mind here Suzanne Keller's idea developed in *Beyond the Ruling Class: Strategic Elites in Modern Society* (New York: Random House, 1963), that different groups are able to gain disproportionate power because their social position gives them more leverage in political or economic competition than that possessed by other potential leaders.

2. Educational service centers are a new organizational phenomenon on the education scene that have been little studied. They began primarily as part of the reform of special education, but in the last quarter century they have become firmly entrenched as entrepreneurial multiservice centers for schools. See Weiss, Norling, and Kimberly, "The Development and Effectiveness of Educational Service Centers," and Weiss et al., *Managing Cooperation and Complexity in Education.*

3. The most thorough discussion I have seen of entrepreneurship among the leaders of small social service organizations is Dennis Young's work on entrepreneurship among nonprofit organizations. His case studies show the importance of aggressive, unfettered leadership if these small organizations are to pursue new opportunities and creatively develop new programs. Although educational service centers are publicly sponsored, they face the same organizational problems as small social service nonprofits. See Dennis Young, *If Not for Profit, For What? A Behavioral Theory of the Nonprofit Sector Based on Entrepreneurship* (Lexington, MA: Lexington Books, 1983); and Dennis Young, *Casebook of Management for Nonprofit Organizations: Entrepreneurship and Organizational Change in the Human Services* (New York: Haworth Press, 1984).

4. See Milofsky, "Neighborhood-based Organizations," for a discussion of cash flow problems in other small social service organizations.

5. I encountered a similar arrangement of psychological services in my earlier study of learning disability programs in California elementary schools. See Milofsky, *Special Education,* 49–61.

6. See Beck, *Introduction to the Rorschach Method.* This manual was the bible of ACORN in-service training sessions.

7. Most of my observations of in-service training sessions were conducted with the advice and supervision of Fred Strodtbeck. Strodtbeck relied heavily on the observation techniques pioneered by and the research tradition initiated by Robert Freed Bales. See, for example, Bales's *Personality and Interpersonal Behavior.*

8. For Talcott Parsons's theory of the professions, see "Social Structure and Dynamic Process." For Everett Hughes, see "Professions." For an influential recent treatment of similar issues, see Paul Starr, "The Consolidation of Professional Authority, 1850–1930," and "Escape from the Corporation, 1900–1930," in *The Social Transformation of American Medicine: The Rise of a Sovereign Profession and the Making of a Vast Industry* (New York: Basic Books, 1982), 79–144, 198–232.

9. The most thorough dismantling of Parsons's theory of professions is Eliot Freidson, *Profession of Medicine: A Study of the Sociology of Applied Knowledge* (New York: Harper & Row, 1970). See also Freidson's *Doctoring Together: A Study of Professional Social Control* (New York: Elsevier, 1975), for an empirical study of *non*control that contrasts with the organizational dynamic I describe here. Another important critique of the moral theory of professions is Bucher and Strauss, "Professions in Process."

10. Although most sociologists have attacked the notion that there is serious scrutiny of practice and control of error among professionals, an important exception is Charles Bosk, *Forgive and Remember: Managing Medical Failure* (Chicago: University of Chicago Press, 1979). Bosk focused primarily on how doctors define what an error is, but one has the impression that not all medical establishments are as careful as are the one he was observing. Bosk, working in an elite medical school hospital, reports that senior physicians emphasized pa-

tients in the facility received scrupulously high-quality care. It was essential to convince area physicians that this hospital provided the best care available, and that when they doubted their own competence in handling a case, they could be sure that a patient referred to University Hospital would receive the best care possible. Maintaining the reputation as *the* elite medical facility in the area was essential to institutional survival and created special pressure on staff to maintain the highest standards of competence. Although physicians generally receive pressure to maintain high quality of care, there are notorious examples where blind or alcoholic physicians were allowed to continue practicing. Thus, what Bosk describes seems to represent the situation of a particular medical institution attempting to protect its organizational turf, rather than the general conditions of medical practice.

11. Paul Peterson, *School Politics Chicago Style* (Chicago: University of Chicago Press, 1976), describes policymaking in the Chicago Public Schools very much in terms of this clash of large, city-wide interest groups. Remember that Chicago has long been the epitome of urban machine politics. Edward C. Banfield, *Political Influence* (Glencoe, IL: Free Press, 1961), describes how important it is to Chicago politicians to assemble large interest blocs to support political decisions. This is the political climate that Peterson describes in his book. Although my vantage point was at the grassroots level rather than the pinnacle of power, I would suggest that in a political culture as sensitive to constituencies and power blocs as that of Chicago, a small, poorly represented group like school psychologists are likely to find it difficult to have their parochial interests or point of view represented.

12. Where Peterson's book suggests the image of large, well-organized interest groups bloodying each other to secure political advantages, another image that fits the situation of low-level employees of a huge school system like that in Chicago is Berger's notion of stratum mobility (Bennett Berger, *Working Class Suburb* [Berkeley and Los Angeles: University of California Press, 1960]). Although political pluralism may accurately describe the activities of leaders in the school system, the low-level employees are likely to feel powerless, pawns of decisions made in a distant administrative center. At the grass roots level, it does not much matter what political or economic action one undertakes. One's fate is the same as other people at one's level. If one moves ahead or suffers a decline of fortunes, everyone else in one's immediate surroundings are likely to suffer the same fate because the factors that affect decisions are only defined at the highest levels of power. In a mass system, the individual actions of little people do not count. This may be alienating for people who, like Berger's subjects, see themselves unavoidably thrown into a stratum moving up or down in status terms at a glacial rate. Their equivalent in schools are probably classroom teachers. In such a system, those who are outsiders are likely to feel doubly helpless to affect their social and political situation. If "normal" people have no power, trying to enhance one's position by building influence with those people is hopeless. Worse, one may be noticed as a dangerous person in a system that forces conformity on everyone. The safest practice is to seem like

everyone else and to benefit from the slow gains or the moderated declines of the stratum with which one has affiliated. So school psychologists try to hide and seem normal as winds of change blow in the school system.

Chapter Seven

1. For a review of the literature on test bias, see Sattler and Theye, "Procedural, Situational and Interpersonal Variables in Individual Intelligence Testing"; and Cole and Bruner, "Cultural Differences and Inferences about Psychological Processes."

2. Senate Report 94-168, 2 June 1975, Education for All Handicapped Children Act.

3. For Pennsylvania, see Kuriloff, Kirp, and Buss, *When Handicapped Children Go to Court;* and Dworkin, "Reference Group Orientation and Role Definition of School Psychologists in Educational Bureaucracies." For California, see my earlier book, *Special Education;* Kirp, Buss, and Kuriloff, "Legal Reform of Special Education"; and the judicial opinion in *Larry P. v. Riles,* 343 F Supp. 1306, 502 F. 2nd. 963 N.S. Cal, 1979.

4. *P.A.S.E. v. Hannon,* 74C 3586, N.D. Ill., 1980.

5. Shortly after I left Chicago to teach at Yale, Richard Berk gave a talk where I worked at the Institution for Social and Policy studies about his research on Chicago student classification records. He was carrying out that work with Bill Bridges and Anthony Shih in cooperation with the plaintiffs in *P.A.S.E.* When I told him about this research, he advised me to stop talking unless I wanted to be subpoenaed. I did stop talking, mainly because I was obliged to protect the Chicago psychologists who took me into their confidence, although the conclusions of this research suggest that perhaps the plaintiffs were correct in their complaints.

6. Everett C. Hughes, "Good People and Dirty Work," in *The Sociological Eye: Selected Papers on Institutions and Race* (Chicago: Aldine-Atherton, 1971), 87–97.

7. Merton, *Sociological Ambivalence.*

8. Carrier, "Sociology and Special Education"; Milofsky, "Is the Growth of Special Education Evolutionary or Cyclic?"; Carrier, "Reply to Milofsky's Comments on 'Sociology and Special Education'"; and Carrier, *Learning Disability.*

9. In addition to Mercer, *Labeling the Mentally Retarded,* and Carrier, see Sally Tomlinson, *A Sociology of Special Education* (London: Routledge & Kegan Paul, 1982).

10. See, for example, Waller, *Sociology of Teaching;* Gertrude McPherson, *Small Town Teacher* (Cambridge, MA: Harvard University Press, 1972); L. M. Smith and W. Geoffrey, *The Complexities of an Urban Classroom* (New York: Holt, Rinehart & Winston, 1968); Arthur L. Stinchcombe, *Rebellion in a High School* (Chicago: Quadrangle Books, 1964); Philip Jackson, *Life in Classrooms* (New York: Holt, Rinehart & Winston, 1968); and Charles A. Valentine, "Defi-

cit, Difference and Bi-Cultural Models of Afro-American Behavior," *Harvard Educational Review* 41 (May 1971):137–157.

11. See, for example, National Institute of Education, *Violent Schools-Safe Schools: The Safe School Study Report to the Congress* (Washington, DC: U.S. Government, National Institute of Education, 1978).

12. See Milofsky, "Special Education and Social Control."

13. In addition to my *Special Education,* see McIntyre, "Two Schools, One Psychologist."

14. See Bowles and Gintis, *Schooling in Capitalist America.*

15. Two discussions of the meritocracy are Becker, *Human Capital;* and Young, *Rise of the Meritocracy.* Discussions of how ideas of meritocracy come to convince people that inequality is legitimate are in Pierre Bourdieu, "Cultural Reproduction and Social Reproduction," in Jerome Karabel and A. H. Halsey, eds., *Power and Ideology in Education* (New York: Oxford University Press, 1977), 487–511; Pierre Bourdieu, "The Forms of Capital"; and Paul DiMaggio, "Cultural Capital and School Success: The Impact of Status-Culture Participation on the Grades of US High School Students," unpublished paper (New Haven: Yale University, n.d.).

16. This is demonstrated in James Rosenbaum, *Making Inequality* (New York: Wiley, 1976), 29–80.

17. Following Carrier, *Learning Disability,* one might well argue that the whole idea of special education is a social construction intended to serve symbolic rather than "real" needs, since most of the data on the reliability of diagnosis suggests we cannot conclusively identify these handicaps with the most sophisticated methods, and studies of the efficacy of intervention programs show that special education classes do little good for the children they teach. These findings, of course, share the difficulties of all efficacy research in education.

18. Paul J. DiMaggio and Walter W. Powell, "The Iron Cage Revisited: Institutional Isomorphism and Collective Rationality in Organizational Fields," *American Sociological Review* 48 (April 1983):147–160.

19. Robert K. Merton, "Manifest and Latent Functions," in Robert K. Merton, *Social Theory and Social Structure* (Glencoe, IL: Free Press, 1949), 21–82.

20. Tomlinson, *Sociology of Special Education;* and Milofsky, *Special Education.*

21. Carrier, "Sociology and Special Education"; Berk, Bridges, and Shih, "Does IQ Really Matter?"

22. Berk, Bridges, and Shih, "Does IQ Really Matter?"

23. Charles E. Lindblom, "The Science of 'Muddling Through'," *Public Administration Review* 19 (Spring 1959):79–87; and *The Policy Making Process,* 2d ed. (Englewood Cliffs, NJ: Prentice-Hall, 1980).

24. Harold Garfinkel, *Studies in Ethnomethodology* (Englewood Cliffs, NJ: Prentice-Hall, 1967).

25. George Homans, *The Human Group* (New York: Harcourt, Brace & World, 1950), 48–155.

26. This, again, is Lindblom's notion of incrementalism (personal communication). He emphasizes that policymakers rarely produce an intervention that is institutionalized the first time around. There usually are successive approximations to a solution as the political process operates and the practicalities of problem solution force revisions of the original intervention. Lindblom sees these successive adjustments as necessary to fit an intervention to the contexts it is meant to change. In suggesting this adaptive process, however, Lindblom does not mean to suggest that there "really" are such things as social problems. Social problems are identified by consensus or by powerful actors in a society, a culture, or a political system. They are problems because people identify them as such. Issues cease being problems when the public consensus that identified them breaks up and dissolves. When this happens, solutions may continue on if they have been institutionalized in formal organizations or the governmental system, or if an economic or political interest group is prepared to maintain the intervention on its own—perhaps by forming a business or nonprofit organization. In the absence of institutionalization, solutions aimed at the solution of social problems wither away as the problems become nonproblems. Thus, we no longer have a War on Poverty because we as a society are no longer committed to a global attack on poverty. Individuals may be unhappy about this turn of events, and it is still easy to find lots of people who do not have enough money. But poverty in the sense it was defined in the early 1960s has ceased to be a social problem for the society in the sense that attacking it is not presently on the political agenda in a meaningful sense. In addition to Lindblom, "The Science of 'Muddling Through';" and Lindblom, *Policy Making Process;* see Lindblom and Cohen, *Usable Knowledge.*

27. David Kirp, *Just Schools: The Idea of Racial Equality in American Education* (Berkeley and Los Angeles: University of California Press, 1982); 3–12.

Bibliography

Addams, Jane. 1910. *Twenty Years at Hull House*. New York: Macmillan.

Anastasi, Anne. 1976. *Psychological Testing*, 4th ed. New York: Macmillan.

Bales, Robert Freed. 1970. *Personality and Interpersonal Behavior*. New York: Holt, Rinehart & Winston.

Banfield, Edward C. 1961. *Political Influence*. Glencoe, IL: Free Press.

Beck, Samuel J. 1937. *Introduction to the Rorschach Method: A Manual of Personality Study*. New York: American Orthopsychiatric Association.

Becker, Gary. 1975. *Human Capital: A Theoretical and Empirical Analysis, with Special Reference to Education*. New York: National Bureau of Economic Research, distributed by Columbia University Press.

Becker, Howard S., Blanche Geer, Everett Hughes, and Anselm Strauss. 1961. *Boys in White*. Chicago: University of Chicago Press.

Berger, Bennett. 1960. *Working Class Suburb*. Berkeley and Los Angeles: University of California Press.

Berk, Richard A., William P. Bridges, and Anthony Shih. 1981. "Does IQ Really Matter? A Study of the Use of IQ Scores for the Tracking of the Mentally Retarded." *American Sociological Review* 46:58–71.

Binet, Alfred, and Th. Simon. 1914. *Mentally Defective Children*. Trans. W. B. Drummond. New York: Longmans, Green.

Bosk, Charles. 1979. *Forgive and Remember: Managing Medical Failure*. Chicago: University of Chicago Press.

Bourdieu, Pierre. 1977. "Cultural Reproduction and Social Reproduction." In Jerome Karabel and A. H. Halsey, eds., *Power and Ideology in Education*. New York: Oxford University Press.

———. 1986. "The Forms of Capital." In John G. Richardson, ed., *Handbook of Theory and Research for the Sociology of Education*. New York: Greenwood Press.

Bowles, Samuel, and Herbert Gintis. 1976. *Schooling in Capitalist America*. New York: Basic Books.

Bucher, Rue, and Joan Stelling. 1969. "Characteristics of Professional Organizations." *Journal of Health and Social Behavior* 10:3–11.

Bucher, Rue, and Joan Stelling. 1977. *Becoming Professional.* Beverly Hills, CA: Sage.

Bucher, Rue, and Anselm Strauss. 1961. "Professions in Process." *American Journal of Sociology* 66:325–334.

Campbell, Ernest Q., and Thomas F. Pettigrew. 1959. "Racial and Moral Crisis: The Role of Little Rock Ministers." *American Journal of Sociology* 64: 509–516.

Caplan, Gerald, and Marie Killilea, eds. 1976. *Support Systems and Mutual Help: Multidisciplinary Explorations.* New York: Grune & Stratton.

Carrier, James G. 1983. "Masking the Social in Educational Knowledge: The Case of Learning Disability Theory." *American Journal of Sociology* 88: 948–974.

———. 1986. "Sociology and Special Education: Differentiation and Allocation in Mass Education"; "Reply to Milofsky's Comments on 'Sociology and Special Education'. " *American Journal of Education* 94 (May):281–327.

———. 1986. *Learning Disability: Social Class and the Construction of Inequality in American Education.* New York: Greenwood Press.

Chicago Board of Education. 1960. *The Bureau of Child Study.* Chicago: Board of Education, Bureau of Child Study.

Clark, Burton. 1956. *Adult Education in Transition.* Berkeley and Los Angeles: University of California Press.

Cole, Michael, and Jerome Bruner. 1971. "Cultural Differences and Inferences about Psychological Processes." *American Psychologist* 26:867–875.

Coleman, James S., Ernest Q. Campbell, Carol J. Hobson, James McPartland, Alexander M. Mood, Frederic Weinfeld, and Robert L. York. 1966. *Equality of Educational Opportunity.* Washington, DC: Office of Education, National Center for Educational Statistics, U.S. Government Printing Office.

DeCharms, Richard. 1968. *Personal Causation: The Internal Affective Determinants of Behavior.* New York: Academic Press.

Deutsch, Martin, J. A. Fishman, L. Kogan, R. North, and M. Whiteman. 1964. "Guidelines for Testing Minority Group Children." *Journal of Social Issues* 20:127–145.

Dexter, Lewis Anthony. 1964. *The Tyranny of Schooling: An Inquiry into the Problem of "Stupidity."* New York: Basic Books.

DiMaggio, Paul. (n.d.) "Cultural Capital and School Success: The Impact of Status-Culture Participation on the Grades of U.S. High School Students." Unpublished paper. New Haven: Department of Sociology, Yale University.

DiMaggio, Paul J., and Walter W. Powell. 1983. "The Iron Cage Revisited: Institutional Isomorphism and Collective Rationality in Organizational Fields." *American Sociological Review* 48 (April):147–160.

Dworkin, Bruce. 1976. "Reference Group Orientation and Role Definition of School Psychologists in Educational Bureaucracies." Ph.D. diss. University of Pennsylvania. *Dissertation Abstracts Index,* 37/07A:4644.

Edgerton, Robert B. 1967. *The Cloak of Competence: Stigma in the Lives of the Mentally Retarded.* Berkeley and Los Angeles: University of California Press.

————. 1970. "Mental Retardation in Non-western Societies: Toward a Cross-Cultural Perspective on Incompetence." In H. C. Haywood, ed., *Social-Cultural Aspects of Mental Retardation*. New York: Appleton-Century-Crofts.

Elstein, Arthur S., Lee S. Shulman, and Sarah A. Sprafka. 1978. *Medical Problem Solving: An Analysis of Clinical Reasoning*. Cambridge: Harvard University Press.

Etzioni, Amitai. 1964. *Modern Organizations*. Englewood Cliffs, NJ: Prentice Hall.

Exner, J. E., Jr. 1966. "Variations in WISC Performances as Influenced by Differences in Pre-test Rapport." *Journal of Genetic Psychology* 74:299–306.

Feuerstein, Reuven. 1970. "A Dynamic Approach to the Causation, Prevention and Alleviation of Retarded Performance." In H. C. Haywood, ed., *Social-Cultural Aspects of Mental Retardation*. New York: Appleton-Century-Crofts.

Freidson, Eliot. 1970. *Profession of Medicine: A Study of the Sociology of Applied Knowledge*. New York: Harper & Row.

————. 1975. *Doctoring Together: A Study of Professional Social Control*. New York: Elsevier.

Freud, Sigmund. 1938. "The Psychopathology of Everyday Life." In A. A. Brill, ed., *The Basic Writings of Sigmund Freud*. New York: Modern Library.

Garfinkel, Harold. 1967. *Studies in Ethnomethodology*. Englewood Cliffs, NJ: Prentice-Hall.

Goffman, Erving. 1959. *The Presentation of Self in Everyday Life*. Garden City, NY: Anchor Books.

————. 1961. "The Moral Career of the Mental Patient." In *Asylums, Essays on the Social Situation of Mental Patients and Other Inmates*. Garden City, NY: Doubleday, Anchor.

Goldner, Fred. 1967. "Role Emergence and the Ethics of Ambiguity." In Gideon Sjoberg, *Ethics, Politics, and Social Research*. Cambridge, MA: Schenkman.

Goslin, David A. 1967. *Teachers and Testing*. New York: Russell Sage.

Grant, W. Vance, and Leo J. Eiden. 1982. *Digest of Educational Statistics, 1981*. Washington, DC: National Center for Educational Statistics.

Grant, W. Vance, and Thomas D. Snyder. 1982. *Digest of Educational Statistics, 1983–84*. Washington, DC: National Center for Educational Statistics.

Hassell, Christine M. 1981. "A Study of the Consequences of Excessive Legal Intervention in the Local Implementation of PL 94-142." Berkeley: University of California with California State University, San Francisco. Ph.D. dissertation. *Dissertation Abstracts Index*, 42/07-A:3105.

Heber, Rick. 1959. "A Manual on Terminology and Classification in Mental Retardation." *American Journal of Mental Deficiency*. 64.2 Monograph Supplement.

Heberlein, Thomas A., and Robert Baumgartner. 1978. "Factors Affecting Response Rates to Mailed Questionnaires: A Quantitative Analysis of the Published Literature." *American Sociological Review* 43:447–462.

Henry, William E., John H. Sims, and S. Lee Spray. 1971. *The Fifth Profession*. San Francisco: Jossey-Bass.

Heyns, Barbara L. 1978. *Summer Learning and the Effects of Schooling*. New York: Academic Press.

Hill, Kennedy T., and Seymour B. Sarason. 1966. "The Relationship between Test Anxiety and Defensiveness to Test and School Performance over the Elementary Years: A Further Longitudinal Study." *Monographs of the Society for Research in Child Development*, Serial #104, v. 31 #2.

Hirsch, Jerry. 1981. "To 'Unfrock the Charlatans'." *Sage Race Relations Abstracts* 6 (May):1–67.

Homans, George. 1950. *The Human Group*. New York: Harcourt, Brace & World.

Hughes, Everett C. 1971. "Good People and Dirty Work." In *The Sociological Eye: Selected Papers on Institutions and Race*. Chicago: Aldine-Atherton.

———. 1971. "Professions." In *The Sociological Eye: Selected Papers on Work, Self, and the Study of Society*. Chicago: Aldine-Atherton.

Hurley, Roger. 1969. *Poverty and Mental Retardation: A Causal Relationship*. New York: Vintage Books.

Huse, Edgar, and James L. Bowditch. 1973. *Behavior in Organizations: A Systems Approach to Managing*. Reading, MA: Addison-Wesley.

Hutt, Max L. 1977. *The Hutt Adaptation of the Bender-Gestalt Test*, 3d ed. New York: Grune & Stratton.

Jackson, Philip. 1968. *Life in Classrooms*. New York: Holt, Rinehart & Winston.

Jastak, J. F., S. R. Jastak, and S. W. Bijou. 1965. *Wide Range Achievement Test*, rev. ed. Austin, TX: Guidance Testing Associates.

Jencks, Christopher, M. Smith, H. Leland, M. J. Bane, D. Cohen, H. Gintis, B. Heyns, and S. Michelson. 1972. *Inequality: A Reassessment of the Effect of Family and Schooling in America*. New York: Basic Books.

Jensen, Arthur. 1969. "How Much Can We Boost IQ and Scholastic Achievement?" *Harvard Educational Review* 38, Reprint Series 2:1–123.

———. 1972. "A Theory of Primary and Secondary Familial Mental Retardation." in *Genetics and Education*. New York: Harper & Row.

Kahn, R., D. M. Wolfe, R. P. Quinn, J. D. Snoek, and R. A. Rosenthal. 1964. *Organizational Stress*. New York: Wiley.

Kamin, Leon. 1974. *The Science and Politics of IQ*. Potomac, MD: Lawrence Erlbaum.

Kanner, Leo. 1964. *A History of the Care and Study of the Mentally Retarded*. Springfield, IL: Charles C. Thomas.

Kaplan, Robert M., and Dennis P. Saccuzzo. 1982. *Psychological Testing: Principals, Applications, and Issues*. Monterey, CA: Brooks/Cole Publishing.

Katz, D., and R. Kahn. 1966. *Social Psychology of Organizations*. New York: John Wiley & Sons.

Keller, Suzanne. 1963. *Beyond the Ruling Class: Strategic Elites in Modern Society*. New York: Random House.

Kirk, S. A., and W. D. Kirk. 1971. *Psycholinguistic Learning Disabilities: Diagnosis and Remediation*. Urbana: University of Illinois Press.

Kirp, David. 1982. *Just Schools: The Idea of Racial Equality in American Education.* Berkeley and Los Angeles: University of California Press.

Kirp, David, William Buss, and Peter Kuriloff. 1974. "Legal Reform of Special Education: Empirical Studies and Procedural Proposals." *California Law Review* 62:40–155.

Kirp, David L., and Donald N. Jensen. 1983. "What Does Due Process Do?" *Public Interest* 73 (Fall):75–90.

Kuriloff, Peter. 1985. "Is Justice Served by Due Process?: Affecting the Outcome of Special Education Hearings in Pennsylvania." *Law and Contemporary Problems* 48 (Winter):89–118.

Kuriloff, Peter, David Kirp, and William Buss. 1979. *When Handicapped Children Go to Court: Assessing the Impact of the Legal Reform of Special Education in Pennsylvania,* National Institute of Education Project Neg.-033-0192 (Washington, DC: U.S. Government, National Institute of Education), ERIC Document ED196256.

Labov, William. 1972. "The Logic of Nonstandard English." In *Language in the Inner City.* Philadelphia: University of Pennsylvania Press.

Levin, Lowell S., and Ellen L. Idler. 1981. *The Hidden Health Care System: Mediating Structures and Medicine.* Cambridge, MA: Ballinger.

Lighthall, Fred F. 1963. "Social Psychology: An Alien Guild." *Elementary School Journal* 63:361–374.

———. "A Social Psychologist for School Systems." *Psychology in the Schools* 6: (1969):3–12.

Lighthall, Fred, and J. W. Braun. 1975. *The Twenty-Second Case.* Final Report, NIMH Project 5-T21-MH-11217. Chicago: Department of Education, University of Chicago.

Lindblom, Charles E. 1959. "The Science of 'Muddling Through'." *Public Administration Review* 19 (Spring):79–87.

———. 1980. *The Policy Making Process,* 2d ed. Englewood Cliffs, NJ: Prentice-Hall.

Lindblom, Charles E., and David Cohen. 1979. *Usable Knowledge.* New Haven: Yale University Press.

Linton R. 1936. *The Study of Man.* New York: Appleton-Century-Crofts.

Lipsky, Michael. 1980. *Street-level Bureaucracy: Dilemmas of the Individual in Public Services.* New York: Russell Sage.

Lubov, Roy. 1969. *The Professional Altruist: The Emergence of Social Work as a Career, 1880–1930.* New York: Atheneum.

McIntyre, Donald. 1969. "Two Schools, One Psychologist." In Frances Kaplan and Seymour Sarason, eds., *The Psycho-Educational Clinic.* Community Mental Health Monograph Series, v. 4. Boston: Massachusetts Department of Mental Health.

McPherson, Gertrude. 1972. *Small Town Teacher.* Cambridge, MA: Harvard University Press.

March, James G., and Johan P. Olson. 1976. *Ambiguity and Choice in Organizations.* Bergen-Oslo-Troms: Universitetsforlaget.

Masling, Janet. 1959. "The Effects of Warm and Cold Interaction on the Administration and Scoring of an Intelligence Test." *Journal of Consulting Psychology* 23:336–341.

————. 1960. "The Influence of Situational and Interpersonal Variables in Projective Testing." *Psychological Bulletin* 57:65–86.

Mead, George Herbert. 1962. *Mind, Self, and Society.* Charles W. Morris, ed. Chicago: University of Chicago Press.

Mercer, Jane. 1973. *Labeling the Mentally Retarded.* Berkeley and Los Angeles: University of California Press.

Merton, Robert K. 1949. "Manifest and Latent Functions." In *Social Theory and Social Structure.* Glencoe, IL: Free Press.

————. 1976. "The Ambivalence of Physicians." In Merton, *Sociological Ambivalence.*

————. 1976. *Sociological Ambivalence.* New York: Free Press.

Merton, Robert K., with Elinor Barber. 1976. "Sociological Ambivalence." In Merton, *Sociological Ambivalence.*

Milofsky, Carl. 1974. "Why Special Education Isn't Special." *Harvard Educational Review* 44:437–458.

————. 1976. *Special Education: A Sociological Study of California Programs.* New York: Praeger.

————. 1986. "Is the Growth of Special Education Evolutionary or Cyclic? A Response to Carrier." *American Journal of Education* 94, 3:313–321.

————. 1986. "Special Education and Social Control." In Richardson, *Handbook of Theory and Research for the Sociology of Education.*

————. 1987. "Neighborhood-based Organizations: A Market Analogy." In Walter W. Powell, ed., *The Nonprofit Sector: A Research Handbook.* New Haven: Yale University Press.

Mitchell, Dave, Cathy Mitchell, and Richard Ofshe. 1980. *The Light on Synanon.* New York: Seaview Books.

Mullen, Frances A. 1949. "Fifty Years of Service to the Mentally Handicapped Children of the Chicago Schools." *Chicago Principal's Club Reporter* 39: 11–17.

Murnane, Richard. 1975. *The Impact of School Resources on the Learning of Inner City Children.* Cambridge, MA: Ballinger.

National Institute of Education. 1978. *Violent Schools-Safe Schools: The Safe School Study Report to the Congress.* Washington, DC: U.S. Government, National Institute of Education.

Neal, David, and David L. Kirp. 1985. "The Allure of Legalization Reconsidered: The Case of Special Education." *Law and Contemporary Problems* 48 (Winter):63–87.

New York Times, 17 December 1983.

Nurco, David N., Norma Wegner, Philip Stephenson, Abraham Makofsky, and John W. Shaffer. 1983. *Ex-Addicts' Self-Help Groups: Potentials and Pitfalls.* New York: Praeger.

Pancoast, Diane L., Paul Parker, and Charles Froland. eds. 1983. *Rediscovering Self-Help: Its Role in Social Care.* Beverly Hills, CA: Sage.

Parsons, Talcott. 1951. "Social Structure and Dynamic Process: The Case of Modern Medical Practice." In *The Social System*. New York: Free Press.

Perrow, Charles. 1972. *Complex Organizations: A Critical Essay*. Glenview, IL: Scott, Foresman.

Peterson, Paul. 1976. *School Politics Chicago Style*. Chicago: University of Chicago Press.

Pittenger, John C., and Peter Kuriloff. 1982. "Educating the Handicapped: Reforming a Radical Law." *Public Interest* 66 (Winter):72–96.

Pressman, Hope Hughes. 1975. *A New Resource for Social Reform: The Poor Themselves*. Berkeley: Institute of Governmental Studies, University of California, Berkeley.

Rosenbaum, James. 1976. *Making Inequality*. New York: Wiley.

Rudy, David. 1986. *Becoming Alcoholic: Alcoholics Anonymous and the Reality of Alcoholism*. Carbondale and Edwardsville: Southern Illinois University Press.

Saliterman, Gail. 1971. The Politics of Decision-making in an Incompletely Bureaucratized Organization: A Study of Textbook Selection in Public School Systems." Ph.D. diss., Department of Political Science, American University. *Dissertation Abstracts Index*, 33/02-A:803.

Sameroff, A. J. 1975. "Concepts of Humanity in Primary Prevention." Paper prepared for the Vermont Conference on the Primary Prevention of Psychopathology, Burlington, VT (June).

Sarason, Seymour. 1976. "The Unfortunate Fate of Alfred Binet and School Psychology." *Teachers' College Record* 77:579–592.

Sarason, Seymour, and John Doris. 1979. *Educational Handicap, Public Policy, and Social History: A Broadened Perspective on Mental Retardation*. New York: Free Press.

Sattler, Jerome, and Fred Theye. 1967. "Procedural, Situational, and Interpersonal Variables in Individual Intelligence Testing." *Psychological Bulletin* 68:347–360.

Schrag, Peter, and Diane Divoky. 1975. *The Myth of the Hyperactive Child and Other Means of Child Control*. New York: Pantheon.

Science 1978. "California Court is Forum for Latest Round in IQ Debate." v. 201:1106–1108.

Scott, W. Richard. 1981. *Organizations: Rational, Natural, and Open Systems*. Englewood Cliffs, NJ: Prentice Hall.

Selznick, Philip. *Leadership in Administration*. New York: Harper & Row.

———. 1966. *TVA and the Grassroots*. New York: Harper & Row.

Shapiro, Joan Hatch. 1971. *Communities of the Alone*. New York: Association Press.

Shils, Edward. 1975. *Center and Periphery Essays in Macrosociology*. Chicago: University of Chicago Press.

Shore, Kenneth. 1986. *The Special Education Handbook: A Comprehensive Guide for Parents and Educators*. New York: Teachers College Press.

Shuey, Audrey M. 1966. *The Testing of Negro Intelligence*, 2d ed. New York: Social Science Press.

Simon, Kenneth, and W. Vance Grant. 1973. *Digest of Educational Statistics, 1972.* Washington, DC: National Center for Educational Statistics.

Skolnick, Jerome. 1967. *Justice Without Trial.* New York: Wiley.

Slater, Robert. (1980). "The Organizational Origins of Public School Psychology." *Educational Studies* 1:1–11.

Smith, L. M., and W. Geoffrey. 1968. *The Complexities of an Urban Classroom.* New York: Holt, Rinehart & Winston.

Spiegel, John. 1971. *Transactions: The Interplay between Individual, Family, and Society.* New York: Science House.

Starr, Paul. 1982. *The Social Transformation of American Medicine: The Rise of a Sovereign Profession and the Making of a Vast Industry.* New York: Basic Books.

Stinchcombe, Arthur L. 1964. *Rebellion in a High School.* Chicago: Quadrangle Books.

———. 1974. *Creating Efficient Industrial Administrations.* New York: Academic Press.

Taylor, Ronald L. 1984. *Assessment of Exceptional Students: Educational and Psychological Procedures.* Englewood Cliffs, NJ: Prentice Hall.

Tomlinson, Sally. 1983. *A Sociology of Special Education.* London: Routledge & Kegan Paul.

Tuddenham, Read D. 1962. "The Nature and Measurement of Intelligence." In Leo D. Postman, ed., *Psychology in the Making.* New York: Knopf.

———. 1969. "Intelligence." In Robert L. Ebel, ed., *Encyclopedia of Educational Research,* 4th ed. London: Collier-MacMillan.

United States Senate. 1975. Senate Report 94-168, "Education for All Handicapped Children Act." 2 June.

Valentine, Charles A. 1971. "Deficit, Difference and Bi-cultural Models of Afro-American Behavior." *Harvard Educational Review* 41 (May):137–157.

Vellutino, Frank R. 1987. "Dyslexia." *Scientific American* 256, 3:34–41.

Waller, Willard. 1932. *The Sociology of Teaching.* New York: Wiley.

Weatherley, Richard, and Michael Lipsky. 1977. "Street-level Bureaucrats and Institutional Innovation: Implementing Special-Education Reform." *Harvard Educational Review* 47, 2:171–197.

Weatherley, Richard A. 1979. *Reforming Special Education: Policy Implementation from State Level to Street Level.* Cambridge, MA: MIT Press.

Weber, Max. 1978. *Economy and Society.* Ed. Guenther Roth and Claus Wittich. Berkeley and Los Angeles: University of California Press.

Wechsler, David. 1974. *Manual for the Wechsler Intelligence Scale for Children,* rev. New York: Psychological Corporation.

Weick, Karl. 1976. "Educational Organizations as Loosely Coupled Systems." *Administrative Science Quarterly* 21:1–19.

Weiss, Janet A., Frederick Norling, and John Kimberly. 1981. "The Development and Effectiveness of Education Service Centers: A Study of JACS." Unpublished report. New Haven: School of Organization and Management, Yale University.

Weiss, Janet A., Frederick Norling, and Mark Hymel. 1984. *Managing Cooperation and Complexity in Education: The Case of Educational Service Agencies. Final Report*. Ann Arbor, MI: Institute for Social Research. ERIC Document ED242098.

Williams, Robert L. 1971. "Danger: Testing and Dehumanizing Black Children." *School Psychologist* 25:11–13.

Wolff, Theta H. 1973. *Alfred Binet*. Chicago: University of Chicago Press.

Yablonsky, Lewis. 1967. *Synanon: The Tunnel Back*. Baltimore: Penguin Books.

Young, Dennis. 1983. *If Not for Profit, For What? A Behavioral Theory of the Nonprofit Sector Based on Entrepreneurship*. Lexington, MA: Lexington Books.

———. 1984. *Casebook of Management for Nonprofit Organizations: Entrepreneurship and Organizational Change in the Human Services*. New York: Haworth Press.

Young, Michael. 1971. *The Rise of the Meritocracy*. Baltimore: Penguin Books.

Index